Covering Up Luther

VERITAS

Series Introduction

"... the truth will set you free." (John 8:32)

In much contemporary discourse, Pilate's question has been taken to mark the absolute boundary of human thought. Beyond this boundary, it is often suggested, is an intellectual hinterland into which we must not venture. This terrain is an agnosticism of thought: because truth cannot be possessed, it must not be spoken. Thus, it is argued that the defenders of "truth" in our day are often traffickers in ideology, merchants of counterfeits, or anti-liberal. They are, because it is somewhat taken for granted that Nietzsche's word is final: truth is the domain of tyranny.

Is this indeed the case, or might another vision of truth offer itself? The ancient Greeks named the love of wisdom as *philia*, or friendship. The one who would become wise, they argued, would be a "friend of truth." For both philosophy and theology might be conceived as schools in the friendship of truth, as a kind of relation. For like friendship, truth is as much discovered as it is made. If truth is then so elusive, if its domain is *terra incognita*, perhaps this is because it arrives to us—unannounced—as gift, as a person, and not some thing.

The aim of the Veritas book series is to publish incisive and original current scholarly work that inhabits "the between" and "the beyond" of theology and philosophy. These volumes will all share a common aspiration to transcend the institutional divorce in which these two disciplines often find themselves, and to engage questions of pressing concern to both philosophers and theologians in such a way as to reinvigorate both disciples with a kind of interdisciplinary desire, often so absent in contemporary academe. In a word, these volumes represent collective efforts in the befriending of truth, doing so beyond the simulacra of pretend tolerance, the violent, yet insipid reasoning of liberalism that asks with Pilate, "What is truth?"—expecting a consensus of non-commitment; one that encourages the commodification of the mind, now sedated by the civil service of career, ministered by the frightened patrons of position.

The series will therefore consist of two "wings": (1) original monographs; and (2) essay collections on a range of topics in theology and philosophy. The latter will principally by the products of the annual conferences of the Centre of Theology and Philosophy (www.theologyphilosophycentre.co.uk).

Conor Cunningham and Peter Candler, *Series editors*

Covering Up Luther

How Barth's Christology Challenged the
Deus Absconditus that Haunts Modernity

RUSTIN E. BRIAN

CASCADE *Books* · Eugene, Oreg

COVERING UP LUTHER
How Barth's Christology Challenged the *Deus Absconditus* that Haunts Modernity

Veritas 9

Cascade Books
An Imprint of Wipf and Stock Publishers
199 W. 8th Ave., Suite 3
Eugene, OR 97401

www.wipfandstock.com

ISBN 13: 978-1-62032-173-7

Cataloging-in-Publication data:

Brian, Rustin E.

Covering up Luther : how Barth's christology challenged the *deus absconditus* that haunts modernity / Rustin E. Brian.

Veritas 9

xii + 202 p.; 23 cm—Includes bibliographical references and index.

ISBN 13: 978-1-62032-173-7

1. Barth, Karl, 1886–1968. 2. Luther, Martin, 1483–1546. 3. Jesus Christ—Person and offices. 4. Theology, Doctrinal—History—20th century. I. Title. II. Series.

BT203 .B75 2013

Manufactured in the USA.

To Lauren: my wife, my best friend, and my partner on this crazy journey. Thank you for all the sacrifices you made and all that you put up with to see me complete my dissertation. I absolutely could not have accomplished this without you. You are an ever-present source of God's grace in my life.

Love Always,
Rusty

"The hands of the king are the hands of a healer, and so shall the rightful king be known . . .

And when he could labour no more, he cast his cloak about him, and slipped out of the City, and went to his tent just ere dawn and slept for a little. And in the morning the banner of Dol Amroth, a white ship like a swan upon blue water, floated from the Tower, and men looked up and wondered if the coming of the King had been but a dream."

—J. R. R. Tolkien, *The Return of the King*

"Then I saw a new heaven and a new earth; for the first heaven and the first earth had passed away, and the sea was no more. And I saw the holy city, the new Jerusalem, coming down out of heaven from God, prepared as a bride adorned for her husband. And I heard a loud voice from the throne saying,
   'See, the home of God is among the mortals.
   He will dwell with them;
   They will be his peoples,
   and God himself will be with them;
   he will wipe every tear from their eyes.
   Death will be no more;
   mourning and crying and pain will be no more,
   for the first things have passed away.'"

—*The Apocalypse* according to John

From the Web site of the Karl Barth Archives in Basel, and used with permission from Herr Drewes and Dr. Peter Zocher. I am grateful to Matt Jenson for tipping me off to this photo's existence, to Professor John Webster for his help in locating this photo, and to Dr. D. Stephen Long for speaking to Herr Drewes about my use of this photo. Photo can be found online: http://karlbarth.unibas.ch/index. php?id=52. Copyright by the Karl Barth-Archiv.

Contents

Contents

Acknowledgments

THANK YOU FIRST AND foremost to the God who revealed His scandalously ridiculous love for creation in the Son, Jesus of Nazareth. Thank you for your continued faithfulness to a most unfaithful people, of which I am very much a part.

This book would not exist without the help of so many. Thank you to my parents, Randy and Barbara, to whom I owe the deepest debt of gratitude for your constant love and support. Thank you for always believing in me and helping me accomplish my dreams. Chapters 3 and 4 were written at your kitchen table. Thanks are also in order to John Wright, who taught me how to read Scripture. The real foundation for this book began while I was an MDiv student at Nazarene Theological Seminary, studying and serving as a Teaching Assistant for John Knight Jr. Thank you for commuting from Chicago each week to teach students like me, and for placing almost unrealistic reading expectations upon your students!

This book truly found its shape and scope during my years as a PhD student at Garrett-Evangelical Theological Seminary as my dissertation. Thanks are in order to D. Stephen Long for his faithful help as my advisor throughout the PhD process. Thank you, Steve, for showing interest in a young student at Point Loma Nazarene University and for suggesting the possibility of a future PhD to me. I am deeply indebted to you for your demands for excellence, your academic rigor, and your careful and calculated advising throughout—despite having moved on to Marquette. Perhaps most of all, thank you for your friendship. I'm proud to call you my advisor and friend. Thanks also to Brent Waters, who served as a secondary advisor and who, in the wake of Steve's departure, hired me to be his Teaching and Research Assistant. I learned so much from you, Brent, and am very appreciative of your affirmation of my work. For serving on my exam committee, I also owe a debt of gratitude to George

Kalantzis and Brent Laytham. Thank you for your graciousness and your challenging questions and recommendations. Thanks also to the folks at the University of Aberdeen, and to Professors John Webster and Brian Brock, in particular. I know my coming to Aberdeen did not work out as any of us had planned, but for what it's worth, this book would not exist were it not for your advising, John. Thank you for meeting with me weekly, and for being willing to continue to answer my questions even after leaving Scotland.

Thank you to everyone at Bentonville Church of the Nazarene who supported me through the end of the writing process. Thank you for the graciousness, flexibility, and prayers as I completed my PhD. It is not usual to have a youth pastor completing a PhD, and you made it an experience that I treasure. Thanks for letting me flesh out my theological training in a local church—where theology is meant to be done. Aside from chapters 2 and 3, this book was completed in Bentonville while working as a full-time pastor.

Beyond this, I would like to thank the many professors who helped shape and mold this young theologian, and who not only taught me, but also shared life with me. Thanks to Andy Johnson, Michael Lodahl, Steve McCormick, Tom Noble, Sam Powell, Herb Prince, Bob Smith; thanks especially to Ron Benefiel, who has served as a professor, a mentor, and a friend over a span of many years. Your continued support, guidance, and wisdom are invaluable to this young pastor and theologian. I am also deeply indebted to my many friends and colleagues: Jimmy Cooper, the late Tom Findlay, Ryan Hansen, Matt Jenson, Charlie and Kara Lyons-Pardue, Steven Martinez, Ken Oakes, Brent Peterson, Christy Sim, Ben Suriano, Justin Stratus, Josh and Nell Becker-Sweeden, Derrick and Dayna Thames, Greg Voiles, and Geordie Ziegler, to name only a few.

Finally, I owe a huge thank you to Conor Cunningham and to Peter M. Chandler Jr. for believing in this work and including it in the *Veritas Series*. I am deeply humbled by this honor. And, of course, thanks to Eric Lee for suggesting my work to Conor and Pete. Eric, I'm so glad that I ventured over to your room and was able to see beyond the crazy "death metal"—and that you saw past my arrogance—those many years ago. Though we haven't lived in the same place for many years, I truly thank you for your friendship.

1

Introduction

KARL BARTH'S LIBRARY IN his home in Basel, Switzerland, is host to a curious site. There, amidst Barth's many books, hangs an ornately decorated rug. One typically puts rugs on the floor, of course, where they provide a soft matte for one's feet, as well as add to the aesthetic balance and overall décor of the room. This rug serves a decidedly different purpose, however. So ornate that it could have been woven for an Indonesian king, this rug hangs over a particular section of books—books that Barth called his "Pandora's box"—protecting them and keeping them from view. It was placed there by Karl Barth himself; the author of the works he was covering up: Martin Luther.[1]

Karl Barth shared many interests and theological convictions with the great Reformer. Both were biblical theologians of the highest order, and both unabashedly pursued a *theologia crucis,* or a theology of the cross. Both placed Christology as central to all of theology, understanding the fundamental revelation of God to be the incarnation, death, resurrection, and ascension of the Son in the person of Jesus of Nazareth.[2] Finally, both believed the Church to be in dire need of reform, and both were willing to speak, write, and act in such a way as to attempt to bring about such changes.

1. Busch, *Karl Barth,* 409.

2. I hold it to be very important to go to the trouble of listing all four of these "events" within the "Christ event" in hopes of being holistic and theologically sound. Neither author, necessarily, chose to utilize this wording, though I believe both intended the inclusivity that I'm trying to assume by writing, "incarnation, death, resurrection, and ascension."

That being said, Martin Luther and Karl Barth possessed many distinctive qualities as well. Moreover, they lived in very different time periods, which led to their having drastically different worldviews and emphases. Perhaps most importantly, Barth did not inherit the psychological and cosmological issues that Luther did. In particular, Barth had to face up to the end results of Luther's attempt at reform—both the intended and unintended results. Finally, and perhaps most importantly, Karl Barth was witness to the rise of the Nazi Party in Germany, to World War II, and to the Nazi concentration camps and Russian gulags.[3] Barth was witness to the crumbling of the structure the foundation of which Luther helped, in large part, to lay. Barth looked at what many believed to be pure, unbridled potential for goodness and witnessed, instead, unspeakable horrors and intellectual hollowness.

And so, though Barth and Luther indeed share many commonalities, as time went on—and Barth saw the devastating end toward which Protestant Reformed theology was headed, or had in fact already arrived at—Barth made an intentional decision to distance himself from the theology of Martin Luther. A quick, practical reminder of this theological distancing was to literally cover up Luther by placing a rug over his works. This volume is an attempt to understand why and how Barth sought to distance himself from—and, indeed, to cover up—Martin Luther. It is my contention that one of the reasons, if not the primary reason, why Karl Barth distanced himself theologically from Luther, and quite literally covered him up, is the lingering influence of Luther's primary way of understanding God: the *Deus absconditus*.[4]

3. The latter being less influential on Barth than the former.

4. It is true to say that Luther wanted to maintain equality between the *Deus absconditus* and the *Deus revelatus*. In fact, in one of Barth's earliest attempts at critiquing natural theology, Barth cites Luther on this very point (Barth, *Die Christliche Dogmatik*, 179). Barth was rightly concerned that if the *Deus absconditus* is understood to be larger or more prevalent than the *Deus revelatus*, the result would be a remainder, or a completely unknown aspect to God beyond God's revelation in Christ Jesus. Barth understood this to lead directly to nominalism. But while early on Barth would see in Luther the means to reject such a remainder, I do not believe it to be the case that he maintained such optimism for very long. Throughout volume IV of his *Church Dogmatics*, Barth is rather free in his criticisms of Luther. In particular, Barth believed he was now witness to the end to which Lutheran theology logically leads. It was not that Barth believed Luther himself to intentionally go in this direction, but that his theology inevitably led there anyway. One of these ends, and perhaps the one that worried Barth the most, was "speculative anthropology." In *Church Dogmatics* IV.2, Barth critiques Luther's theology as leading (though unintentionally) to "speculative

This volume is not a careful examination of the life and work of Martin Luther, but rather of the theological works of Karl Barth. As such, Karl Barth and his works will receive primary attention. Indeed, much of the present work consists of careful, pointed examinations of vast amounts of Karl Barth's theological work. This attempt occurs primarily in chapters 3 and 4, where my goal to is to let Barth "speak for himself." I believe that the overwhelming amount of material, and the consistency of Barth's arguments therein, prove that Barth's God is not the *Deus absconditus*, and that he rejects the logic of such a theological position. I believe that the *Deus absconditus* became (unintentionally) the dominant theological position of modernity, and that this was accomplished through the utilization of the logic of dialectic. The logic or philosophy of dialectic, I will argue as a secondary point, is completely contrary to the Gospel of our Lord and Savior Jesus Christ, which reveals a fundamentally non-competitive relationship between God and creation.

Toward this end, in chapter 2, I will discuss modernity and its theological presuppositions. Here, I will argue that modernity, which

---

anthropology" as a result of what Barth calls Luther's "open door" Christology. The connection, for Barth, can be traced through the works of Feuerbach and Hegel, in particular. Barth believed that while Christology plays a very large, visible role in Luther's theology, its role is more accurately described as "exemplary," in that it was a consolidation of what was essentially an anthropological or mystico-anthropological tendency and *schema* that allowed the ancient Alexandrian *idiomata* to be coupled with German idealism in favor of anthropology. Thus, "Luther and the older Lutherans did in fact compromise—at a most crucial point—the irreversibility of the relationship between God and man, long before the message of the Church was similarly affected by a secular human self-understanding which drew its nourishment from a very different quarter. Their successors necessarily find themselves embarrassed and defenseless in face of this secular humanism, and if modern Protestant theology could and has become essentially anthropology, this was not so much due to external pressure as to its own internal entanglement. It was also not an accident that the opposition to this tendency which arose about 1920 came from the Reformed side." Barth, *Church Dogmatics* IV.2, 82–83. For Luther as well as for Barth, the discussion of both the *Deus absconditus* and the *Deus revelatus*, as well as their relationship to each other, is a christological discussion. Early on Barth saw great promise in Luther's christocentric theology, especially his *theologia crucis*. As time passed, though, Barth was forced to look again at Luther's Christology. When he did so, Barth determined that Luther did in fact leave a "door open." The door might well have been left open unintentionally, but nevertheless, it allowed philosophers such as Feuerbach and Hegel to turn Christianity into "speculative anthropology." I believe that open door, in large part, was the *Deus absconditus*. In the next chapter, it will be argued that the further removed God is from the cosmos—that the more unknown God is—the larger the role that humanity takes on for itself, eventually taking over even the place of God.

many claim to be an eschewing of theology altogether, is, in fact, a careful and calculated adoption of a very different type of theology, one in which God is removed from the cosmos and humanity and nature are granted a quasi-divine status. I will argue that this slow development is made possible, in large part, by Martin Luther, and in particular by the nominalism that he inherited from the likes of William of Ockham and Duns Scotus, among others. I will argue that the God of nominalism is the *Deus absconditus* and that the logic that holds this entire system together is dialectic. It is very much my contention that modernity exists still today. In fact, I would argue that it is inescapable until the *eschaton* and the preceding *parousia*. As such, what many call postmodernity or postmodernism I will discuss as being a stance or epistemology within, and only intelligible within, modernity. Thus, I have given this work the subtitle *How Karl Barth's Christology Challenged the* Deus Absconditus *that Haunts Modernity* (the use of the present tense, *haunts*, is quite intentional). The *Deus absconditus* lingers on, and is indeed the dominant theology of many, if not most, moderns. In Karl Barth's Christology lies a possible way forward, a different way forward than what many have experienced within modernity. At the end of chapter 2, I will briefly examine the notion that much of Roman Catholicism can claim an alternate experience of modernity, one that is not characterized by the conflict and strife of dialectic and, I would argue, the *Deus absconditus*. This argument is put forth skillfully by John Milbank, in particular. I will conclude this work by returning to this argument in chapter 5, bringing the end result of my research into Karl Barth's theology to bear on the discussion.

As I have previously stated, chapters 3 and 4 are long, careful examinations of many of Barth's primary works. Before addressing Barth's primary work, however, I deem it necessary to engage one of the world's leading Barth scholars, Bruce McCormack, and his most interesting and powerful thesis about Karl Barth. As an excursus, then, I will set up chapters 3 and 4 by providing a critical review of McCormack's important work, *Karl Barth's Critically Realistic Dialectical Theology: Its Genesis and Development (1909–1936).* It is my belief that whether one agrees with McCormack's positions or not, he is one of the world's leading Barth scholars, and his positions in this work, in particular, have come to dominate much of the theological world—both English- and German-speaking. I will offer a quick and yet careful review of *Karl Barth's Critically Realistic Dialectical Theology,* and I will hone in on one point in particular. To make his argument, McCormack states that the two primary aspects of

Karl Barth's theology are 1) the distinction that God is God and the world is the world, and 2) the knowledge of God. He will further argue that both of these points fall under the heading of Christology for Barth. I whole-heartedly agree with McCormack here. That being said, McCormack will use these positions to go on and argue that Karl Barth was (and remained always) a dialectical theologian. I take great issue with this argument, and refuting this claim is a secondary concern of this present work.[5] So, I will accept McCormack's argument about the primary aspects of Barth's theology, and I will attempt to examine these primary aspects in light of the argument that Barth rejected the *Deus absconditus*, and with it, Luther and nominalism as a whole.

In chapter 3, therefore, I will examine both the position that God is God and the world is the world, as well as the knowledge of God in Karl Barth's theology. In this discussion, it will be helpful to also include topics such as the knowledge/knowability of God and natural theology, as well as Barth's views on the *analogia entis*, limiting my discussion of each to how it pertains to the present work. Here, I will examine eight primary sources, attempting to understand just how Barth dealt with these concepts and the resulting theology and cosmology that developed in Barth. I believe that these works reveal, increasingly so, that Barth's God was not hidden but revealed, not veiled but unveiled—that Barth's God does not ultimately speak a "No" to creation in general and humanity in particular, but rather a "Yes." Barth's arguments are complex, but I believe that the results of this detailed examination reveal Barth to be quite contrary on these matters than the way he is often depicted by both proponents and critics. In short, Barth is often portrayed as essentially being much more similar to Luther than he really was. What similarities are there quickly disappear the later one looks in Barth's theological works.

Building upon the findings of chapter 3, in chapter 4 I will examine Barth's Christology. In particular, I will examine Barth's more "mature" Christology, specifically volume IV of his *Church Dogmatics: The Doctrine of Reconciliation*. As McCormack himself argued, both the notion that God is God and the world is the world, as well as the knowledge of God, are ultimately, for Barth, christological categories or issues. With this in mind, chapter 4 is an attempt at a close examination of Barth's last works, which are, consequently, his greatest christological works. My

---

5. It is my hope that this easily connected argument will help and not hinder the present examination. It is my further hope to pick up this topic, with greater focus and clarity, in a future work.

goal here is to show the result of a theology like Barth's, one that is so heavily christocentric. My contention is that for Barth, all that we can know about God has been unilaterally and decisively revealed in the person of Jesus of Nazareth. As a result, we cannot speak about an unknown or hidden God. Instead, God is revealed, once and for all, in Christ Jesus. Barth's theology, then, being rooted in his Christology, is ultimately one of revelation, one of universal election, one of unity amidst a greater distinction. Here, I believe, more than anywhere else, Barth employs the logic of what I call paradox, which I take to mean the coincidence of two seeming opposites in a noncontradictory manner, in which an overall meaning is achieved through a fundamental unity that is both beyond, and yet contains within itself, all distinction. Furthermore, I will demonstrate that Barth's understanding of paradox is that of the "absurd possibility of the absurd." I will utilize this as a short working definition.

Due to Barth's Alexandrian Christology—and by that I mean the way he views the relationship between the two natures in the person of Jesus—Christ Jesus is shown to define both God and humanity. The rejection of dialectic and the adoption of more paradoxical language, in my opinion, increases chronologically in Barth's work. It is nowhere more apparent and necessary than here, in volume IV, which is Barth's most highly christological work. God and the world are fundamentally distinct in every way, and yet the two are revealed to be in one harmonious, noncompetitive relationship through the person of Christ Jesus. This is most pointedly seen in the relationship between the divine and the human in Jesus. Unity defines the distinction, and not the other way around. Surely, the view of God that results from this highly paradoxical theology is not the hidden, terrible God known by the title *Deus absconditus*.

Finally, after concluding two lengthy chapters in which I engage Barth's primary texts, I will conclude this work in chapter 5 with what I intend to be a more constructive argument than the preceding chapters. The final chapter is an attempt to answer the following three questions: So what? What do we do with this? Where can we go from here? In particular, I have Barth scholarship in mind when I ask and attempt to answer these questions. I believe there are many potential ways forward for Barth scholarship, but one in particular rises to the top as a result of this work. In this work, I will examine the *Deus absconditus*, which I will claim is the God of modernity. Included with this theology is a critique of dialectic, which I have claimed is contradictory to the Christian message. I will begin chapter 5, therefore, by briefly examining Barth's ethics, explaining how I think Barth's rejection of the *Deus absconditus* informs his ethics and provides a positive way forward for the Church. It is my opinion that had he been able to write volume V of the *Church Dogmatics,* it would have been the premier contemporary work in theological ethics.

Then, having attempted to show concrete examples of how Barth rejects such theology, I will return to the concluding section of chapter 2 by proposing that the best way forward for Barth scholarship is alongside of, and in dialogue with, Roman Catholicism. Agreeing that Roman Catholicism had a somewhat alternate experience of modernity than did most in the West, Protestants more than any, I see many similarities in the theology of Karl Barth. In his rejection of so much of the framework that makes up modernity, Barth provides a viable pathway for Protestants to reengage Roman Catholics with conversation and fellowship. I believe this makes sense in light of Barth's increasing preoccupation with Roman Catholicism, something that has been grossly underdeveloped, if not virtually ignored, by much of Barth scholarship. Though deeply critical of the Roman Church, he is, in fact, more critical of the Protestant Church. Driven by the desire to faithfully proclaim the unity of the Church, Barth almost seems to be preoccupied with the Roman Catholic Church and his Roman Catholic colleagues and critics. This is a point that, again, is grossly underdeveloped in most Barth scholarship. I believe that all signs in Barth point his theological followers to the rich and diverse dialogical possibilities with Roman Catholicism, stemming from Barth's theology. Roman Catholics have already grasped this, and indeed one could argue that they have reformed their Church around many of Barth's leading points of praise and critique. Barth has left a profound influence on the Roman Catholic Church through his discussions, his criticisms, and by simply staying current and connected to much of Roman Catholic scholarship. It is time for the Protestant Church to do the same. As Karl Barth says, ultimately both sides, Roman Catholic and Protestant, need to be converted to Christ. My hope is that building upon Barth's rejection of the *Deus absconditus*—as well as his rejection of the logic of dialectic in favor of something different, something I'm calling paradox—such conversations and perhaps even such conversions can begin to happen on both sides.

2

Modernity and Its Theological Presuppositions

The little boy of an African parable, who had played for long enough with a prettily and faithfully carved wooden lion—it might have been an excellent dogmatics!—was dreadfully frightened one day when he saw a real living and roaring lion approaching. If we have never seen the Gospel approaching as a real and living lion, we must not even imagine that we can ever point others to, or prepare them for, that astounding light, that two-edged sword, the decision which is forced on them or the unequivocal way in which it must be made. How can they be expected to take seriously what we ourselves have not taken seriously, or have done so only in the form of a lion which, however savagely it speaks and acts, is only carved out of wood? And if we have not taken it seriously, how can we be usable in the service of Jesus Christ?[1]—Karl Barth

He is not at all a tame lion.[2]—C. S. Lewis

Ask the question, "What is modernity?" and you will receive a myriad of answers covering enterprises such as technology, art, fashion, architecture, and science, just to name a few. Ask the question, "When did modernity begin?" and you will receive such a diverse and perplexing array of answers as to elicit profound confusion. The question

1. Barth, *Church Dogmatics* IV.3.2, 660.
2. Lewis, *Lion, the Witch and the Wardrobe*, 194.

of modernity's origins is often approached through a discussion of seminal thinkers or characters in the development of modernity. Traditional names that surface in this discussion are Galileo, Newton, Descartes, Bacon, Locke, Montaigne, Hobbes, Luther, Cervantes, and even fictional characters such as Sophocles' Oedipus and Homer's Odysseus. The simple truth is that modernity is complex. Complexity is to be expected in the case of any totalizing vision of human life, possibility, and the very cosmos itself.

In my reading of the subject, an oversimplified but almost universally agreed upon definition of modernity is "progress" or "overcoming." Giovanni Vattimo states it thus: "The idea of 'overcoming,' which is so important in all modern philosophy, understands the course of thought as being a progressive development in which the new is identified with value through the mediation of the recovery and appropriation of the foundation-origin."[3]

Modernity equals progress, development, and the overcoming of all things that stand in the way of such progress. We could perhaps further parse this definition out as "progress for progress' sake." However one might define modernity, that definition will always entail a conquering or overcoming of an old way of thinking or doing in favor of a way that is more efficient or effective, and certainly in a way that is more reasonable. Modernity is about the overcoming of things such as superstition and tradition, in favor of that which is more reasonable, and thus more capable of producing the desired results. Modernity is "clearing away the underbrush that stands in the way of knowledge,"[4] according to John Locke. Moreover, modernity is the act of "standing on the shoulders of giants," as so many modern thinkers have articulated.[5] Modernity is thus a way of using and mastering the best of what has come before in order to gain a more privileged position than was previously thought possible.

Modernity begins with a nod of acknowledgment to those who have come before and yet is characterized primarily by a great sweeping aside of the past in favor of the present. In this way, modernity is

---

3. Vattimo, *End of Modernity*, 2. Vattimo argues persuasively for an understanding of modernity as progress and overcoming, contrasting these positions with the attempt to get free of such notions of development in postmodernism.

4. Quoted in Toulmin, *Cosmopolis*, 3.

5. First attributed to Bernard of Chartres, one of the first self-proclaimed "*moderni.*" This statement was made a bit more famous by Sir Isaac Newton. Gillespie, *Theological Origins of Modernity*, 3–4.

an ever-increasing fetishization of the present and of the new. When the wheel of progress begins to roll, it does not stop. Rather, the wheel of progress gains momentum and force until it spins out of control. This is the testimony of the modern world. With a more positive affirmation of the human mind and spirit came the defamation of the divine. With electricity came nuclear weapons. With powered water taps and water purification came the machine gun, landmines, and so-called smart bombs. And with modern art and architecture came the fragmentation of human society—and thus loneliness and severe depression. Women and men continue to pay a devastating price and to accept horrific side effects in exchange for the wonderful benefits of modernity.

According to many, if not most, contemporary scholars, the horrific side effects of modernity—seen in the form of war, urban poverty, natural disasters, and the ever-increasing gap between the developed and so-called developing nations—called modernity's progress into question and subsequently caused modernity to crumble and implode. For these thinkers, a new age or era has been born out of the rubble of disbelief, skepticism, and anger over modernity's inability to deliver on its promise of progress and, ultimately, paradise or utopia. This new epistemological stance or position, for lack of a better term, is called "postmodernity."[6] For the purposes of the present work, however, it must be stated clearly that the author assumes the continuation of modernity, and thus "postmodernity" is merely a stance or position made possible and intelligible only within modernity, as a critical reaction to modernity.

The debate still rages as to what this thing called "postmodernity" really is. At the fore of the debate stands the issue of whether "it" is really even an "it," a substance truly distinct and definable over and against modernity. Some point to specific events such as the destruction of the Berlin Wall, while many others point toward World War II and, specifically, the Nazi prison camps, the Russian gulags, and the two atomic bombs dropped on Hiroshima and Nagasaki by the United States as cultural and historical events that brought about the end of modernity.

6. Again, I take the position that postmodernity is not an age or era that comes after the "new," but rather that it is the recognition of what modernity is even when it cannot be overcome. Thus that which is postmodern is only intelligible within a broader framework that is itself modernity. I believe that it is commonplace to treat postmodernity as if it were an age or era succeeding modernity, but I affirm the logic of those such as Vattimo to the contrary. Thus, "postmodernity" is merely a stance or position made possible and intelligible only within modernity, as a critical reaction to modernity.

Then there are others, preferring literary and artistic works, who point to issues or sentiments that betray the crumbling of modernity and the age of Enlightenment, toward an unstable, decentered time when pessimism and doubt about all things, and especially the existence of God, reign supreme. A sampling of the literature and art utilized by this latter group to display postmodernity include the films *Bladerunner* and *The Matrix* trilogy, literary works such as Cervantes' *Don Quixote* and the dark and disturbing writings of Georges Bataille, paintings such as Velázquez's *Las Meninas*, even the biblical story of Abraham and Isaac, and, without overstating the case, anything French! Indeed, for many thinkers, both positively and negatively, a study in postmodernity is necessarily a study *én Francaise*. As Jamie Smith has put it, "Is the Devil from Paris?"[7] There are still others who say that there really is no such thing as postmodernity or postmodernism, preferring to discuss the current milieu in terms of late or hyper modernity. I would tend to align myself with these folks in asking, "If modernity is characterized by the constant pursuit of the new, then how is postmodernity anything more than the latest upgrade to modernity?" Finally, a study in postmodernity reveals that identifying postmodernity is not nearly as simple as the brief description that I have just laid out. Most philosophers, theologians, and literary scholars who deal in this strange arena are often very ambiguous and carefully eclectic in their sources and theories, so that one can never be too sure exactly what is really going on. As Morpheus, that most prominent of the postmodern guides, said to Neo, "One feels a bit like Alice, tumbling through the looking glass."[8] The dizzying effect experienced in such a study is, perhaps, the telltale sign of postmodernity, as each author seems to want the reader not only to read about this thing called postmodernity but, in fact, to experience it for herself in all its strangeness.

To return to the point at hand, however, this is an examination into modernity, and in particular modernity's theological presuppositions. As tempting as it might be to discuss postmodernity in greater detail, for now it must simply be pointed out that one of the chief principles of postmodernity, however one defines or describes it, is a sense of epistemic crisis, or even schizophrenia in terms of identity. The so-called postmodern person asks the question, "Who am I?" and typically believes the only way to find the answer is to rid herself of the traces and

---

7. Smith, *Who's Afraid of Postmodernism?*, 1–30.
8. Quotation from *The Matrix*.

effects of modernity. Surely the irony is apparent, as this project is exactly the same as the modern project—to sweep aside and rise above the past for the sake of progress. The unity of the modern and postmodern is found in the individual, and thus the two are revealed to be one. At her core, the modern person is the center of the world, of the very cosmos. Perhaps the modern individual is now characterized more by doubt and uncertainty than the belief in pure, unbridled progress, but the true center remains the same: the individual. That individual, which is the supreme gift and curse of modernity, continues today to ask the question that she began asking hundreds of years ago: who am I? (The only true difference between the modern and so-called postmodern person is that the modern person stopped asking that question a long time ago in favor of the question, what can I be?[9]) The modern individual, then, for all of her greatness, forgot who she was and became unable to articulate her own identity because she was too interested in what she might become or accomplish. The so-called postmodern individual still has the same goal of becoming, of progress, only she has begun to realize the need to discover, or perhaps rediscover, her identity in order to move forward.

The question of identity, of who the modern person is, must be asked. In examining who the modern person is, we might come to understand the presuppositions of the modern project—presuppositions that for many have been completely ignored at best or forgotten at worst. Michael Allen Gillespie argues that contemporary Western individuals misunderstand themselves because they do not understand the true guiding principles of modernity. In particular, he argues that modernity, instead of being thought of as being primarily atheistic or non-Christian, should be understood as a *metaphyisica specialis*—that is, that modernity is dependent upon a very distinct and purposeful understanding of God, nature, and humanity. Far from being atheistic or nontheistic, modernity is charged with a very particular and new type of theology.

> Post-Enlightenment thought sought to solve the problem of the contradiction of nature and freedom by erasing the ontic distinction between the natural and the human. Before the Enlightenment, *metaphysica specialis* consisted of theology, anthropology, and cosmology, with man floating somewhere between God

9. Here, "to be" is not to be understood as a metaphysics of presence, wherein being is taken to be coincident with meaning. Rather, the postmodern question of being is much less static or fixed than the modern understanding of being; it is being understood more so in terms of becoming à la Heidegger.

and his other creatures. The Enlightenment eliminated theology
from the mix. Post-Enlightenment thought sought to show in
different ways that there was no distinction between the two remaining ontic realms, that is, that there were no distinct realms
of being as philosophy had hitherto imagined.[10]

Thus, what seems to be an eschewing of theology is rather a carefully
calculated adoption of a very different type of theology, one in which
God is removed from the equation and humanity and nature are fused
together and given a quasi-divine status. This is the heart of modernity.[11]

It is argued that Karl Barth is perhaps the greatest modern theologian. To understand his project, then, we must first examine the theological presuppositions of modernity.[12] Seen in this light, it is my hope
that the radical nature of the theological work of Karl Barth will be more
apparent and accessible to the reader. But before we are able to turn to
the work of Karl Barth, or any truly modern thinker, it is necessary first
to examine the origins of modernity in general, and Martin Luther and
his theological reformation (or revolution) in particular. Finally, in order
to properly understand Martin Luther, it is appropriate first to examine

10. Gillespie, *Theological Origins of Modernity,* 280. Note: in all text that is original
to the author, gender neutral language has been employed. In quoted text, however, I
have sought to preserve the original author's language, inclusive or not.

11. Kevin Hart addresses this issue very well in a discussion of the relationship
between Harold Bloom and Maurice Blanchot. Hart sums up Blanchot's position thus:
"the Bible is a work of testimony; it tells us of a covenant formed between God and
human beings. What ties humans and God together is none other than speech. If we
could only detach that testimony from the Bible, remove it from the book, we could
divest it of all traces of a sacred aura and put it to work as ethics. And that, Blanchot
thinks, is exactly what has been slowly happening for centuries and is now emerging
with a particular force." Hart, *Postmodernism,* 125. This is a wonderfully helpful way
of talking about humanity taking over the role once held by God *vis-à-vis* ethics. It
should be further pointed out that Hart describes postmodernity in a very similar way
as I do here. He defines postmodernity as "not a rejection of the modern; it is a series
of reflections on the impossibility of modernity to complete its own projects" (ibid.,
119).

12. This is the position held by theologians such as Bruce McCormack, Paul Jones,
and, oddly enough, Reinhard Hütter. It is not the interpretation of Barth upheld by
the likes of Graham Ward or Stanley Hauerwas, both of whom are hesitant to clas-
sify Barth as a thoroughgoing "modern" theologian. I would venture to say that Barth
is obviously modern in terms of temporality or *Sitz im leben,* but that his theology
displays more than what is commonly characterized as modern. Barth is both modern
and extremely non- or pre-modern. His theology perhaps fits best with the likes of
Athanasius, Cyril, and even Aquinas and Augustine, rather than with Luther, Calvin,
and Moltmann, et al. In this way, Barth's theology is singular and unique.

the radical theological and philosophical shift that took place in the late scholastic period. It is only in understanding this radically new way of conceiving of both God and humanity, known as nominalism, that one can make sense of Luther's peculiarity and his overwhelming anxiety. En route to Barth, therefore, we must delve into the complex history of nominalism, scholasticism, modernity, and Martin Luther.

Nominalism

Nominalism represents a decisive shift, or more accurately, a radical breaking with the theological cosmology out of which it proceeded. Stemming from the work of William of Ockham in particular, who was himself heavily influenced by Duns Scotus, who was in turn influenced by Henry of Ghent and Avicenna, et al., nominalism is founded upon the notion of absolute divine freedom, and in particular power *vis-à-vis* will.[13] Nominalism is thus about the sheer force, reality, and freedom of divine will.[14] Furthermore, "for nominalism, the idea of absolute divine power had as its corollary divine unpredictability."[15] The elevation of God's divine power far above any attempts at human comprehension takes that same power dangerously close to irrationality, non-intelligibility, and even untrustworthiness. For example, "Scotus declared, 'I do not call something contingent because it is not always or necessarily the case, but because its opposite could be actual at the very moment it occurs.'"[16] Consistency, especially on the part of God, simply cannot be counted on.[17] "Nominalism points not toward the dawn of a new enlightenment

13. Frederick Christian Bauerschmidt provides a brilliant and concise description of the shift from the medieval to the modern period, focusing on the role nominalism played in that process. His argument is sophisticated and careful, taking into account the scholarship of especially Heiko Oberman on this subject. Bauerschmidt, *Julian of Norwich and the Mystical Body Politic of Christ*, see esp. ch. 1.

14. Referring to Oberman, Bauerschmidt here points out that however one might parse out the new theological and philosophical positions of nominalism, we should acknowledge that the focus was not human individuality, but "the shared emphasis on the omnipotence of God, and in particular the exploitation of the distinction between God's 'absolute power' (*potentia absoluta dei*) and God's 'ordained power' (*potentia ordinata dei*)." Ibid., 24.

15. Gillespie, *Theological Origins of Modernity*, 66.

16. Quoted in Cunningham, *Genealogy of Nihilism*, 23.

17. Is it any wonder why Descartes would later seek to prove that God was not an omnipotent deceiver?

but toward the dark form of an omnipotent and incomprehensible God."[18] Interestingly, this absolute reverence for divine will stems from a desire to speak positively about human freedom and the human will. To assert human freedom while maintaining absolute divine freedom, many of those in the nominalist school found it helpful to elevate God's power so highly that there was virtually no room left for God in the cosmos. The result of this radical shift in the understanding of both God and humanity shook the very intellectual foundations of the world and arguably continues to do so to this very day.

William of Ockham follows after Scotus and takes nominalism to its logical outcomes. First and foremost, Ockham rejects realism and the scholastic attempt to reconcile theology and philosophy.[19] Philosophy is rejected, naturally, as it is understood to be a human endeavor, one that, moreover, seeks to understand and thus master God. Theology, on the contrary, is understood by Ockham as the reception of divine revelation. God, for Ockham, is completely omnipotent. This further means, for Ockham, that God can and does act directly in the world. God is above every form of rationality, every form of observable law of nature, even previous understandings of God based upon divine revelation. God is completely free in a way that nothing else is. "God is also the only necessary being."[20] For Ockham, it is God that is real, God that is powerful,

---

18. Gillespie, *Nihilism Before Nietzsche*, 23.

19. Ibid., 16.

20. Ibid., 17. Given these claims, it is very curious that on the same page Gillespie makes the claim that "there is no univocity of being [in Ockham's work]." Surely univocity is not Ockham's goal. It might even be arguably true that something more like equivocity is in Ockham's sights. But goal or not, Ockham's system of thought results in a cosmology wherein God's singularity and power are so heavily stressed that God and creatures appear to be utterly unconnected, to the point that God cannot really be apprehended by humanity. The result is a cosmology according to which humans are essentially lost in an abyss of uncertainty, incapable of knowing anything for certain, even something clearly revealed by God. In this system, even something clearly revealed by God—that God is love, for example—must be understood in light of God's radical omnipotence, and so God can and probably will act completely contradictorily toward humanity at any given point. Thus there is no certainty, no universals, no overarching connection between creatures—and certainly not between creatures and their creator, and thus not even a hierarchy of Being. Given all of this, it would seem that despite possibly the best intentions, Ockham's system leads precisely to a univocity of being, for how can any real distinction be made between beings according to the system he has laid out—be they creaturely or divine? No distinction can be made between creatures and certainly not between creation and God, because there is only one real category for Ockham, and that category is God or Being. The only way

and it is God's will upon which everything hangs. While this is orthodox Christian theology, in Ockham we are able to see the result of stretching the limits of orthodoxy in uneven ways. Ockham's legitimate and orthodox concern with emphasizing God's singular necessity and power, however, lead him to dangerous conclusions.

Scotus and those such as William of Ockham who followed after him were concerned that the theological and philosophical systems of many of their colleagues left no room for God's omnipotence or absolute freedom and power. To oversimplify things, Scotus, Ockham, and their followers were concerned that their scholastic contemporaries had domesticated God. Whether or not their point was valid is for another discussion. What is presently important are the two primary outcomes of nominalism. On the one hand, some argue that the nominalism birthed by Scotus and Ockham, as I have briefly shown, leads directly to univocity.[21] Ockham's rejection of realism, as well as any form of overarching connection or relationality between beings, in addition to his rejection of metaphysical community, leads directly and dangerously to a false accounting of individual creatures or beings. Though his intended outcome is to affirm a radicalized autonomy, wherein he can affirm the distinctive will of individual creatures and God, in actuality Ockham is left with only the ability to affirm one reality rather than many separate and distinct realities. Cunningham calls this an "ontology of indistinction," or an "impervious singularity."[22] Such a system is surely not able to affirm the overall picture of God—or humanity, for that matter—elicited from Scripture. In particular, univocity cannot give an account for the covenantal relationship between God and creation articulated and affirmed throughout Scripture.[23] Furthermore, we would do well to heed

---

of accounting for difference, then, would simply be difference of intensity of Being within an overall univocity. Conor Cunningham argues this point very forcefully in his *Genealogy of Nihilism*.

21. Conor Cunningham is representative of this group. Gillespie takes issue with this position, though not directly with Cunningham, as the former's work preceded the latter's.

22. Cunningham, *Genealogy of Nihilism*, 17.

23. The overarching theme in all of Scripture is that of a covenantal bond, like that of marriage, between God and God's people Israel, of which the Church is very much a part—for example, the covenantal promises of Genesis 12 and 17; the entire Gospel according to Matthew, wherein Jesus is portrayed as the fulfillment of the covenant made with the people of Israel; or the account of the day of Pentecost in Acts 2, where the Spirit of the Lord falls on all present, in fulfillment of Jesus' promises.

the warning that univocity, via nominalism, leads directly to nihilism and thus should be avoided at all costs.[24]

Another primary result of nominalism, one with which I am more keenly concerned in the present work, is the type of God that emerges from such a privileging of divine power and will above all else. The God of the nominalists is a mighty, loving, and terrible rogue, a God that cannot be trusted. That God could be thought of in such a way was due almost exclusively to this new revolution of thought which allowed for God's absolute freedom (and power) above all else. As a result, God was so far removed from humanity by the abyss of confusion separating God from creation that God became simply an afterthought, or a formal principle, and thus God lost all real reality. "At the end of the Middle Ages," therefore, "nominalist theology effectively removed God from creation."[25]

And yet God did remain, but in what sense? Some chose to think of God as a formal necessity, as a first cause, or a watchmaker. For these, God was necessary to the world, but only as a first cause, or as an initiator. Accordingly, humanity was now in charge of the world and came to be of central importance.[26] Human freedom and free will became paramount. This was the preferred route taken by many humanist intellectuals of the Renaissance and Enlightenment periods. Opposite to this path, though sharing many similarities indeed, others chose the powerful, erratic, untrustworthy, and even terrible God of the nominalists as the only way to faithfully proclaim God's sovereignty in light of human freedom.[27] It was precisely this God, birthed in large part from the work of Scotus and Ockham, that haunted and plagued a young monk named Martin Luther. In the hands of Luther, the nominalist revolution took on the form of a full-on schism. Virtually nothing would be the same in the Western world after Luther's revolt against the stale corruption of the Church of his day. Wracked by fear and anxiety over the seeming disparity between law and grace, between God's justice and God's love, Luther

24. Drawing upon thinkers from the Radical Orthodoxy sensibility, in general, and John Milbank, in particular, Conor Cunningham has argued this point more forcefully than anyone else. While the particular genealogy is commonly critiqued, I do not believe that the overall move is as contestable as some would like to argue. James K. A. Smith provides a brief but thorough account of many of these critics of Radical Orthodoxy and their positions in his *Introducing Radical Orthodoxy*, 49–60.

25. Dupré, *Passage to Modernity*, 3.

26. Seemingly, there is a natural progression from deism to humanism to nihilism.

27. Notice that God's sovereignty must be affirmed "in light of" human freedom. Humanity, human freedom in particular, is seen as primary within nominalism.

rejected the neat, orderly God of scholasticism in favor of the wild, erratic, and dangerous God of the nominalists.[28] And thus, "only when the early humanist notion of human creativity came to form a combustive mixture with the negative conclusions of nominalist theology did it cause the cultural explosion that we refer to as modernity."[29]

Gerard Manley Hopkins' description of Scotus as the "unraveller" is surely accurate.[30] Scotus and Ockham, et al., successfully unraveled

28. Heiko Oberman goes to great lengths to show the diversity that existed within the "school" of nominalism. Oberman, *Harvest of Medieval Theology*, 196–206.

His discussion of Gregory of Rimini is a case in point. He interprets Gregory as a "right-wing" nominalist, along with Bradwardine, as opposed to the "left-wing" nominalists such as Robert Holcot and Adam Woodham. Further proof of this diversity can be seen in Oberman's discussion of the four "schools" of nominalism in his article "Some Notes on the Theology of Nominalism."

It should be further pointed out that Oberman famously argues for the catholicity of nominalism. His claim is that nominalism is, ultimately, unable to avoid the snares of Pelagianism. That being said, Oberman believes that nominalism reflects a late medieval quest to interpret and appropriate Augustine, and that in the end, aside from the nominalist doctrine of justification, "Nominalism can be regarded as the forerunner of the Tridentine formulation of the relation of Scripture and Tradition and is therefore in agreement with the beliefs basic and characteristic for what has come to be known as Roman Catholicism." Despite its many "problems," therefore, nominalism, according to Oberman, maintains catholicity. Oberman, *Harvest of Medieval Theology*, 423–28. I would argue that Oberman is, of course, correct to point out the complexity and diversity within nominalism. Likewise, he is right to say that nominalism is a quest to understand and appropriate Augustine, and that as such, much of nominalism was in line with the positions of the Church at the time of key figures such as Ockham and Biel, as well as the present-day Church. But to argue that nominalism itself maintains catholicity is surely a bit of a stretch. Perhaps it is better to say that the pursuit that is nominalism, or the questions raised by nominalism, are catholic, but the system that results from this search is not. Given the range and variety of nominalism, so adeptly explicated by Oberman, there are likewise many positions within nominalism as a whole that are catholic, but to then argue for the catholicity of the entire movement is surely too much. The same could be said of the theology of Mormons and Jehovah's Witnesses, or perhaps of the Knights Templar and the Free Masons. To argue that overall these groups maintain catholicity, though, is simply preposterous. Regardless, Oberman's work stands as perhaps the finest of its kind and is surely more right and more helpful than the contrary. Nominalism is certainly part of the Church's internal quest for faithfulness, orthodoxy, and solidarity with early thinkers such as Augustine. I would argue, however, that the end result does lie outside the parameters of catholicity, despite Oberman's superbly argued thesis.

29. Dupré, *Passage to Modernity*, 3.

30. From Hopkins, "Duns Scotus' Oxford," cited by Cunningham, *Genealogy of Nihilism*, 22. Of course, being a modern, Hopkins predicates this title upon Scotus in praise of his focus on singularity, or *haecceity*, which he reads in Scotus' *Ordinatio* II, d.3.1.2.48.

the dominant understanding of the relationship between God and the world. The result of this unraveling, as Dupré has noted, was a great cultural explosion that we have since come to know as modernity. Without exploring its theological origins, this cultural explosion simply cannot be understood.

The (Not So) Hidden Theology of Modernity

Having briefly examined nominalism, it remains now to examine just how nominalism contributed to the development of, and perhaps even the logic of, modernity. Michael Allen Gillespie has masterfully connected the dots from then to now in his *Theological Origins of Modernity*. To round out our understanding of nominalism and the suppositions of modernity, therefore, let us examine Gillespie's text in more depth.

Modernity, according to Gillespie, did not arise out of nothing. Neither did it develop out of medieval thought. Rather, there was an enormous crisis between the medieval and modern periods. In the middle of this crisis occurred the nominalist revolution, the Renaissance, and the Enlightenment. These three movements in history participated in the destruction of the dominant cosmology of the medieval period. Only out of this rubble could something like modernity spring forth. And yet modernity often veils itself in an essential atheism or non-theism, and thus a form of *creatio ex nihilo*. Gillespie argues that nothing could be further from the truth. He asserts that rather than being atheistic or non-theistic, modernity arose as a result of a significant theological and metaphysical shift and that to understand modernity as somehow being devoid of, or free from, a specific theological metaphysics is to fundamentally misunderstand modernity. "To understand the shape of modernity as it has come down to us, we thus need to examine carefully the origins of modernity, to look behind the veil that modernity itself has drawn to conceal its origins. The origins of modernity therefore lie not in human self-assertion or in reason but in the great metaphysical and theological struggle that marked the end of the medieval world and that transformed Europe in the three hundred years that separate the medieval and the modern worlds."[31]

In particular, says Gillespie, modernity was (or is) "a series of attempts to answer the fundamental questions that arose out of the

---

31. Gillespie, *Theological Origins of Modernity*, 12.

nominalist revolution."[32] "Modernity in this sense was the result of an ontic revolution within metaphysics that accepted the ontological ground that nominalism established but that saw the other realms of being through this new naturalistic lens. . . . Thus, while modern metaphysics began by turning away from both the human and the divine toward the natural, it was able to do so only by reinterpreting the human and the divine naturalistically."[33]

Gillespie's thesis should be clear. Modernity is and has a distinct metaphysics and thus a theology. Modernity is not the eschewing of all theology, but only of a particular type of theology, and the critical appropriation of both humanism and nominalism in particular. Modernity, in short, is an attempt to answer the question of how God and creatures are related. The answer to that question would have devastating cultural, political, and religious effects—effects that are still being felt today.

As has already been demonstrated, a conversation over the first modern person or thinker is a somewhat unfruitful enterprise, for there are typically as many answers to this query as there are questioners. For his part, Gillespie poetically dodges this difficulty by choosing a rather arbitrary day on which it is believed that three dominant figures in the birth of modernity happened to gather in the same place for the same event, calling this the birthplace of modernity. That place, says Gillespie, was the Cathédrale Notre-Dame des Doms in Avignon, the year was 1326, and the three men were Petrarch, William of Ockham, and Meister Eckhart.[34] Each man, in his own way, challenged the premises of scholastic metaphysics in a way that would have long-standing consequences.

Petrarch was one of the first to emphasize human identity in purely autonomous terms. The human being, for Petrarch, was central in that humans could at least know, trust, and rely upon themselves.[35] William of Ockham, taking this a step further, emphasized the great gulf between God and God's creation. Ockham would ultimately argue that the result of this chasm between God and creation is that humans cannot truly

32. Ibid., 261.

33. Ibid., 262. These other realms being human and divine, or, to be more specific, human freedom and divine will.

34. Ibid., 3, 34, 43. This is not to say that Gillespie believes any of these three men to be the most important thinker in modernity or the founder of modernity. Rather, he points to these three in such a way that places a certain shared responsibility for the development of modernity primarily, though not exclusively, onto their shoulders.

35. As opposed to God, for whom the same cannot be said.

know God, who is understood to be hidden, mysterious, and even terrifying. Finally, Eckhart seeks to explore this chasm in mystical terms, and thus provides a logical bridge between Petrarch and Ockham. Eckhart embraces a nominalist understanding of God, and so for him, "God is pure willing, pure activity, or pure power, and the world in its becoming is divine will, is this God . . . the world is the incarnation, the body of God, and he is in the world as the soul is in the body, omnipresent as the motive principle."[36] The resulting mixture of these three men would lead almost directly to Luther.

Francesco Petrarch

For more than a millennium, the tripartite cosmological view and its resulting effects on the political milieu held firm. God was above, hell was below, and the earth—and the city or state in particular—was in between. But as the medieval period began to crumble, so too did the orderly hierarchical view of God and human society begin to erode. Emperors and popes began to argue and even make war against one another, political strife reigned, and diseases grew into epidemics. During this time, Francesco Petrarch "looked not to the city, God, or the cosmos for support but into himself, finding an island of stability and hope not in citizenship but in human individuality."[37] Petrarch reflected on the reality of the world around him and, drawing upon Heraclitus, saw all life, and human life in particular, in terms of strife. Looking inward, Petrarch believed that "far greater is the war that takes place within our souls."[38] To achieve victory in the persistent war within, Petrarch looked back to the ancients such as Virgil, Horace, Cicero, and Seneca. In the ancients, Petrarch found the appropriate way to order one's desires or loves around the love of fame. It was the love of fame, according to Petrarch, that was "the strongest spur to virtue."[39]

For Petrarch, the love of fame, and the resulting pursuit of the virtues, was the key towards a future life in heaven. In Petrarch's understanding, humans—indeed all creatures—are mortal and must perish. Virtue, however, maintains one even after death and ushers one into heaven. As

36. Gillespie, *Theological Origins of Modernity*, 35.
37. Ibid., 46.
38. Ibid., 49.
39. Ibid., 53.

a result, Petrarch's view of Christianity was more classic than scholastic. Petrarch's Christianity, which can easily be contested, was very much mediated by a Platonic and Stoic reading of Augustine, and especially the *Confessions*.[40] Thus, Petrarch's understanding of Christianity was more about the classical understanding of contemplation than it was about charity, for example. Human individuality, and the reflective retreat into the interiority of the mind, was paramount for Petrarch. This is so much the case that Petrarch even viewed nature as strange or alien. "His actual experience of nature, then, appears to have consisted in little more than horror at the sight of the huge, formless space below."[41] Petrarch does, arguably, gravitate more toward Christianity later in his life, especially the doctrine of the Trinity, but the human individual, and the mind in particular, was always at the center of his religious and intellectual pursuits.

Amidst a world wracked by strife, an increasingly corrupt Church, and chaotic theology, Petrarch offers a similar and yet drastically different vision of human life than that which was commonly espoused by the Church of his day. Essentially, argues Petrarch, "we cannot control God but we can control ourselves." As a result, the best thing that one could do with one's self was to study oneself rather than God. Following Petrarch, there was a significant decrease in emphasis on the fallen view of humanity, and an increase in the view of humanity as the *imago Dei*.[42] Out of this shift came the monumental movement known as humanism, the origins of which Petrarch is almost single-handedly responsible for.

> Petrarch set his contemporaries on a twofold journey. The first phase of this journey led inward to the unexplored territory of a self filled with passions and desires that were no longer something mundane and unspiritual that had to be extirpated or constrained but that were instead a reflection of each person's individuality and that consequently deserved to be expressed, cultivated, and enjoyed. The second phase of the journey led backwards to an ancient but now suddenly relevant past filled with courageous and high-minded individuals who had won fame and a kind of immortality by cultivating their own individuality.[43]

40. Ibid., 55–57.

41. Dupré, *Passage to Modernity*, 45. Here Dupré is citing Petrarch's rather curious move to describe not the view from the top of the mountain, but rather that which is interior to himself in his account of his ascent of Mount Ventoux.

42. Gillespie, *Theological Origins of Modernity*, 71.

43. Ibid., 70.

As Gillespie notes, Petrarch's originality can certainly be debated, and he is often forgotten today, but his marked importance in the birth of humanism should not be overlooked.

William of Ockham

It can perhaps be said that Duns Scotus is to blame for nominalism. Many genealogies of modern social and religious thought make this claim. And though perhaps it is fair to say that Scotus certainly got the proverbial ball rolling, Gillespie is correct to point out that it is William of Ockham who takes Scotus's work and critically appropriates the arguments of Roscelin, Abelard, and Henry of Ghent, to take nominalism to its logical conclusion.[44] For Ockham, and his famous "razor," there can be no universals, and so we as humans should seek to employ as few universals as possible.[45] Ockham does believe that we as finite beings cannot "make sense of the world without universals."[46] Since there are no true universals, however, Ockham claims that humanity remains closer to the real the fewer universals it makes use of. So, according to Ockham's famous illustration, God did not have to send God's Son in the form of a man. He could have just as easily sent Him in the form of a rock or even a donkey! Assuming that God's Son had to be a man is to assume a universal category or constant, which will, eventually, assume priority even over God. Only God's will, which is ultimately unknowable, can be understood to be universal.

Ockham challenged everything. Nothing could be counted on, as everything was ultimately unstable, disconnected, and rather arbitrary. The revolutionary quality to Ockham's thought can be seen even more clearly in his view of human freedom in regard to morality. Ockham rejected scholasticism's teleological view of nature. Nature, accordingly, does not help humanity in any way to move toward beatitude or the good. Humans simply are; we simply exist in the world. Moreover, human agency becomes ultimately an unimportant category, for according to Ockham,

44. Ibid., 22.

45. Ibid., 23. Gillespie points out the varying ways that Ockham employs his so-called razor: 1) Do not multiply universals needlessly. 2) "No plurality should be assumed unless it can be proved by reason, or by experience, or by some infallible authority." 3) "One should affirm no statement as true or maintain that something exists unless forced to do so by self-evidence, that is, by revelation, experience, or logical deduction from a revealed truth or a proposition verified by observation."

46. Ibid.

surely God is not moved or convinced in any way of humanity's goodness or sinfulness based upon human actions in the world. In this way, God does not save or damn based upon anything that humans do. Whatever divine logic is behind salvation and damnation may as well be thought of as arbitrariness for Ockham, because the idea that somehow human decisions force God's hands in one way or the other is preposterous. Thus, for Ockham, "there is no utilitarian motive to act morally," and therefore "the only reason for moral action is gratitude."[47]

The implications of these views are astounding. Ockham would have been shocked by the notion that his teachings, which he believed to elevate both human and divine freedom, actually result in univocity, nihilism, and/or atheism. Likewise, the notion that his teachings would eventually serve as the catalyst for the sundering apart of the largest and most powerful organization on the planet, the Catholic Church, would have seemed outlandish. But surely these charges must be levied against him. As early as 1326, Ockham's teachings were censured—and from 1339 to 1347 repeatedly condemned. "But his influence continued to grow," writes Gillespie, "and in the one hundred and fifty years after his death nominalism became one of the most powerful intellectual movements in Europe."[48]

Ockham, primarily utilizing Scotus, effectively removed God from the cosmos, resulting in the collapsing of divinity and humanity in upon itself. Moreover, due to the radical way in which Ockham understood universals, humanity was "free" to do as it pleased in the moral arena due to its utter inability to affect its own end either way. The result is either a God who is vacant from the cosmos, on the one hand, or one who is hidden altogether and therefore terrifying, on the other.

47. Ibid., 24. Ockham states, "For every righteous will is conformed to right reason. But the will by which God predestines this person and not another is righteous. Therefore, it is conformed to right reason. Therefore, there is a reason why He predestines this person and not another. But the reason is not in God, since for His part God is equally related to all, inasmuch as He does not play favorites. Therefore, there is a reason in something else, and only in the predestinate person. Therefore, etc." William of Ockham, *Ordinatio* I, d.41,q.u. Likewise, "In some cases, foreseen good use of free will is a reason for predestination in the predestinate; and in other cases, there is no reason for predestination in the predestinate, but they are predestined simply because God wants to give them eternal life." Quoted in McCord Adams, *William Ockham*, 2:1331. If some are predestined for redemption and others for eternal punishment, therefore, both are shown to be God's grace. Thus, the only reason for one to act morally whatsoever is gratitude—but surely not requirement.

48. Gillespie, *Theological Origins of Modernity*, 27.

Meister Eckhart

Meister Eckhart's work is best understood as an attempt to worship the unknown, hidden God of nominalism. For Eckhart, as God is the only true being, creaturely beings are only real in that either they "are" God or God somehow is "in" them.[49] The result of this is a curious version of panentheism that ends up looking a great deal like animism. Essentially, God cannot be equated with the quiddity of creatures, for to equate God with creaturely substance would be to limit God. This is not a problem, in that it is reflective of orthodox Christian theology. The problem is that Eckhart takes this to the extent that creaturely existence is either understood as a part of God, or God is understood to be animating creatures.[50] Eckhart contends that God is not the "what" but the "how" of creaturely existence. Much like in George Lucas's *Star Wars* saga, God is the pure will, power, or force behind all existence. In addition to panentheism, Gillespie points out that Eckhart's theology actually lends itself rather well to materialism, even atheistic materialism at that. Basically, if one takes the God of nominalism as articulated by Ockham, and then affirms that this God is in everything, as articulated by Eckhart, then one ends up with a system of pure, unnecessary, non-purposeful motion. In the end there is no real difference between a nominalist cosmology and an atheistic one. "The existence or nonexistence of God is irrelevant for the understanding of nature, since he can neither increase nor decrease the

49. Ibid., 35.

50. Recently, John Milbank has put forth a very original and curious argument in favor of Eckhart, and what Milbank calls his "radicalization of orthodoxy" in particular. Milbank defines this as "saying that *both* pantheism and acosmism are true: or that it is true both that 'there is only the world' (but including worlds of which we may not know) and that (1) God 'needs me'; I myself can judge God or see all that God sees; and that (2) in its innermost ground, the created soul (and, indeed, the Augustinian 'seminal reason' of every created thing) is identical with the uncreated deity." John Milbank and Slavoj Zizek, *Monstrosity of Christ*, 189. Basically, Milbank likes Eckhart (though Milbank's Eckhart is as far from nominalism as is possible) because he sees in him the possibility, with a bit of creativity, of a theology based in paradox. In essence, Milbank believes that Eckhart's theology can allow for a more robust philosophy of immanence than even atheistic materialism can offer, as well as a more robust theology of transcendence than most Christian theology can offer. Understood in this way, a radically immanentized world can coexist with a radically transcendent God, in a non-conflictual manner. I see much possibility in this argument, and am obviously a proponent of a theology of paradox. That being said, I'm unsure as to whether Eckhart is really the best choice here, and if he can truly be freed from his nominalist "baggage," in order to successfully do what Milbank wants him to do.

chaos of radical individuality that characterizes existence. Science thus does not need to take this God or Scripture into account in its efforts to come to terms with the natural world and can rely instead on experience alone. *'Atheistic' materialism thus has a theological origin in the nominalist revolution.*"[51]

As Cunningham points out, Eckhart even instructs his readers to "love God as 'non-God.'"[52] Moreover, Bernard McGinn argues that Meister Eckhart is the chief exponent of divine nothingness, because for Eckhart, "there is no 'God,' at least as humans could ever conceive him."[53] The emphasis on human imperceptibility is clear, but the effect of the position that there is no "God" is also quite apparent as well.[54]

It would seem that God or no God, Eckhart's system remains the same.[55] God was everywhere for Eckhart, and thus God was nowhere— or God is everything and thus nothing is God, or God is (no-)thing. And thus Eckhart provides the logical framework that would allow nominalism to spread like wildfire amidst the flourishing of modernity, be it in the religious or atheistic camp.[56] With each new condemnation, the logic of nominalism grew and grew. Soon, nominalism was in fact the dominant religious or nonreligious mindset. In this way, nominalism became the seed for and the very logic of modernity. And yet, even as modernity began to rise and grow in stature, it began to crack and crumble under the weight of corruption and skepticism. The result of this was an unbelievably volatile religious and political climate in Europe. Into this

51. Ibid., 36. Atheistic materialism is not identical with The Secular, but the former is certainly a significant factor or agent within the latter. And so, this is surely very similar to the point that is powerfully argued by John Milbank, that the Secular is the bastard child of Christendom or the Church. See Milbank, *Theology and Social Theory*.

52. Cunningham, *Genealogy of Nihilism*, 260.

53. McGinn, "*Vere tu es Deus Absconditus*," 103.

54. It is important to note that McGinn argues that for Eckhart, the resulting situation should not produce fear and anxiety. Rather, it is the cessation of all experience.

55. In this way, Eckhart surely played a seminal role in the development of agnosticism.

56. Gillespie masterfully shows how the thinking of Petrarch, Ockham, and Eckhart led to Francis Bacon, who, as perhaps the most important modern thinker, essentially gave birth to the two dominant schools of thought on modernity. On the one hand, Gillespie shows how Bacon led to Descartes, who in turn led to Leibniz, Malebranche, Spinoza, Kant, Fichte, Hegel, Schopenhauer, and most of the rest of Continental philosophy. On the other hand, Gillespie shows how Bacon led to Hobbes, who in turn led to Locke, Hume, Mill, and the rest of the Anglo-American philosophers.

darkening landscape came Martin Luther, perhaps the most important nominalist of them all.

Luther and His Hidden God: The *Deus Absconditus*

Born in 1483, Luther's life and work stand as a signpost for the crumbling of medieval Europe, and the subsequent and inevitable rise of modernity. Luther was a fiery, insatiable young man, unwilling to accept the theological and practical stagnation of so much of Christendom. He was preoccupied with personal piety, as well as a robust (to say the least) view of hell, the devil, and the latter's involvement in the world—and with Luther in particular. Luther was a restless, emotional, and passionate man. He was both fearless and plagued by fear. He was, in short, a man for whom the world has since found no equal.

Luther was born "the son of a Mohra peasant who became a Mansfield miner, a husky, hardworking, frugal, humorless, choleric anticleric who loathed the Church yet believed in hell—which, in his imagination, existed as a frightening underworld toward which men were driven by cloven-footed demons, elves, goblins, satyrs, ogres, and witches, and from which they could be rescued only by benign spirits."[57]

The child of a very different era than our own, Luther was frequently punished by both his parents in a fashion that by any definition seems to verge on child abuse. It is safe to say that Luther inherited from his parents and his upbringing many of the character traits that can be used to caricature him to this day. Luther could not help inheriting the pagan or common mystical beliefs of the age, which very much included a preoccupation with the devil and hell. As a matter of fact, Luther's writings, especially his more personal writings, are filled with descriptions of personal conflicts with the devil—some spiritual, but most physical.[58] Moreover, though he would indeed become a very pious, spiritual man,

---

57. Manchester, *World Lit Only by Fire*, 137.

58. Perhaps my favorite of such stories of personal physical conflicts with the devil is the story related by William Manchester of the feces fight that took place between Luther and the devil. Manchester claims that while many pious Luther scholars say that it was an ink fight, Luther himself used the term *Scheiss* or shit, according to Philipp Melanchthon, saying that afterwards, "having been worsted . . . the Demon departed indignant and murmuring to himself after having emitted a crepitation of no small size, which left a foul stench in the chamber for several days afterwards." Manchester, *World Lit Only By Fire*, 139.

it is safe to say that Luther inherited the misgivings of his parents toward the church—a view that was quite reflective of many common people of the time. Finally, from a psychological perspective, the constant fear in which Luther lived as a child would continue on into adulthood, only the fear would be directed toward a different, more powerful father figure: God.[59]

Luther spent much of his early academic career at the university in Erfurt, which had a long tradition of nominalism. In fact, just four years prior to Luther's matriculation at Erfurt, two professors there, Jodokus Trutfetter and Bartholomaeus Arnoldi, held a public debate at which "they succeeded in formulating the common core of nominalism and of developing its fundamental principles into a cohesive program," thus uniting the two dominant trends of nominalism into one school.[60] Luther would spend four years at Erfurt, where he would eventually finish second out of seventeen candidates for the degree of master of liberal arts. Then, as the result of a somewhat rash vow made to St. Anne during a severe thunderstorm in the year 1505, Luther entered a monastery in the Augustinian order. His vow might have been rash, but it was kept with great tenacity. Luther was known for being incredibly devout. In fact, he so fully threw himself into his new profession that later in life, he came to believe that the strong asceticism he adopted during these years, which included almost continuous fasting and self-mortification, had done his body permanent harm.[61] Despite the young Luther's extreme asceticism, he remained restless in his faith. A trip to Rome did more harm than good, for in Rome Luther came face to face with the some of the worst corruptions of the late medieval Church. And so, racked by fear, anxiety, and doubt, Luther transferred to Wittenberg, hoping to find solace and spiritual refreshment. There, Luther met Johann von Staupitz, a man who, unlike all others, seemed to be able to understand and guide Luther in a beneficial way. After a good deal of counsel, teaching, and prayer,

59. I will not address this and other issues of Luther's personality. I mention them because perhaps more than anyone else in the history of the world, Luther's peculiar idiosyncrasies helped changed almost everything about the Western world, if not the entire world. He was a complex man, and such issues—and their effects upon Luther as well as the world that we moderns or postmoderns inherit—need to be investigated.

60. Oberman, *Luther*, 118.

61. González, *History of Christian Thought*, 3:30.

Staupitz decided that Luther was best suited to study, become a Doctor, and teach at the university.[62]

Luther found himself to be well suited for academic study, and he poured himself into languages and especially biblical study. Luther found many answers to the problems he faced in his engagement with Scripture, yet he also faced new dilemmas. Perhaps most important, during this time, Luther came to understand that his biggest theological problem was "one of sin and grace, or of justice and love."[63] Luther was preoccupied by the question, How could sinful, broken humanity please the holy, righteous God? Luther saw God and the world as opposites, and therefore his theology takes on the form of juxtaposition and conflict. He was quick to juxtapose the theology of the cross with the theology of glory. Luther also drew a sharp distinction between the law and grace, and so he was almost Marcion-like in his elevation and preference of the New Testament over the Old Testament.[64] These and other examples demonstrate that Luther was a mystical theologian, a dialectical theologian, and a nominalist.

Luther inherited a theological world that was shattering under the demise of the medieval or Thomistic synthesis between the mind and the world. The cosmos was no longer understood in terms of harmony. Rather, incongruence, discord, and even strife were increasingly common ways of conceiving of the cosmos and of humanity's place therein. The nominalists greeted alleged universals as mere names, or *nomina*.

> The followers of the via moderna dared to tread a new, uncertain, and controversial path: sensory perception of reality does not lead to the cognition of universal realities but to abstract thought. Universals are the result of such abstractions and are devoid of independent reality. What is real is the individual, the human person as a unique entity perceived by the senses. It is the human intellect that assembles the many perceptions of individual persons into the universal concept of "mankind." "Mankind" as a universal concept is not a real entity existing outside the human mind; it is a "name" (*nomen*) conceived by the mind and based on convention. Such names or concepts provide the scientist or philosopher with comprehensible systems for ordering the wealth of particular phenomena. Since

62. Ibid., 32.

63. Ibid.

64. Luther's similarity to Marcion can perhaps best be seen in his juxtaposition of the law and the Gospel, and as a result, his juxtaposition between Moses and Christ. This is explained well in Pelikan, *Christian Tradition*, 4:166–82.

these systems are constructs of reason and based on experience, they possess no independent reality; and being models, they always require verification—by means of the sensually perceivable reality of the particular. If abstract concepts are allowed to develop lives of their own, the link between thought and reality becomes either speculative or dangerously ideological—and usually both at once.[65]

As a result of nominalism, reality no longer made sense as it had previously. One could no longer take for granted that what the mind perceived was identical to what was really there. In fact, one could no longer take for granted that the "real world" was real at all.[66] Nominalism called reason itself into question, for reason, as beautiful and magnificent as it might be, was not free from the traces of sin. As such, according to Luther, reason "remains under the power of the devil."[67] As a result, Luther, like the nominalists before, was forced to call everything into question. Luther's elevated view of faith, as well as his mysticism, allowed God's existence to remain unquestioned. Although God's existence was not questioned, God's relationship to the world was, as was the ability of humanity to know and depend upon God.

For the highly biblically minded Luther, the effects of nominalism were to be seen primarily in the relationship between God and the world, between sin and grace, and between the individual person—namely, Luther—and his personal relationship with God.[68] It is safe to say that if the world, despite one's personal experience of it, is virtually unknown due to the fact that it cannot be trusted even to be real, the same must be said for God. And so for Luther, while we can know God, this knowledge is only partial or limited, in that God is hidden and essentially unknown. What

65. Oberman, *Luther,* 117.

66. In a very real sense, nominalism broke apart the world and made it necessary for someone like Descartes to come and put it all together again—something that for some was accomplished quite well in Descartes' famous *cogito ergo sum,* and for others was only made worse by the philosopher's dictum.

67. Luther, "Disputation Concerning Man," 138–39 (thesis 24).

68. I do not intend the phrase "personal relationship" here in the way it is commonly used today by many evangelical Christians. Such a usage would surely be anachronistic. Rather, I am referring to the very personal nature of much of Luther's writing, especially as he depicts himself and his relation to the cosmos and to God. As the quote above from Oberman indicates, nominalism made it increasingly difficult to talk about humanity or mankind as a whole, and so the nominalist Luther would often talk about the one person he knew to be real and who was having the experiences of the world and of God that he wanted to convey: himself.

we can know of God, God has revealed in Jesus Christ, but that revelation itself should cause humanity to grovel and confess its own sinfulness and ignorance. The revelation of God in Christ, for Luther, is a revelation of God's grace, but due to human sin, it is, in actuality, a revelation of God's wrath. We cannot claim to know God truly, as God is God and we are not. What we can know, however, is our utter imperfection and sinfulness.

In the fiery, devout person of Martin Luther, these types of theological and philosophical concerns grew to dominate the Western world. No longer did the cosmos fit together in an orderly fashion. No longer was humanity permitted to speak about God as if it could "know" God completely. That which can be known of God derives solely from the revelation of God in Christ, and specifically the *theologia crucis*. Practically speaking, apart from the cross, God is unknown, and that which has been revealed should cause humanity to tremble in fear. God's judgment and wrath, directed perhaps more than anywhere else at the Church, became paramount subjects for preachers and theologians, who, like Luther, had grown tired of the idolatry and whoredom of so much of the contemporary Church. In Luther, reform came not only to the Church and to the world, but also to the very intellectual makeup of the Western mind. The primary theological and philosophical position that shaped and formed these reforms was nominalism, with the logic of this new system being, for the most part, dialectic.

At this point I should note that in the preceding pages, Martin Luther, one of the most singularly important figures in the entire history of Christianity, has been examined and discussed in an almost mercenary fashion. By this I mean to say that for the purposes of the present work, only a very quick sketch of Luther's life and work has been provided. The goal is purely and simply to show that Luther was a nominalist, that the way he envisioned God was therefore the *Deus absconditus*, and secondarily, that this position carries with it, and depends upon, the logic of dialectic. Taken for granted, therefore, is Luther's immense effect upon the Western world, indeed the entire world. The reform that Luther sought to bring about in a Church mired in corruption was surely necessary, and his translation of the Bible into the vernacular of the people helped pave the way for many good and important changes in both the Church and the world. Luther himself was essentially an event, which like other great world events is a marker of the changing of the times and of thought. It is precisely for these reasons that I have skipped over so much of Luther—of work that has already been done, and done very well. It is my belief that along with the great catalogue of world-changing sermons, lectures, written works, and disputations that Luther passed along to future generations, necessarily came nominalism and the *Deus absconditus*. These two philosophical and theological positions—which I believe together form a comprehensive cosmology—aided by dialectic, of course, became the dominant theological and philosophical framework for burgeoning modernity and would eventually lead to, among other things, nihilism.

Excursus: Roman Catholicism's Alternate Modernity

Nominalism and its effects are not exclusive to Protestantism. Of course, nominalism arose long before the idea of a split in the Roman Church ever existed. For the most part, however, those who would remain faithful to the Roman Church after the Reformation were highly critical of nominalism. Moreover, as Luther and his theological progeny gained momentum, the Roman Church's Counter-Reformation solidified its position as primarily anti- or non-nominalist.[69] Within the Roman Church, though, there has always been, and will always be, much room for diverging philosophies. Still, the Roman Catholic Church, after the Reformation, struggled more with the false doctrine of pure nature than with the cosmos-splitting nominalism of Luther, Ockham, and Scotus.[70]

69. In this way, it might be argued that nominalism, rather than the more popular doctrines of *sola fide* and *sola scriptura*, is actually the core doctrine of Protestantism. This of course does not mean that all Protestants are therefore nominalists, just as all Protestants do not subscribe to *sola scriptura* or *sola fide*, nor does it mean that those who do commonly affirm these doctrines mean the same thing when they affirm said doctrines. Rather, it is more plausible to say that nominalism played a crucial role in the inception and development of Protestantism. It would further mean, therefore, that nominalism will always be a point of temptation for Protestants. Being a nominalist and being tempted by nominalism are two very different things, and I would venture to say that it is never wholly wrong or regrettable to wrestle with a doctrine that one cannot ultimately affirm.

70. Henri de Lubac makes this argument about pure nature in his book *Surnaturel*. Cardinal de Lubac later reworked his thesis, after being chastised by the Vatican in the papal encyclical *Humani Generis* (1950), and released it in two volumes in 1965: *Augustinianism and Modern Theology*, and *The Mystery of the Supernatural*. Pope Pius XII's *Humani Generis* (August 12, 1950) may be found online: http://www.vatican. va/holy_father/pius_xii/encyclicals/documents/hf_p-xii_enc_12081950_humani-generis_en.html. Pure nature, which is a perversion of Thomism and Augustinianism, claimed Henri de Lubac, is a modern development, derived primarily from the Thomistic commentators, and not from Thomas (or Augustine) himself. Pure nature, according to de Lubac, is the view that human nature, *on its own*, is capable

Thus, as the non-Roman Catholic world was struggling with nominalism and its effects, the Roman Catholic world was dealing with very different issues. Rather than wrenching the cosmos apart, many Roman Catholics struggled with collapsing it in upon itself.[71]

This very different struggle helped draw further distinctions between Roman Catholics and Protestants. As a result, I would argue that the Roman Catholic world has had a very different experience of modernity than its Protestant counterparts. As we have seen, modernity, at least for most Europeans and North Americans,[72] has been framed

of achieving its proper end, beatitude, without the necessity of divine assistance. The argument goes, as it is put forth in *Humani Generis*, paragraph 26, et al., that it is to limit God's sovereignty to believe that God could not and did not create creatures completely capable of achieving beatitude on their own. Played out to its logical conclusion, pure nature would create a world of pure immanence, where secular atheistic humanism would be on par with Catholic humanism, in that neither has any need of transcendence. This world of pure nature, then, would be a purely equivocal or univocal world as well, in that human language would in no way be able to point toward or participate in anything greater than the given moment for the former, or human language would have only one sense or meaning, in that the supernatural and natural would be completely collapsed in upon each other, creating only one field of meaning in the case of the latter. As opposed to pure nature, de Lubac argues for a sort of grace-nature wherein human creaturely existence and *telos* is a pure gift of grace. Nature, then, authentic, pure nature, naturally desires for supernatural fulfillment, which it cannot achieve on its own. It is indeed just as St. Augustine said at the very beginning of his *Confessions*: "You stir man to take pleasure in praising you, because you have made us for yourself, and our heart is restless until it rests in you" (I.i.1). Humanity apart from God, therefore, is a lonely, toiling, *restless* creature. Humanity, however, with God's assistance, may achieve beatitude *in God alone*. Human nature, then, exists always already in need of supernatural grace to achieve the end it naturally desires: beatitude. Grace-nature, for de Lubac, is always longing and searching for that which it cannot attain on its own. In this way it is not a mere passive receptacle but something quite active. Like its counterpart, nominalism, pure nature represented a dangerous temptation for Roman Catholics. De Lubac and the rest of the French *Ressourcément* theologians recognized this and sought to ensure that such a teaching would not take hold of the Church. The result, Vatican II, was perhaps the greatest shift in the Roman Catholic Church since the time of the Reformation.

71. Clearly this temptation can be understood as a form of univocity, and pure nature certainly can be labeled as such. It is interesting, then, given Cunningham's thesis that nominalism, which would seem to be equivocity rather than univocity, is in fact a subtle and insidious form of univocity that leads inevitably toward nihilism. It might be safe to conclude, then, that played out to its logical conclusion, equivocity and univocity result in one and the same end, that being nihilism.

72. This is surely a very "Western" argument, in terms of the modern world and the cultural, religious, and political barriers that separate much of the "West" from the "East." Interestingly, it is being argued by many that a similar reformation is taking

by a belief in a wild and unpredictable God, a God whose love, even, evokes a strong sense of fear and anxiety. Thus the bulwark for much of the modern world is fear and anxiety about God and one's salvation. This is certainly the case for much of Protestantism. For many, including Luther, this framework offers great incentive for piety. With time, however, and with the steady increase of political and religious strife and conflict, it became easier to simply leave God out of the cosmological equation altogether.[73] The resulting dominant philosophy for modernity can therefore be said to be dialectic. Dialectic helps make sense out of a wholly unknown (and possibly terrifying) God and that God's relationship to creation. This becomes evident in the influential work of Hegel, who of course inherits this propensity toward dialectic from Luther. The leaning toward dialectic can be traced further back through all the great nominalists and finally to Heraclitus and Thucydides, who conceived of all existence as struggle and ultimately war.[74] Thus, for Protestants, conflict became the dominant epistemological category for understanding existence.[75] The overarching framework for this shift, which takes place primarily within Protestantism, is nominalism, which provides the logic for dialectic.

Dialectic, of course, existed long before nominalism; we may trace it back to Plato. With the inception of modernity, however, and

place right now within Islam. If this is the case, one can only wonder how great the results of this reformation will be, as Islam continues to grow in numbers and strength across the globe.

73. Charles Taylor has documented this wonderfully in *A Secular Age*.

74. Hobbes would develop a large-scale political system based upon this same observation a few millennia later.

75. David Bentley Hart argues this masterfully in his book *The Beauty of the Infinite*. Hart, of course, is concerned with much more than just modern Protestantism. Hart's contention is that the Church, especially the Western Church, has been seduced by its ancient foe, Gnosticism—and through Gnosticism, dialectic, and nominalism, it has traded its ontology of peace for one of conflict and violence. Hart argues time and again in his book that theology must be liberated from "apologetic dialectic, in which it has no ultimate stake, and calls it again to its proper idiom: a proclamation of the story of peace posed over against the narrative of violence, a hymnody rising up around the form of Christ offered over against the jubilant dithyrambs of Dionysius, the depiction of an eternal beauty advanced over and against the depiction of a sempiternal sublime" (93). Nietzsche, argues Hart, is the diagnostician *par excellence* of this metaphysical embrace of violence on the part of the Church. Hart's book, I would argue, is in a very real way a work of apologetics (in the very best sense of the term) written toward "elite" postmodern philosophers and those within the Christian fold who are tempted by their work.

its dominant logic of nominalism, dialectic takes on a whole new role. Rather than remaining simply a mode or method of argument, in modernity, dialectic became the dominant epistemological approach to God and can therefore be said to be the dominant cosmology for most within the modern world. Dialectic provided Christendom with a logical web connecting the hidden, unknown God of nominalism with everyday life. Because God was now the "Wholly Other," all reference to God—univocal or analogical—was inadequate. In other words, whatever is said of God must at the same time be unsaid.

Contrary to this dominant mindset, John Milbank argues that Roman Catholics, at least many Roman Catholics, have had a decisively different experience of modernity, one that is not based upon dialectic and its inherent nominalism. What they experienced certainly was modernity, but it was, according to Milbank, a modernity that was contrary or counter to the one that was commonly experienced and articulated by the majority of those in the Western world.[76] Milbank argues that this counter-modernity is best articulated by a French Roman Catholic named Maurice Blondel in his important book, *L'Action*. In *L'Action*, Blondel offers a very different notion of dialectic, one in which conflict and violence do not dictate the relationship between the participants of the equation. The traditional dialectical synthesis or *aufhebung* (sublation) entails a conflict between the thesis and antithesis that needs to be "solved." This conflict is usually "solved" through the negation or destruction of one

76. This is important to note, as surely there can be no escape from modernity. Individualism and progress, much like the light bulb, cannot go away once witnessed or experienced. Modernity is the greatest totalizing vision that humanity is capable of on its own, and it is precisely for this reason that I have argued that so-called postmodernity is nothing other than a new "upgrade" or "version" of modernity. Modernity, or enlightenment, is a speeding train that never arrives at its intended destination. As Horkheimer and Adorno have stated, liberal society is driven by "shooting off with the speed of a rocket from A (where one is anyhow) to B (where everything is just the same.)" Horkheimer and Adorno, *Dialectic of Enlightenment*, 149. As such, the core of modernity is revealed to be that "nothing remains as of old; everything has to run incessantly, to keep moving" (134). There is no way to stop the rocket of progress and incessant movement, except to destroy it. This is surely the cause taken up by terrorist groups such as the Islamic extremist group al-Qaeda, in their terrible acts of destruction and chaos such as the bombing of the World Trade Center and the bombings in the UK shortly thereafter. That 9/11 could be understood symbolically, philosophically, and even artistically, as an attempt to destroy modernity, or at least modern capitalism, is discussed masterfully in a special issue of the South Atlantic Quarterly devoted to the events of September 11, 2001. See Hauerwas and Lentricchia, Special Issue of *South Atlantic Quarterly*.

or both former moments in the equation en route to the *aufhebung*.[77] Blondel, however, argues for a "version" of dialectic resulting in synthesis or mediation and not destruction or negation. Conflict is not the logic of Blondel's dialectic, but rather love.

> For the ground holding together the products of our action is not substance, but an intuited harmony, the combining together in infinite unity of disparate elements. Likewise, successful action is sacrifice, our offering of ourselves to others, so that the action constitutes a "bond" between us. . . . Mediating action, then, is the key to the mysterious *vinculum substantiale* of Leibniz: only when *love* is affirmed do we have an ontology, and only when sin is acknowledged as the theoretical inhibition of action, or the abstract withholding of assent to the inevitable meaning of action, do we have any epistemological criterion for "untruth," or theoretical as well as practical falsity. . . . Blondel is able to weld together the stoic approach to the cosmos, and the unity of theory and practice, with the Aristotelian approach to ethical *praxis*, because he contends that all thought is participation in divine creative action, the force of origination, and, at the same time, that all creation is *kenosis*, a self-emptying mediation. Hence the finite series of reality seeks the *telos* of the Father's full self-realization in the *logos*, and at the same time it is precisely this end which preserves simply the series, the endless interplay of creative mediation. Blondel seeks to expound an ontology of supernatural charity, and he is quite explicit: "Down to the last details of the last imperceptible phenomenon, mediating action makes up the truth and the being of all that is. And it would be strange indeed to be able to explain anything apart from him without whom nothing has been made, without whom all that has been falls back into nothingness."[78]

For Blondel, then, synthesis, sublation, a way forward, can be made without resorting to violence, contradiction, or negation. Much like the birth of a child—or perhaps more accurately, much like the eternal generation of the Son by the Father and the Spirit, who in turn is eternally spirated by the mutual love of the Father and the Son—mediation can be

77. The traditional Hegelian example is the relationship between Being and Nothingness. The sublation of the two results in becoming, which in a way involves both the former but more fundamentally, negates both Being and Nothingness, for something which is becoming, is certainly not identical with Being and it is likewise certainly something rather than nothing.

78. Milbank, *Theology and Social Theory*, 214–15.

based upon love, and not violence; that is, it can birth something new, without calling into question the existence of the two previous elements or moments in the "equation." This is only possible, it must be said, within a framework that allows for a participatory ontology, which Milbank grounds rather nicely in the sheer unique claim of Christian theology for an "ontological priority of peace."[79]

Milbank's theses have been critiqued, and surely any attempt at so neatly packaging so much political and intellectual history into one work will fall short at times, as well as make overgeneralizations. The singularity and force of Milbank's argument, however, cannot be discarded so easily. Milbank's work, and his analysis of Blondel's significance in particular, offers an option, a contrary possibility for how to live and be in modernity. Blondel and the tradition that he represents reveal an alternate route through modernity. Conflict does not have to be the primary descriptor of existence. Humanity need not fear a loving but dreadfully terrifying unknown God. Luther was right to contest much about Roman Catholicism. Indeed, much must still be contested and reformed. If one wants to undertake Christian theology, however, there is something very important to be gained from Milbank's argument about much of Roman Catholicism's experience of a counter-modernity.

Conclusion

For my part, in this work I accept Milbank's thesis about Roman Catholicism's experience of a counter-modernity as articulated by or predicated upon the "version" of dialectic affirmed by Blondel. I hope to return to it at the end by creatively demonstrating that the theological work of Karl Barth has much more in common with this counter-modernity described by Milbank than has previously been demonstrated. Karl Barth rejected the *Deus absconditus* and the dialectical and nominalist theology such a doctrine needs in order to survive. Perhaps it is best to consider his work in the light of others who share this rejection. Luther's *Deus absconditus*, after all, is arguably the common understanding of God for most people today, and it has been so throughout the modern period.[80]

79. Ibid., 363ff. This is perhaps Milbank's most monumental claim in this work. It is only because Christianity does not affirm any form of dualism in its origins that it can ultimately avoid a dialectical, or conflict-oriented, metaphysic.

80. God, for modernity, is very much like the Wizard in *The Wizard of Oz*, a figure—great or small—hiding behind a veil, unknowable and unintelligible to most, if

Martin Luther's view of God was wracked by fear and anxiety. The gross corruption of so much of the Church of his day surely did not help. As a result, Luther accepted the theological inheritance of nominalist thinkers such as William of Ockham and Duns Scotus, who sought to stress God's distance from creation, or God's wholly otherness. The sheer force and determination with which Luther put forth his theological convictions enabled this marginalized and officially condemned theological position to take root in Protestant thought. For good reasons, Luther sought to distance God from the corruption of the Church. Luther did such a good job, however, that God became almost irrevocably removed from the cosmos itself. The unknown, fearful God of power and might that resulted from nominalism via Luther is the *Deus absconditus*.

The result of the *Deus absconditus* has been shown to lead to atheism and, most likely, nihilism. Therefore any theology predicated upon such a doctrine is doomed to fail. As a result, much of modern theology, especially Protestant theology, was headed for a dead-end. Karl Barth was keenly aware of this fact when he stepped onto the theological stage. Though he of course inherited a nominalistic framework and would be forever tempted by nominalism, Barth's theological work was founded solely upon Scripture.[81] In this way, he was indeed the Reformation's truest son. Barth so thoroughly and forcefully returned to Scripture—and therefore did not bow at the altar of nominalism—that he was able both to return to and to build upon the ancient dogmatic teachings of the Church in a way that is both critical of, and yet indebted to, all Protestant and Roman Catholic theology that came before him.

Barth's significance has only begun to be appreciated by the Church, be it Protestant or Roman Catholic. This is largely due to the sheer immensity of his written canon. Getting at Barth, and then allowing him

not all. One might argue that the logical conclusion to such a theology can be seen in Philip Pullman's *His Dark Materials* trilogy, wherein God, who essentially vacated the cosmos eons ago, dies a feeble, helpless old man, anticlimactically—indeed, virtually unnoticed, with no effect upon creation. Another example can be seen in the recent film *The Book of Eli*, a film full of theological content and import and yet, strangely, devoid of God (the Son, in particular), grace, and the Christian community altogether. God, in this film, fits into the neat categories of individualism and nationalism, and is, moreover, an uninvolved, vengeful God.

81. Aside from the temptation and influence presented to Barth via Luther, Barth very much inherited this framework from the Reformed doctrine of the eternal decrees, in general, and from Calvin and his understanding of double predestination, in particular.

to "speak for himself," is no easy task, and yet that is precisely my intention in the following chapters. The two most important aspects of Barth's theological work are his writings on the knowledge of God and his Christology.[82] It is in examining these two aspects of Barth's theology, then, that we will be able to observe whether and to what extent Barth adopts the nominalist categories of Luther, Ockham, and Scotus, particularly in regard to the view of God as the *Deus absconditus*. It is my contention that understanding Barth's acceptance or rejection of this most important doctrine of God is paramount to a true understanding of Barth and his theological convictions. Barth's theology is an attempt to take seriously, and therefore to be of service to, the God revealed in Jesus Christ. For Barth, this was always a very real and very living God.

Much like the boy with the wooden lion had to experience a real lion in order to fully appreciate and understand it, so too must we, according to Barth, experience the living and true God in order for us to fully appreciate and understand God. It is to this discussion—that of the experience and articulation of God—that we now turn.

82. This position is held by Bruce McCormack and will be examined in the excursus that follows.

Rediscovering Henning Schroër's Original Terminology: *"Paradoxie"* and Not *"Dialektik"*

BRUCE MCCORMACK'S *KARL BARTH'S Critically Realistic Dialectical Theology* is surely one of the greatest examples of contemporary Barth scholarship. McCormack's incredible knowledge of the particulars of Barth's life, along with his vast familiarity with not only English-language but also German-language Barth scholarship, results in a profound and compelling work. I would argue that any work on Karl Barth written today must take seriously, and dialogue with (either positively or negatively), this important work by McCormack, as it is perhaps the most important and influential piece of Barth scholarship of the last twenty years. For that reason I find it necessary to provide a review of McCormack's work as a point of entry into my examination of Barth's primary texts. In what follows, therefore, I will offer a brief critical summary of McCormack's important work, focusing specific attention on the places that are central to his argument in regard to Barth's enduring use of the dialectical method. Throughout this brief critical review, the focus will necessarily be limited to McCormack's discussion of Barth's allegedly dialectical theology. This is neither a critique of McCormack's description of Barth's theology as both critical and realistic nor a critique of McCormack's work as a whole.

There is much about McCormack's argument that I find convincing, but I take issue with one of his central tenets, namely, that Karl Barth's theology was always dialectical. Even on this point I am in agreement with much of McCormack's argument, and so in many ways my thesis might be seen as an attempt at splitting hairs, so to speak. Ultimately, however, I believe that McCormack is wrong to argue that Barth remained always a "dialectical theologian," that he fails to treat Barth's own statements in rejection of dialectic with proper seriousness, and that, in general, he fails to consider the insidious effects and assumptions that accompany a dialectical position. My argument is that, ultimately, dialectic is not compatible with Christian theology, and that Barth was increasingly aware of this same truth himself.

At the outset, McCormack makes his argument very clear. McCormack's driving focus is the rejection of any sort of "periodization" thesis in regard to Barth's theology. In particular, McCormack is highly critical of Hans Urs von Balthasar's thesis that Barth's book on Anselm marks a significant shift in Barth, a move away from a dialectical approach to theology in favor of an analogical approach to theology. Some have referred to this supposedly new way of doing theology with the term "neo-orthodoxy." McCormack believes, however, that this is an inaccurate, and ultimately dangerous, misreading of Barth's work. McCormack adamantly asserts that Barth did not turn to "neo-orthodoxy." Rather, even before his break with liberalism in 1915, Barth was a "critically realistic dialectical theologian" and remained that way until death.[1] McCormack's thesis is surely quite bold, and he spends the rest of the book building his defense for this argument.

McCormack begins by roughly tracing the lines of von Balthasar's two attempts at a periodization of Barth's work. The first periodization places Barth's book on Anselm at its core. The argument goes that up until the year 1931, Barth employed dialectical reasoning in his writings. After this point, von Balthasar says, and specifically with the publication of Barth's book on Anselm, Barth moved to analogical reasoning. In short, the real issue is what these two positions mean for the relationship between God and the world. The former position would argue that there is a deep and fundamental difference between God and creation. Unity, in this position, would necessarily be the result of the overcoming of this difference.[2]

---

1. McCormack, *Karl Barth's Critically Realistic Dialectical Theology*, vii.

2. In this case, especially, the overcoming of the difference will always favor one side or the other. So, for example, God will be shown to be mightier than humanity, or perhaps humanity would be shown to be the dominant one. Either way, the model has to reference the weakness of one, in light of the strength of the other. Conflict must occur in order for this process to be effective.

The second of von Balthasar's periodization theses allows for a gradual change from dialectic to analogy over a period of twelve years (1927–1938), which is only completed in the years following 1938.[3] McCormack believes that this three-part assessment of Barth's work was von Balthasar's preference, but that the former has dominated English scholarship. McCormack attempts to do justice to von Balthasar by showing that he preferred a much more gradual understanding of this alleged change in Barth's way of thinking. Niceties aside, however, McCormack makes it quite clear that he does not agree with von Balthasar.

Similarily, Eberhard Jüngel believed that Barth's way of thinking shifted on or around the time of Barth's letter to Erik Peterson, in which Barth dismisses dialectics, saying, "The revelation of which theology speaks is not dialectical; it is no paradox. . . . this scarcely needs to be said."[4] Barth's concern here is that the revelation of God (in Christ) be understood as capable of speaking for itself. Barth wants to reject any way of understanding revelation as needing something else to be truly effective. For Jüngel, this early rejection of dialectics sheds light on a burgeoning change in Barth's thought.[5] McCormack disagrees with this interpretation of Barth's thought as well, which here means disagreeing with Barth himself![6]

McCormack cuts to the chase very quickly. In fewer than ten pages, he has rejected the various periodization theses and has already begun to offer his support and argument for the consistency of dialectic in Barth's work. He states that much of his argument can be traced back to two contemporary German scholars, Ingrid Spieckermann and Michael Beintker. Spieckermann is credited with discovering a form of analogy that is present as far back as Barth's revised commentary on Romans (*Romans* II).

3. McCormack, *Karl Barth's Critically Realistic Dialectical Theology*, 4.

4. Quoted in ibid., 6. It is curious and must be pointed out that here Barth uses dialectic and paradox almost interchangeably. I believe that at this point in time, Barth either does not understand or simply does not develop the distinction between the two concepts. It seems to me that this statement is made to deny that there is an ultimate distinction or incompatibility between God and humanity, between the Knower and the known, etc. From my reading of Barth, I would argue that this conflation of dialectic and paradox is relatively isolated.

5. Jüngel states that in 1925 it was already apparent how much Barth had changed on the issue of dialectic in general, and in Barth's *Der Römerbrief* in particular, as a result of Peterson's critiques. Jüngel, *Barth-Studien*, 144.

6. This is only one of a myriad of instances in which McCormack feels justified in rejecting Barth's own statements, descriptions, memories, and concerns.

She argues that the "analogy of the cross" that she discovers in *Romans* II "provided the 'ground and limit' of all dialectically constructed theological witness to God in His Self-Revelation."[7] The reason for McCormack's appeal to Spieckermann is that she shows that Barth did not discover analogy in his research for his book on Anselm, but rather that analogy was always there in his thought and works. Still, McCormack states that Spieckermann nonetheless places too much importance on Barth's book on Anselm, and thus ends up assisting the periodization thesis that Mc-Cormack wants so desperately to disprove.

McCormack's true praise is reserved for Beintker's profound work *Die Dialektik in der "dialektischen Theologie" Karl Barths*. In this book, Beintker distinguishes between several different types of dialectic, arguing that Barth's use of dialectic is much more nuanced than just simple, straightforward dialectic. McCormack states that Beintker demonstrates that Barth makes use of as many as four different types of dialectic even before Romans II. Beintker agrees with Spieckermann as well, arguing that Barth demonstrates both analogy and dialectic from very early in his academic career and that he will continue to do so until the end of his life.[8] Following closely in Beintker's footsteps, McCormack's position is that Barth's theology is very much alive and changing, but that it is always in line with one form or another of dialectical thought. McCormack and Beintker want to stretch the way that dialectic is traditionally understood. In addition, they both want to say that while analogy can be found very early in Barth, dialectic is found very late as well.[9] It would seem that by stretching the way dialectic is understood, McCormack hopes to show that Barth's thinking remained always dialectical, even if Barth himself disagreed. The stretched dialectic that emerges, I would argue, cannot ultimately handle the weight of Barth's mature theology.

Finally, as a further means of introducing McCormack's fine book, it is important to point out that his approach is very much that of a critical historian. McCormack places much emphasis on the historical events of Barth's life as well as his particular social context. McCormack argues that the rise to power of the Nazi Party, for example, should never be separated from Barth's writings. Barth's particular social and political

7. Quoted in McCormack, *Karl Barth's Critically Realistic Dialectical Theology*, 8.

8. Surely the argument that Barth utilizes analogy, albeit in a selective manner, all the way up until the end of his life, presents a problem for the argument that Barth was and always remained a dialectical theologian.

9. McCormack, *Karl Barth's Critically Realistic Dialectical Theology*, 13.

concerns, McCormack believes, were ever present and necessarily had an effect upon his writings, despite his best attempts to prevent this. Thus, McCormack states that the true importance of Barth's book on Anselm lies not in a breakthrough during his theological learning process (as Barth himself states), but rather is the result of his falling out with Gogarten, Bultmann, and Brunner, as well as the political climate in Germany.[10] McCormack believes that the social and historical events of Barth's life play a much greater role than Barth himself will admit. McCormack will even go so far as to disagree with Barth's autobiographical statements, and especially with his reflections upon his reasons for writing particular works or for engaging in particular arguments. This is nowhere more apparent than in regard to Barth's book on Anselm, which McCormack is determined not to give a central role in Barth's body of work. McCormack displays this tendency most tellingly near the end of his book, where he writes, "Barth's book on Anselm is not a wholly reliable guide to his own theological method—regardless of what he might say on the subject later—unless it is read dialectically."[11] McCormack's argument is powerful, but the brashness with which he so easily dismisses even Barth's own statements in order to build his case for how best to understand Barth is surely suspect at best and condemning at worst. Introductory remarks aside, we will now examine the parts of McCormack's argument that are so vital to the present endeavor.

McCormack believes that Barth's theology did not initially translate very well into the English-speaking world. Essentially, McCormack argues that Barth's acceptance by the English-speaking world came at the price of his dialectical theology. Barth was an anomaly; his was a strange mixture of early medieval and Reformed orthodox theology that left readers a bit puzzled. McCormack believes that it was only by truncating Barth's theology and placing it within the confines of so-called neo-orthodoxy that he gained a foothold in the English-speaking world.[12] McCormack states that there were four basic central themes to Barth's theology that gave rise to this problem: "the 'infinite qualitative distinction' between God and humankind, the sole normativity of God's Self-revelation in Christ, the rejection of natural theology, [and] the love of paradoxes and dialectic."[13] McCormack goes on to demonstrate multiple examples of the

10. Ibid., 15.

11. Ibid., 434.

12. Ibid., 24.

13. McCormack, *Karl Barth's Critically Realistic Dialectical Theology*, 24. It is

highly critical reception of Barth's work by English-speaking scholars. These references reveal that for many, Barth's theology was simply too complex and that its refreshing uniqueness was ultimately perceived to be more of a problem than a benefit.

Of the utmost importance for Barth was the distinction between God and humanity, a distinction that is characterized on the human end by utter sinfulness, and on the divine end by equal and opposite utter goodness. The human condition, according to Barth, is one of pride in the face of an almighty benevolent Creator. The Gospel, moreover, reveals that this difference is not total and that human sinfulness cannot triumph over divine grace. Barth states, then, at the beginning and end of his career, that the overall goal and nature of his theology can be summed up with the phrase *Veni Creator Spiritus*, or "Come Creator Spirit."[14] This doxological core of Barth's theology should not be overlooked. It makes sense, then, from this perspective to argue that the primary assumption of Barth's theology is that God will and has already come to redeem creation. The starting point, the main character in this story, according to Barth, is God. God, who is completely other than creation, makes God's own self known to creation in the person of Jesus of Nazareth. Thus, despite the otherness of God, God can be known. McCormack calls this central principle "critical realism," as God can be known as one who is real and whole, "in itself apart from and prior to the knowing activity of human individuals."[15] It is precisely because God is real and whole in a truly autonomous way that McCormack classifies Barth's theology as "critical realism." God, according to this line of thought, is real in a way that is unique and ultimately definitive of what it means to be real. Only God exists as God exists. Hence, humans exist *really* in a very different way than God. I find nothing objectionable in the idea of critical realism, based as it is in the cry *Veni Creator Spiritus,* except that McCormack uses the principles of what he has called "critical realism" to claim that Barth views the relationship between God and the world as a fundamental *diastasis*, paving the way for his next claim, which is that Barth is ultimately a dialectical theologian.

---

important to note the way McCormack groups "paradoxes" and "dialectic" together. I would argue that this is an early indicator that McCormack does not properly distinguish between the two, and that he ultimately does not take paradox seriously as a category of its own.

14. Ibid., 32.

15. Ibid., 129.

McCormack says of Barth, "He conceived of the relation of God to the world in terms of a fundamental *diastasis* (i.e., a relation in which the two members stand over against each other with no possibility of a synthesis into a higher form of being)."[16] It is true that there is no possibility of a "synthesis into a higher former of being," as it would be impossible for there to be a higher form of being than "that than which nothing greater can be conceived." But was it even suggested that the goal was to achieve a "higher form of being"? God is the ultimate Supreme Being, and great as humanity might be, we do not share or participate in being as if it were a common substance uniting God and humanity. God and humanity are different by more than simply varying degrees or intensities of being. McCormack points out that for Barth, "the world remains world. But God is God."[17] This is, in essence, the practical working out of the Kierkegaardian "infinite qualitative distinction." For Barth, the world and God are completely and totally different. Yet how does this complete and total difference or distinction necessarily result in dialectic, let alone reveal that dialectic is the ultimate quality or method of Barth's theology throughout his entire life? Is it not proper to dialectic to require a synthesis of some sort, born out of the conflict of the thesis and antithesis? Moreover, does that synthesis not stand upon the ashes left after the destruction of the first two moments? God remains God and the world remains the world, this is true. Yet, according to Barth, this is only secondary knowledge about God and the world—secondary in that it can only be understood and affirmed in and through the person of Jesus Christ, the God-man. We cannot know this difference first, or else our knowledge is based upon something other than the fundamental revelation of God in Christ. On the contrary, we know Christ, and therefore we are able to understand the sheer difference between God and humanity, which makes the unity of the two all the more striking. This is unlike any dialectic I am familiar with.

Surely the so-called *diastasis* between God and humanity is more aptly understood in light of the way Barth addresses the relationship between God's judgment and love. McCormack rightly points out that Barth believes that while God's "judgment is eternal and definitive," so is God's love "eternal and definitive." He further quotes Barth as saying, "the two things contradict each other, do they not? Yes, but only in our

16. Ibid.
17. Ibid.

thoughts."[18] Here we see that what we perceive to be contradiction is only so due to the limitations of human understanding. God's judgment and God's love are eternal and definitive: both stand firm and unwavering as a testament to the confounding complexity of the mystery of God. The two are not in conflict, and any perceived conflict is merely a product of human understanding and has no real substance. Surely this is the exact same logic that is on display in Barth's total distinction between the world and God. Both remain utterly different, and yet the difference is not characterized by conflict but rather by a deep, paradoxical unity.

In the third chapter of McCormack's book, he attempts to support his claim that the two best examples of Barth's critically realistic dialectical theology are "the world is the world but God is God," and the knowledge of God. McCormack is accurate to point out the importance of these two motifs in Barth's theology. However, while I agree with the centrality of both of these in Barth's work, I will argue, contrary to McCormack's well-argued thesis, that these two issues reveal precisely why Barth is not a dialectical theologian. In my reading of McCormack, his entire argument hangs on whether or not these two issues—"the world is the world but God is God," and the knowledge of God—can be shown to be the basis for dialectic in Barth.[19] For this reason, subsequent chapters of this work will examine these issues (chapter 3) as well as Christology (chapter 4), which is the dominant "heading" that they both ultimately fall under for Barth, in hopes of showing that each reveals that rather than utilizing the logic of dialectic, Barth's theology reveals the logic of something much more complex, something I call paradox.

As I have briefly examined the former motif, and will indeed return to the issue at great length, it should be pointed out that in my estimation, this issue of the distinction or difference between God and the world is ultimately a christological matter. Jesus Christ is always to be our starting point if we are to embark upon specifically Christian theology, argues Barth. Thus, the incarnation, God dwelling among humanity, taking

18. Quoted in McCormack, *Karl Barth's Critically Realistic Dialectical Theology*, 94.

19. Note that I did not say that these two reveal Barth's indebtedness to the dialectical method. Neither do I think that McCormack would make this statement. Rather, for both myself and Professor McCormack, Barth does not begin with any method, be it dialectic or paradox (or something else entirely), but rather with Scripture and the revealed Word of God. Whether Barth's theology should best be classified as dialectical, paradoxical, or something else is a descriptive endeavor, a way of classifying the complex work of the great theologian from Basel. Method can never be said to be first for Barth.

upon himself true flesh and true blood, that is, becoming truly human, is the foundation for everything that we can know about God as well as everything we can know about humanity. Barth makes this point very clear throughout his writings: Jesus Christ is the ultimate and definitive revelation of both God and humanity. Explaining how this is the basis for his adoption of Kierkegaard's "infinite qualitative distinction," Barth says, "The philosophers call the crisis of human knowing *Ursprung*. The Bible sees at the same crossroads Jesus Christ."[20] Here Barth reveals that Christology is key to both the discussion of the human possibility of the knowledge of God as well as the distinction between God and the world. It is as if in the person of Jesus of Nazareth, and especially in His crucifixion and resurrection, an intersection or crossroads is made between two utterly distinct and parallel roads. Utilizing the terms of this metaphor, the two roads are not parallel as two equals separated only by a distance, but as two completely separate entities and realities altogether, one completely dependent upon the other for its very existence. Therefore, an intersection or crossroads is unthinkable. To claim that these two paths would cross is illogical at best and utterly foolish at worst. Yet this is precisely what is claimed in the incarnation of the eternally begotten Word of God in the flesh and blood of Jesus of Nazareth. The crossroads marking the intersection between the divine and the human is none other than Jesus Christ. The logic of this crossroads, much like all of divine logic, is unthinkable for mortals, and thus it is only through the gratuitous gift of self-revelation that God makes God's knowledge our knowledge. McCormack rightly describes Barth's position on this matter, saying, "True knowledge of God is a knowledge in which 'our logic' is renewed by being brought into conformity with the 'logic of God.'"[21] Thus it is clear that the two big examples of what McCormack calls Barth's "dialectical theology"—the distinction between God and the world, and the knowledge of God—are both fulfilled and explained in Jesus. Barth's Christology, then, is key to addressing both issues. Though we will come to different conclusions, both McCormack and I can agree on this important point.

20. Quoted in McCormack, *Karl Barth's Critically Realistic Dialectical Theology*, 224.

21. Ibid., 159. Here McCormack is discussing Barth's distinction between *Kenntnis* and *Erkenntnis* in *Romans* I. The former, says McCormack, is knowledge that can be acquired through the law. The latter, he goes on to say, is personal, participatory knowledge, which can only be given by God Himself. The issue of the possibility of human knowledge of God, for Barth, is always an issue of *Erkenntnis*, as it is always a christological matter.

To understand the way in which McCormack understands the dialectical theology he sees in Barth, it is important to understand the complex distinction of dialectical approaches as laid out by Michael Beintker. In particular, McCormack depends upon Beintker's distinction between two critically different types of dialectic, a distinction that he makes in hopes of explaining Barth's first commentary on Romans.[22] The first type of dialectic is "supplementary dialectic," which Beintker defines as follows: "One member of a pair predominates in value and potency over the other. As a consequence of this 'imbalance' the predominant member is able to overcome the other. At some point, the stronger member takes up the weaker into itself with the result that the weaker member is either cancelled out altogether or is perhaps taken up into the other in a higher synthesis. In either case, an initial situation of simple opposition gives way to reconciliation. Thus a 'supplementary dialectic' is one that admits of a certain progress."[23]

In this type of dialectic, one of the two parties is stronger and more valuable than the other in every way. As a result, the stronger and more valuable party "overcomes" the weaker and less valuable party either by cancelling it out or swallowing it up. McCormack, following Beintker, calls this "reconciliation." Reconciliation, here, is the eradication or engulfing of the weaker party by the stronger. This reconciliation, if indeed it can be called that, is more like a one-sided slaughter. In the conflict that

22. McCormack, *Karl Barth's Critically Realistic Dialectical Theology*, 162. It is very important to refer to McCormack's footnote number 149 on the page in citation. Here, McCormack says, "Beintker is here modifying a distinction originally coined by Henning Schröer between 'supplementary' and 'complementary' paradoxes." Again, it is clear that McCormack is heir to a tradition of using the terms, and thus the concepts, of paradox and dialectic interchangeably. I believe that this is an important and costly mistake. Now, I must point out that Barth himself does this periodically. This is important to point out for two reasons. First, though I disagree with McCormack's reading of Barth on this subject, it certainly does have some basis in Barth, especially in his earlier writings. Second, and more important, this serves as a helpful reminder that I am not arguing that Barth intentionally adopted a philosophical strategy or methodology called paradox over and against dialectic. Barth intentionally adopted no overarching methodology or strategy, except the obedient interpretation of Scripture. My argument, to the contrary, is that while this is clear, Barth clearly rejected dialectic as false and dangerous to Christian theology in his later, more mature work. Thus, my constructive suggestion is to understand Barth's theology, especially his mature theology, as having a paradoxical shape and logic, rooted firmly in Barth's Christology. The argument is for a helpful and productive way of reading and understanding Barth, not for Barth's own intentional strategy or method.

23. McCormack, *Karl Barth's Critically Realistic Dialectical Theology*, 163.

is supplementary dialectics, a vastly superior party confronts a party that is inferior in every way with what is essentially a Hobson's choice: "conform and lose your identity completely or be eradicated and erased." In this "reconciliation," it must be logically stated that nothing of the weaker party remains. The progress that Beintker and McCormack claim for this dialectic is a progress born of destruction. Surely this mode of thought cannot be equated with the revelation of God in Christ.[24]

Beintker calls the second type of dialectic "complementary dialectic." In complementary dialectic, as Beintker defines it, "the two members stand over against each other in a relation of open contradiction or antithesis. No reconciliation or synthesis between the two is admitted; therefore, such movement as exists has the character of a ceaseless to-ing and fro-ing between the two without any real progress."[25]

This type of dialectic, unlike the previous type, achieves no progress. One way of conceiving of a complementary dialectic is as the encounter between two equals, which, like the classical opposition of the irresistible force to the immovable object, gets nowhere. Another way of conceiving of this type of dialectic is as one in which the two parties are so completely dissimilar that they are not able even to interact with one another, let alone achieve any sort of synthesis, be it through a peaceful or antagonistic encounter. Neither Beintker nor McCormack believes that this type dialectic is compatible with the Christian message. I would wholeheartedly concur.[26]

But before moving on, there is one major problem with McCormack's use of Beintker, who is in turn using the work of Henning Schröer: Beintker mistakenly conflates the terms *Dialektik* and *Paradoxie*. Beintker, in examining what he calls the *Dialektik* of Barth's *Krisismotiv*, states that in terms of the divine "Yes" and "No," "a permanent back and forth between the 'Yes' and the 'No' is to be excluded despite the phenomenological polarity of both. The divine 'Yes' is kept to the last word, the actual movement of the 'No' to 'Yes' is therefore ontologically seized [locked

24. It would seem to me that the best possible theological cosmology that could arise from this way of thinking would be pantheism, wherein creatures are denied not only freedom but even autonomy, as all are really just God.

25. McCormack, *Karl Barth's Critically Realistic Dialectical Theology,* 163.

26. Surely the best type of theological cosmology that could come out of such a view of things would be some sort of process theology or philosophy. On the opposite end of the spectrum, a very unorthodox form of Deism might be compatible with this view as well. Neither of these is, in my opinion, a viable option for a Christian theologian.

into place]—irreversibly."[27] There is, then, according to Beintker, genuine *Spannung* or tension as between two equals on the phenomenological level, while at the same time, the "Yes" clearly prevails ontologically. I would argue that in this we have moved beyond the limits of dialectic, into the realm of paradox. Beintker, however, instead of keeping the two in overall unity, breaks them apart, seeing the former as an example of complementary dialectic, and the latter as an example of supplementary dialectic. He does so because he is following Henning Schroër's argument, except that Schroër's argument was stated in terms of *Paradoxie* and not *Dialektik*. "Schroër differentiates in his analysis of the term 'paradox' between complementary and supplementary paradox. While the complementary paradox implies a contradiction, within which thesis and antithesis face each other equivocally, within the supplementary paradox there exists 'the prevalence or dominance of a member [of the two] or thesis.'"[28]

Beintker then goes on to demonstrate how Barth demonstrates this supplementary *Dialektik* throughout Barth's first edition of *Der Römerbrief*, and McCormack does the same. But why equate the two terms? It is interesting that within the very same section, within the same footnote even, Beintker will use the term *Paradoxie* when quoting Schroër but use the term *Dialektik* when employing Schroër's logic toward Beintker's own argument. McCormack, meanwhile, drops the terminology of *Paradoxie* altogether. As I have argued and will argue, this is a sloppy move, as the two terms surely are different from one another. In examining Schroër's definitional statements, in particular, I can very much understand how such a distinction can be made between various types of paradox, which I take to mean the coincidence of two seeming opposites in a noncontradictory manner, in which an overall meaning is achieved through a fundamental unity that is both beyond, and yet contains within itself, all distinction. That being said, dialectic is conflict. The thesis and antithesis are always in conflict, until one overcomes the other. Synthesis, newness, and resolution are achieved by way of overcoming and, ultimately, destruction. In summary, I find Schroër's distinction of types of *Paradoxie* most helpful, Beintker's conflation or confusion of the term with *Dialektik* confusing and dangerous, and McCormack's use of Beintker sloppy, as

27. Beintker, *Die Dialektik in der "dialektischen Theologie" Karl Barths*, 38. All quotations from Beintker's German text are the work of the author.

28. Ibid. Citation is from Schroër, *Die Denkform der Paradoxalität als theologisches Problem*, 37.

originally the distinction was of the different types of *Paradoxie* and not about *Dialektik* at all.

Moving on, McCormack demonstrates that Beintker uses the *Realdialektik* between "real history" and "so-called history" as well as between "real humanity" (in Christ) and "unreal humanity" (in Adam) to further explain his point.[29] Beintker argues that Barth's theology adheres much more closely to the rules of supplementary dialectic than complementary. These two *Realdialektiks* are the primary two dialectical relationships that Beintker sees on display in *Romans* I, and therefore they allow him the opportunity to asses Barth's early theology. Beintker and McCormack believe that Barth's early theology displays the logic of supplementary dialectic in that God is above and outside of history and that the way of humanity revealed in Christ is above and incompatible with the way of humanity revealed in Adam. God's history—that is, salvation history (*Heilsgeschichte*)—is "real history" in that the turn from the ways of Adam to the ways of Christ has happened in the past tense.[30] "Real history" and "so-called history" have been synthesized in Christ, and thus the newness of all things is not only possible but actual. Likewise, "real humanity" and "unreal humanity" have been synthesized in the person of Christ Jesus, in such a way that the old way of humanity has passed away in light of the new way, the way of Christ. In these two *Realdialektiks*, McCormack argues, "eternity enters once again into time, absorbing it and bringing it to a standstill—which is to say, the enslavement to the law of sin and death which governs temporal existence is momentarily broken."[31] Though there are setbacks along the trajectory from the old way to the new, the overall description of both history and humanity is that of progress: progress from old to new, progress from humanity to God.

Finally, Beintker and McCormack say that the two forms of *Realdialektik* discussed above give birth to a distinct way of thought, or *Denkform*, which is basically a "dialectic of becoming."[32] Beintker describes this *Denkform* in Barth's *Romans* I, saying, "everything depends upon

---

29. Interestingly, Beintker actually juxtaposes Moses with Christ, and not Adam. He is, therefore, working with the tension between law and Gospel, particularly in light of the Lutheran distinction between the two. Beintker, *Die Dialektik in der "dialektischen Theologie" Karl Barths*, 39.

30. McCormack, *Karl Barth's Critically Realistic Dialectical Theology*, 164.

31. Ibid.

32. Ibid.

finding a suitable way to express the *becoming* of the new world of God."[33] The argument here is that in Barth's early writings, especially *Romans* I, Barth's dialectical reasoning was conceived from the standpoint of process. As such, Beintker and McCormack argue that Barth's early theology demonstrated the constant process and progress from old to new and from humanity to God. Whether or not this description is befitting of Barth's early theology is of no consequence, as Beintker and McCormack accurately claim that Barth's *Denkform* quickly changed, eschewing the process paradigm. "The 'dialectic of becoming' as the principle *Denkform* of *Romans* I would quickly give way to a *Denkform* governed by an altogether different kind of dialectic: a dialectic in which the contradiction or antithesis of two magnitudes is steadfastly maintained in order to bear witness to a truth lying beyond both of them."[34]

Moving away from the problematic paradigm of the "dialectic of becoming," Beintker and McCormack claim that Barth embraced a much more radicalized dialectic, one characterized by what I would call tension. This tension is that of two parties standing in total contradiction or antithesis, without hope of a traditional synthesis or reconciliation. The truth and therefore the resolution that this new *Denkform* offers is not arrived at simply. The resolution offered by this new *Denkform* is born of the irresolvable tension between the two parties. One party does not eradicate or consume the other; nor do the two parties stand so infinitely apart that resolution is not possible.[35] Rather, and this is very crucial, the two parties stand in complete contradiction, and their antithesis "bears witness to a truth lying beyond both of them." McCormack and Beintker go on to argue that the transition from the early "dialectic of becoming" to this newer *Denkform* is predicated upon a radical shift in Barth's eschatology.

While the argument regarding the radical shift in Barth's eschatology is an important one,[36] what is more important to this exploration of

---

33. Quoted in McCormack, *Karl Barth's Critically Realistic Dialectical Theology*, 164.

34. Ibid., 165.

35. In many ways, this new *Denkform* that Beintker and McCormack argue for is simply a synthesis of the supplementary and complementary dialectics that they have already described. This new *Denkform*, in my estimation, seems like a way of holding together the best aspects of both understandings of dialectic, while attempting to be rid of the more negative traits of both forms.

36. I would definitely agree that Barth's eschatology changes or matures between *Romans* I and *Romans* II and has a huge bearing upon his later theological works.

Barth's work is the claim that Barth's new *Denkform* is one in which the antithesis between the two parties "bears witness to a truth lying beyond both of them." This statement seems to be fundamentally unstable and completely foreign to Barth's way of thinking from the very beginning. The logic of this statement plays out in such a way that one party does not eradicate or swallow up the other, nor do the two parties stand so drastically separate that there can be no real possible resolution whatsoever. Rather, the logic of this statement is that the two parties, in their absolute distinction and antithesis, discover in their opposition a truth that surpasses either party on its own as well as any synthetic possibilities of the two. Given Barth's aversion to any point of origin or destination other than Christ Jesus, what could this truth that lies beyond either party be? It behooves us to examine this problem in light of the previously stated examples of Barth's dialectical theology. Specifically, Beintker and McCormack say that the two paramount examples of Barth's dialectical theology are the *Realdialektiks* between "real history" and "so-called history," and between "real humanity" and "unreal humanity," and of course, both fall under the most obvious and important dialectic at work in Barth's theology, "The world remains world. But God is God." Surely any definition of Barth's dialectical method would have to be compatible with these most basic examples of Barth's so-called dialectical theology. But I would argue that none of these so-called fundamental dialectics of Barth's are compatible with this new *Denkform*. In the case of "real history" and "so-called history," what would be the truth that lies beyond? Is it not the case that "real history" is the salvation history of God, specifically made manifest in the person and work of Jesus Christ? Thus, "real history" is the eschatological confrontation of the kingdom of God with the kingdoms of humanity. Likewise, "real history" is real precisely in the fact that its basis is Jesus Christ, who reveals to humanity the very reality of human potentiality as well as the actuality of the atonement. To say that this so-called dialectic is "solved" or that it finds resolution in a truth that lies beyond is to say that the revelation of God in Christ is not ultimate, and that "real history" is not quite real enough. Is the same not also true for the so-called dialectic between "real humanity" and "unreal humanity"? If Christ is the real human, while Adam and all those who follow in his sinful footsteps are unreal humans, then what is the truth that lies beyond? Surely the claim that there is a truth that lies beyond

---

Whether or not this change in eschatology results in the dialectical *Denkform* described by McCormack is another matter entirely.

Christ, whom Barth declares emphatically is the ultimate and definitive revelation of both God and humanity, is completely incompatible with Barth's theology. Finally, as is the case with the first two, what truth lies beyond the ultimate dialectic of God and the world? Claiming any truth beyond God completely lays waste to any claims of God's sovereignty. This statement—that Barth's *Denkform* becomes one where the two sides of the dialectic find resolution in a truth that is beyond each, one that arises out of the tension between the two—would be laughable and offensive to Barth.

My argument, on the contrary, is that the so-called dialectical distinctions between God and the world, between "real humanity" and "unreal humanity," and between "real history" and "so-called history" are not dialectical at all, but rather that these tensions are best understood as paradoxes. God, "real humanity," and "real history" are always more real and are thus unquestionably preferred to the world, "unreal humanity," and "so-called history." The former do not simply trump or conquer the latter, however, for agonistics is not the fundamental characterization of the relationship between the parties in this distinction. Rather than conflict, which is the pinnacle presupposition of any form of authentic dialectic, the relationship between God and the world, "real humanity" and "unreal humanity," and "real history" and "so-called history," infinitely distinct as they might be, are characterized not by conflict but rather by unity.[37] Because all that we can know about both God and humanity we learn from Christ Jesus, we know that the distinction between these various positions is always understood only within the unity of divinity and humanity in Christ Jesus. Thus, though God and the world are infinitely and qualitatively distinct, they are in an even greater way unified in complete harmony and noncompetition. The tension between the two remains, yes, and yet paradoxically the resolution comes through this tension by revealing that there is distinction and difference without conflict. God is always God and therefore remains the orienting goal and *telos* of humanity. Yet, humanity remains humanity, despite all the best

37. Of all of these, an argument might be made for a truly dialectical approach to "real humanity" and "unreal humanity." As McCormack later points out, "God creates the new humanity by negating the old" (*Karl Barth's Critically Realistic Dialectical Theology*, 224). While this is certainly true in some ways, God also continues to allow for "unreal humanity" to exist and to flourish in its own darkness and sinfulness. Despite the universal nature of the atonement and election, Barth does not believe that God eradicates, swallows up, or even negates "unreal humanity" unless "real humanity" becomes the desire of the "unreal human."

rules of human logic that would claim otherwise. In short, though there is distinction, and though there is resolution, there is not conflict and neither party is eliminated, eradicated, or absorbed by the other.

McCormack is right to identify the increasing tension manifest in Barth's theology, tension that does not give way to conflict. He is wrong, however, to think that the resolution lies somewhere beyond the two realities. The tension is resolved in the revelation that difference is not bad and that the two utterly distinct parties, God and humanity, can actually dwell with one another in unity and peace, despite God's always being above and beyond even humanity's best potential. Barth's mature theology, which most assuredly begins with *Romans* II, is accurately characterized as a theology of tension, difference, and distinction between God and humanity. This difference, however, is definitely not the tension of dialectic, but rather it is a different kind of tension; it is the resolved and yet persistent tension that is paradox. It is the tension of two seeming opposites coinciding in a noncontradictory manner, in which an overall meaning is achieved through a fundamental unity that both is beyond, and yet contains within itself, all distinction. To see this logic at work, I will now turn to a careful examination of many of Barth's most important texts. I will begin by examining Barth's statement that "God is God. And the world is the world," as well as the knowledge of God. Afterward, I will proceed by examining Barth's mature Christology, the heading under which, along with McCormack, I believe the former two fall. I hope to show that Barth employs not the logic of dialectic, but rather something more strange, more complex—something I would call paradox.

3

The Natural Knowledge of God
in Karl Barth's Theology

For the wrath of God is revealed from heaven against all ungodliness and wickedness of those who by their wickedness suppress
the truth. For what can be known about God is plain to them,
because God has shown it to them. Ever since the creation of the
world his eternal power and divine nature, invisible though they
are, have been understood and seen through the things he has
made. So they are without excuse; for though they knew God,
they did not honor him as God or give thanks to him, but they
became futile in their thinking, and their senseless minds were
darkened. Claiming to be wise, they became fools; and they exchanged the glory of the immortal God for images resembling a
mortal human being or birds or four-footed animals or reptiles.
Therefore God gave them up in the lusts of their hearts to impu-
rity, to the degrading of their bodies among themselves, because
they exchanged the truth about God for a lie and worshiped
and served the creature rather than the Creator, who is blessed
forever! Amen. For this reason God gave them up to degrading
passions. Their women exchanged natural intercourse for un-
natural, and in the same way also the men, giving up natural
intercourse with women, were consumed with passion for one
another. Men committed shameless acts with men and received
in their own persons the due penalty for their error. And since
they did not see fit to acknowledge God, God gave them up to a
debased mind and to things that should not be done. They were
filled with every kind of wickedness, evil, covetousness, malice.
Full of envy, murder, strife, deceit, craftiness, they are gossips,

slanderers, God-haters, insolent, haughty, boastful, inventors of evil, rebellious toward parents, foolish, faithless, heartless, ruthless. They know God's decree, that those who practice such things deserve to die—yet they not only do them but even applaud others who practice them. —Romans 1:18–32.[1]

"What is exegesis?" No one can, of course, bring out the meaning of a text (*auslegen*) without at the same time adding something to it (*einlegen*). Moreover, no interpreter is rid of the danger of in fact adding more than he extracts.[2] —Karl Barth

By the miracle of foolishness it is possible to think of God as not existing. But only by this miracle.[3] —Karl Barth

Introduction

UNFORTUNATELY, KARL BARTH IS perhaps best known for his infamous rejection of fellow German theologian Emil Brunner. After Brunner published an article titled "Nature and Grace" in which he called for a revival of "natural theology," Karl Barth responded in 1934 with his polemical response, "*Nein!*"[4] Barth is also well known for his rejection of the *analogia entis*, about which he said, "I regard the *analogia entis* as the invention of Antichrist, and I believe that because of it it is impossible ever to become a Roman Catholic, all other reasons for not doing so being to my mind short-sighted and trivial."[5] For Barth the *analogia entis*, or analogy of being, equipped Roman Catholicism with the false notion that one could, through the use of pure reason, move analogously from an understanding of creatures to the Creator. As Barth understood it, the *analogia entis* did not sufficiently account for divine transcendence, and

1. All scriptural citations, unless otherwise noted, will come from the NRSV.

2. Barth, *Epistle to the Romans*, ix. Hereafter cited as *Der Römerbrief* to prevent any confusion with Barth's *Shorter Commentary on Romans*.

3. Barth, *Anselm*, 165.

4. Barth, Brunner, and Fraenkel, *Natural Theology*, 65–128.

5. Barth, *Church Dogmatics* I.1, xiii. Hereafter cited as *CD* I.1. Subsequent volumes of *Church Dogmatics* will be cited in the same manner.

It strikes me as quite fascinating that Barth feels the need to add the final phrase to this sentence. As is often the case with Barth's theological writing, he takes away and gives at the same time. In this passage he denounces a key Roman Catholic theological principle as the "invention of Antichrist," and then proceeds to say that if it were not for that one principle or teaching (it is not dogma), one should consider conversion!

thus allowed theology to move in the realm of something more akin to sociology or, more accurately, ontotheology.[6] Though it was surely not the professed use and understanding of this doctrine by Roman Catholics, Barth feared that this analogous relationship between creatures and their creator placed greater importance upon creation than the revelation of God in Christ, in that creation is understood to be analogously "complete." What is at stake for Barth, in both of these strong critiques, is nothing less than the fundamental priority of the revelation of God in Christ as the basis for all knowledge and especially for salvific knowledge. Essentially, Barth rejected the possibility of any form of natural knowledge of God that would do away with the need for Christ Jesus. The complexity of this argument for Karl Barth, as well as for all those who would seek to stand in solidarity with his theological reforms, cannot be overestimated.

It is in light of this complexity that I will attempt in this chapter to examine Barth's seemingly incongruous teachings on the natural knowledge of God. Rather than focus on secondary sources, I will primarily be examining eight of Barth's major works that discuss the natural knowledge of God. These primary sources are 1) *Der Römerbrief* or *The Epistle to the Romans* (6th ed., 1928); 2) the *Göttingen Dogmatics* (1924–25); 3) *Anselm: Fides Quaerens Intellectum* (1931); 4) *Church Dogmatics* I.1 (1932); 5) "Nein!" (1934); 6) Barth's Gifford Lectures, *The Knowledge of God and the Service of God* (1937–38); 7) *Church Dogmatics* II.1 (1940); and 8) *A Shorter Commentary on Romans* (1940–41). I will examine the texts in the order in which they were written, and only on the grounds of the natural knowledge of God (and therefore not exhaustively).

For Barth, the Christian life is about heeding the command of God. This command was given in Christ Jesus, who was crucified and resurrected, of whom Scripture is our witness by the power of the Holy Spirit. Hearing, let alone understanding and obeying the command of God, however, is no easy task. "True apprehension can be achieved only by a strict determination to face, as far as possible *without rigidity of mind*, the tension displayed more or less clearly in the ideas written in the text."[7] Standing in this tension, be it dialectic or paradox, is difficult but rewarding. Situating one's self inside the text in this fashion allows a limited amount of knowledge of the unknowable, and thus allows one, to

---

6. I would argue that stripping theology of divine transcendence also robs theology of the radical possibility of divine immanence. I will examine this in more depth in ch. 4.

7. Barth, *CD* I.1, 8. Italics mine.

a limited extent, to speak about the unspeakable. It is my contention that this is the best framework within which to understand Barth's theology. For this reason, Barth's *Der Römerbrief* as well as his *Shorter Commentary on Romans* will be given a bit more weight than the other texts.[8] The reason for this moderately preferential treatment of Barth's commentaries on the Epistle to the Romans is that the primary biblical defense of the natural knowledge of God, at least for Barth, can be found in Romans 1:18–21.[9]

It is my belief that this type of an examination will reveal the paradoxical shape of Barth's theology. Rather than revealing inconsistencies or logical ineptitude, the shape of Barth's theology is the best witness to his deep faithfulness to the biblical witness of the revelation of the God of

8. It might be more helpful to say "equal weight." I simply mean to avoid the tendency of many scholars to view biblical commentary as secondary to "theology." Specific to Barth, the commentary on the Romans is often not allowed to play as great a role as Barth's *magnum opus*, the *Church Dogmatics*. For Barth, the *CD* was meant to aid pastors as they served their churches each week through the spoken word and a life of service. The only difference, then, between the *CD* and the commentary on Romans, for Barth, was that the latter was commenting on and interpreting one book, whereas the former was trying to do so comprehensively of all of the canon.

Additionally, it should be pointed out that Eberhard Jüngel argues that Barth intentionally distanced himself from his early dialectical theology, of which *Der Römerbrief* is certainly included—as a result of the critiques levied against him by Erik Peterson. Specifically, Jüngel says that this shift takes place in 1925 and that Barth's *Church Dogmatics* represents a whole new direction in theology for Barth from *Der Römerbrief* and his dialectical theology in general. I believe this thesis does not contradict but rather supports my overall argument. With that in mind, my slight elevation of Barth's exegesis of Paul's Epistle to the Romans over the other works in question is purely because it is a very direct engagement with Scripture. I am not making an argument for the supremacy of *Der Römerbrief* over and against Barth's later works. Jüngel's article, therefore, is quite helpful to present Barth studies, and I would generally agree with his overall premise. Jüngel, *Barth-Studien*, 127–79.

Finally, it should also be noted that the examination of Barth's primary works in this chapter concludes with a brief examation of Barth's *Shorter Commentary on Romans*, a work that most certainly was written long after 1925. It is clear there that Barth not only affirms the positions I am engaging in this particular text, but indeed radicalizes them. For these reasons, I believe it to be safe to elevate Barth's direct engagement with this brief passage from Scripture as an example of his tendency to allow Scripture to shape, guide, and even change his theological arguments.

9. Aside from Romans, the other major source for this issue is Paul's speech to the Athenian philosophers at the Aeropagus in Acts 17:22–34. Unfortunately, this passage will not be examined here, though I do believe that the way Barth reads Paul in Romans can be said to apply to the way to read this section about Paul recorded by Luke in Acts.

Abraham, Isaac, and Jacob in Jesus of Nazareth. Seen in this light, what was once thought to be simple and straightforward—Barth's rejection of all forms of natural knowledge of God—may seem to be much more complex. My contention is that this complexity will always be present in a theology that is attempting to stay faithful to Scripture, and especially a theology that is Pauline.

Moreover, it should be abundantly clear throughout this examination of the knowledge of God in Barth's theology that Barth's God is not the hidden, mysterious, dreadful God of Luther. Barth's God is simply not the *Deus absconditus*. The arguments are complex and dispersed throughout a massive amount of text, hence the need for such a lengthy examination. I believe, however, that after studying the material, it is quite evident that Barth's God is not hidden but revealed, not veiled but indeed unveiled; and the fundamental revelation of Barth's God is not a "No," but rather a loud and resounding "Yes."

Der Römerbrief (6th ed., 1928)

Karl Barth first published his commentary on the Epistle to the Romans in 1918 while a pastor in Safenwil. In the preface to the 1918 edition, Barth says that his book is "no more than a preliminary undertaking."[10] Barth had no idea how true this statement would turn out to be. The commentary was published during the time when Barth and his friend Edward Thurneysen were "re-educating" themselves, in light of their increasing dislike of the theology of their youth, Protestant liberalism. The results of this time of re-education can first and foremost be seen in the second edition of *Der Römerbrief*, which Barth published in 1922. The new Barth so thoroughly disagreed with the old Barth that "of the First Edition only the Preface now remains."[11] The second edition was published just as Barth's time in Safenwil was coming to an end and he was preparing for his new position as Professor of Theology at the University of Göttingen. All in all, Barth's commentary on Romans would undergo six revisions, none of which was more drastic than the complete reworking of the book between 1918 and 1921. All subsequent editions included only minor changes as well as a brief revised preface.

10. Barth, *Der Römerbrief*, 2.
11. Ibid., v.

The six prefaces reveal interesting comments about Barth's friends and foes, his hermeneutical positions, and his suppositions about the Epistle and its author, the Apostle Paul. Regarding the second of these suppositions, Barth discusses being labeled as a "Biblicist."[12] Barth does not deny this label, but rather seeks to clarify how he would like it to be used of him. Barth's "Biblicism" is often pitted against the historical-critical method of biblical exegesis, and in particular the *Religionsgeschichtliche Schule* (History of Religions School), which Barth does not hold in very high regard.[13] Barth reads Scripture fairly literally, attempting to stay true to what he finds in the text, rather than to some philosophical system or prolegomena. Barth admits, along with his critics, that there are numerous "uncomfortable points" in Paul's writings, especially in Romans.[14] Nonetheless, Barth endeavors to wrestle with these "scandals to modern thought" in a way that is fitting to the Pauline corpus and the Christian faith. Barth does not claim to have all the answers, nor does he claim an exhaustive knowledge of even the book of Romans.

Finally, regarding the third supposition, that of Paul and the Epistle itself, Barth assumes that in Romans Paul is speaking of and only about Christ.[15] Furthermore, "Paul knows of God what most of us do not know: and his Epistles enable us to know what he knew."[16] This means that for Barth, Paul truly did see the Lord, as is recounted by Paul in 1 Corinthians 15 and by Luke in Acts 22.[17] Paul's encounter with the resurrected Lord shaped every moment of Paul's life from that point forward. Paul's Epistles, therefore, and especially Romans, are fraught with the evidence of Paul's faith in his risen Lord.[18] Furthermore, as Eugene Rogers has pointed out, Paul's Epistles, and especially Romans, are the product of the resurrected Paul.[19] Saul, the zealous persecutor of Jesus' followers, had

12. Ibid., 11–12.

13. Ibid., 1, 6–10.

14. Ibid., 10.

15. Ibid.

16. Ibid., 11.

17. By including this, I am throwing in my lot with Barth against the extreme proponents of the historical-critical method, most of whom would vehemently deny that the story in Acts 22 can be faithfully attributed to Paul (thus Saul), since surely he did not claim this story as his personal testimony in his own Epistles.

18. On this point, N. T. Wright has provided a very persuasive argument as well. See Wright, *Resurrection and the Son of God*, 398.

19. Rogers, *Thomas Aquinas and Karl Barth*, 99.

died, and Paul the apostle was resurrected in his place. "The Prologue [of Romans] has set Paul up as such a 'spiritual person, the measure and rule of human acts.'"[20] Paul's very life, then, is to be a (or more accurately *the)* hermeneutical lens through which to read Paul's writings. This is made clear, at least in regard to the Epistle to the Romans, in chapter 1:1–6. It would seem that this statement could be expanded to include the entire Pauline corpus, and it would seem that Karl Barth would be one of the first to line up in support of this claim. Having addressed some preliminary points of interest from the prefaces of *Der Römerbrief,* I now turn to a brief examination of Barth's comments on Romans 1:18–21.

For the wrath of God is revealed from heaven against all ungodliness and unrighteousness of men, who hold the truth imprisoned in the chains of their unrighteousness.[21] (v. 18)

Barth begins his comments on this section in comical fashion, saying, "In the name of God! We know not what we should say to this."[22] Barth says that Paul is working from a similar framework as Luther when Luther announces the *Deus absconditus.* Yet this hidden God is revealed, and what is revealed is God's wrath. God's wrath is released or revealed against ungodliness and unrighteousness, which is essentially all of the created order.[23] Going on, Paul says that this ungodliness and unrighteousness is primarily seen in humanity, who actually have claim to some possession of truth but who imprison this selfsame truth in their own unrighteousness. All humans are sinners for Paul and Barth; this is the fundamental aspect of our life. What is more, God's judgment is a fact, regardless of our attitude toward it.[24] This imprisoned truth has been chained up by humanity and made into something that it is not. There are many false

20. Ibid. This comment is made amidst an examination of Thomas Aquinas' commentary on this prologue to Romans.

21. In this section I will list verses 18–21 as Karl Barth translated them for use in his commentaries on Romans. I have copied the style from Barth's commentary. Portions not in italics are usually words added to aid the translation from Greek to German (and then to English!) and are usually not discussed by Barth. For further notes on Barth's notation style, see Barth, *Der Römerbrief,* xv.

22. Ibid., 42.

23. But it must be emphasized that this is not what our knowledge of God is based in for Barth, in that the knowledge of God is based upon the revelation of God in Christ Jesus.

24. Barth, *Der Römerbrief,* 42.

names that humanity gives to this imprisoned truth. These false names reveal that humans do not actually see the object that is bound, but merely the apparition that they desire to occupy this position. Thus the false name is a mere negation of the truth that is bound.[25] As false, this thing is a "No-God." Ironically, we have a tendency to call this "No-God" "God," and thus we reveal our further guilt in that we know what it is that we are supposed to see bound up.

The discussion of humanity's worship of the "No-God" as well as the revelation of God's wrath point to the observation that there is some sort of natural knowledge of God. Perception of negation and wrath is still perception. True perception, though, can only take place in and through Christ, the righteousness of God. For surely,

> the wrath of God cannot be His last word, the true revelation of Him! "Not-God" cannot seriously be named "God." Nevertheless: it is, in fact, always God against whom we are thrust. Even the unbeliever encounters God, but he does not penetrate through to the truth of God that is hidden from him, and so he is broken to pieces on God, as Pharaoh was (ix. 15–18)[26] . . . The whole world is the footprint of God: yes, but, in so far as we choose scandal rather than faith, the footprint in the vast riddle of the world is the footprint of His wrath. The wrath of God is to unbelief the discovery of His righteousness, for God is not mocked. The wrath of God is the righteousness of God—apart from and without Christ.[27]

25. Ibid., 43.

26. Clearly Barth has Matthew 21:44 in mind here. After telling the parable of the vineyard owner whose tenants do not execute their responsibilities and even kill the owner's messengers and son (which seems to be the story of God in a nutshell), Jesus says, "Have you never read in the scriptures: 'The stone that the builders rejected has become the cornerstone; this was the Lord's doing, and it is amazing in our eyes'? Therefore I tell you, the kingdom of God will be taken away from you and given to a people that produces the fruits of the kingdom. *The one who falls on this stone will be broken to pieces; and it will crush anyone on whom it falls.*"

27. Barth, *Der Römerbrief*, 43. Herein is the irony: there is no "apart from Christ" for Barth. This could perhaps be said of people such as Pharaoh, but for those who live on the latter end of the incarnation, crucifixion, resurrection, and ascension, there is no such thing—even for the heathen—of "apart from and without Christ." Either Barth is being inconsistent, or, more likely, he is intentionally arguing that we are never meant to remain within a system wherein the knowledge of God is merely of God's wrath.

Hence the unbeliever, in the height of her nihilistic disbelief, is confronted with the truth of God *vis-à-vis* the wrath of God. We begin to go awry, according to Barth, when we think that we know what we are talking about when we say "God." This univocal understanding of God allows the war against God to move to the trap of ontotheology, wherein "we make Him nigh unto ourselves . . . Secretly we are ourselves the masters in this relationship."[28] Eventually, after having supplanted God with ourselves, we trade in this false knowledge for the belief in the "No-God." "Being to ourselves what God ought to be to us, He is no more to us than we are to ourselves."[29] In summary of this verse, as well as Barth's view of humanity apart from Christ, he says, "men have *imprisoned* and encased the *truth*—the righteousness of God: they have trimmed it to their own measure, and thereby robbed it both of its earnestness and of its significance. They have made it ordinary, harmless, and useless; and thereby transformed it into untruth."[30]

Thus far, there can be only two options in terms of Barth's view of the knowledge of the wrath of God. On the one hand, the "knowledge" of the unbeliever is not knowledge in the same way knowledge is usually understood. Rather, the "knowledge" of the unbeliever is some form of embedded assumption or cognition that never makes it out of the dark recesses of the human mind. This "knowledge" can only be explained by the dogmatic assertion that God is the Creator of all things and that creation must somewhere, in some way, know that it is dependent in order to exist. The second and more likely option is that humans are blinded by self-deception. According to this option, humans do see that we have truth bound and imprisoned. Furthermore, it must be said that we do know that the "No-God" is simply a negation, a creative way of distracting ourselves long enough to shove God to the nether regions of the imagination. We have become so good at self-deception that we have simply forgotten, for the most part, that truth is "out there" somewhere. This type of knowledge is not a true knowledge of God, but it does remain, in some twisted way, a form of knowledge nonetheless, a *via negativa* of sorts.

28. Barth, *Der Römerbrief,* 44.
29. Ibid., 45.
30. Ibid.

Because that which may be known of God is manifest to them; for God
manifested it unto them. For the invisible things of him since the creation of
the world are clearly seen, being perceived through the things that are made,
even his everlasting power and divinity; so that they are without excuse: be-
cause that, in spite of knowing God, they glorified him not as God, neither
gave thanks; but became vain in their reasonings, and their senseless heart
was darkened. (vv. 19–21)

Barth asserts that this passage should be read as tragic, as humans should,
and to a certain extent do, already know the truth that is revealed in the
resurrection. He says, "We know that God is He whom we do not know,
and that our ignorance is precisely the problem and the source of our
knowledge."[31] Humanity stands in complete rebellion against its creator,
which is ironically a rebellion against that which is more intimate or immanent to us than we are to ourselves. Barth believes that in some fashion
humanity carries this knowledge of the immanent and yet unknown God
with it always. "He is the hidden abyss; but he is also the hidden home at
the beginning and end of all our journeyings."[32] Here Barth makes reference to Plato's philosophy as a great example of this immanent knowledge
of the transcendent.

In light of this Platonic reference, it would seem that in his commentary on Romans, Barth has a twofold account of natural knowledge.
On the one hand, humanity has a form of negative knowledge that is im-
plicit to existence as such. This "knowledge" is one of God's wrath, which
enables humanity to be free of excuses before God. On the other hand,
Barth allows for this negative knowledge to move to a positive knowledge of sorts, at least in terms of the existence of a Creator or Origin of
all things. Barth reveals this positive knowledge in a statement that will
come as shocking to many of his students. He says, "by calm, veritable,
unprejudiced religious contemplation the divine '*No' can be established*

31. Ibid.

32. Ibid., 46. It is easy to see how perhaps someone might take this to mean that
Barth is advancing the *Deus absconditus*. It is important to note, however, that Barth is
here referring to all of humanity carrying within it some form of inherent knowledge
of the Creator. Had Barth stopped here, the previous accusation might stand. Barth
did not stop here, however. This is not Barth's God. This statement is a statement about
sinful and fallen humanity, and not about God. God, for Barth, is revealed in Jesus
of Nazareth. Thus, it might be said that for Barth, the *Deus absconditus* is the tragic
theology of ordinary men and women, not familiar with Christ, and yet themselves
not free from sin.

and apprehended."[33] And the knowledge of this "No," of God's wrath that renders humanity free of excuse before God, surely cannot remain as such for very long, for there is constant and purposeful movement within the comprehension of the "No" toward the greater and more relevant "Yes." The gift of the knowledge of God is not meant to remain at only the knowledge of a Creator, but rather it is meant to drive or move humanity toward the positive knowledge of God in Christ. And thus neither form of knowledge is in any way complete, and certainly not what some would refer to as "salvific knowledge," but they do both remain, in fact, knowledge. These two forms account for humanity's universal culpability before the Creator.

In conclusion, Barth says that what we can know about God is that "we can know nothing of God, that we are not God, and that the Lord is to be feared."[34] What seems at first glance to be a frustratingly paradoxical statement should be examined more closely, for I believe it holds the key to Barth's musings on this section from Romans. Barth is still attempting to answer the question, what can we know? His answer comes in a sentence composed of three dependent clauses that function as separate answers but are nonetheless dependent upon one another. This interesting structure can best be examined by rewriting the sentence as three sentences, all of which share a common beginning but feature a different ending, with each dependent upon the previous sentence. The purpose of writing this out as three sentences is to see what is at work in the one sentence that Barth has written. My contention is that each clause has meaning on its own, as an answer to the question, what can we know? And yet each answer is unable to stand on its own in light of the witness of the Epistle to the Romans; thus the three are meant to work in cooperation to provide Barth's "answer" to the riddle of what we can know. I take the question mark at the end of the sentence to be further proof of Barth's paradoxical intentions in this sentence.[35]

33. Ibid. Italics mine.

34. Ibid., 47.

35. It should of course be pointed out that the question mark does not appear in the German text. As is often the case, the sentence is much longer than it appears in English and thus the question mark was inserted to help not only translate the sentence, but to interpret it and make the wording more accessible to English audiences. It is clear that this section is a response to the question, what can we know? Barth's answer: we can know that we cannot know God, that we are not God, and that God is to be feared. I believe the translator, Edwyn C. Hoskyns, was quite right, therefore, to make this editorial insertion. Furthermore, prior to the sentence in question, the

"And what does this mean but that we can know nothing of God, that we are not God, that the Lord is to be feared?"

a. "And what does this mean but that we can know nothing of God?"

b. "And what does this mean but that we are not God?"

c. "And what does this mean but that the Lord is to be feared?"

For Barth, human knowledge of God, apart from Christ, can be summed up as follows: we cannot positively know anything about God. We can, however, comprehend that we are not God, which forces us to the negative knowledge that there is a God, and then to the positive apprehension of God's wrath. This should elicit the fear of God, which results in the theological assertion that all are without excuse. The image that Barth employs to illustrate his resulting view of humanity is that it is "wandering in the Night."[36] This "Night" is the Night of God's wrath, and while God is hidden, the fact that it is Night is not. Humanity can and should be able to perceive that it is Night and that this Night does stem from the creator God. Here Barth seems still quite influenced by both Kant and Luther, in terms of the knowledge of the "No-God" or the hidden God. But it should already be clear that both of these concepts, though they are given their due, are not intended to remain. Barth's is not a system plagued by an ever-present, and yet aloof, hidden God. It is my opinion that this will become increasingly clear with each examination of Barth's dealing with the subject of the knowledge of God.

So much for Barth's *Der Römerbrief*. At the end of this examination of Barth's views on the natural knowledge of God, we will return to his work with Romans, this time his *Shorter Commentary on Romans*, to see how his thought has developed over the span of almost twenty years.

German edition includes this very brief transition sentence summing up the previous sentence and introducing the paradoxical sentence that follows: *Gerade das*. Or, "This is straight" or perhaps "straightforward." It might not seem straight or straightforward, but to Barth it was precisely that. Barth, *Der Römerbrief*, 22. All further references to *Der Römerbrief*, unless otherwise noted, are to the English translation.

36. Ibid., 48.

The *Göttingen Dogmatics* (1924–25)

The *Göttingen Dogmatics* represent Barth's first attempt at a proper dogmatics. In preparation for these dogmatics, Barth spent his first few years as Honorary Professor of Reformed Theology at Göttingen teaching about historical Reformed theologians.[37] That being said, Barth nonetheless believed that "holy scripture must be the master in an evangelical dogmatics."[38] He thus sought to pursue a dogmatics that was deeply influenced by and connected to Holy Scripture. In the old Reformers, as well as many Catholic and Orthodox thinkers before the Protestant Reformation, Barth saw just such a commitment to Scripture. He did not, however, believe that this same commitment existed in much of contemporary Protestant Reformed scholarship. And so Barth's first attempt at a dogmatics went against the grain of the formally Reformed theology of so many of his colleagues, and yet embodied the true spirit of the Reformation itself. Barth's was a theology that was constantly changing and forming, based upon his interaction with Scripture and with the way that other Christians throughout time have read and interpreted Scripture. As perhaps the best illustration of this point, the editor of the *Göttingen Dogmatics*, Hannelotte Reiffen, relates the struggle between Professor Barth and the Lutheran theological faculty at Göttingen over the title of the dogmatics. Apparently, the Lutheran faculty insisted that he call the dogmatics "Reformed Dogmatics." Barth, however, thought that this would "call in question the ecumenical character of his lectures by a confessional tag which would run contrary to the history and nature of the Reformed church and its theology."[39] Not wanting to comply with this short-sighted request, and yet recognizing that he was in no position not to, Barth changed the subtitle to the ambiguous "Instruction in the Christian Religion."

This work, as it stands today, is a curious one. In that it originates just a few years after Barth's second edition of *Der Römerbrief,* one can find traces of the early Barth, with his Protestant liberal training as well as his penchant for dialectic. However, one can also see Barth's continued disdain and distancing from the Protestant liberal tradition, as well as his incredibly strong Christology, his comfort with paradoxical reasoning,

---

37. Barth, *Göttingen Dogmatics*, ix.
38. Ibid.
39. Ibid., x.

and his truly Reformed, and therefore catholic, ecclesiology.[40] In the interests of the present work, we will briefly examine the small section of the *Göttingen Dogmatics* in which Barth deals with the "knowability of God." This section (§15) is short and not as rich in terms of the present topic as some other sources, but it will provide a much-needed stair step in between *Der Römerbrief* and Barth's important little book on Anselm.

Barth begins by saying that the very fact that we talk about God at all, that we preach about God, reveals that God is knowable to us, "that he is an object."[41] Here Barth is just stating the obvious, which is that in some strange way God lends God's self to us as an object to be discussed and apprehended. And yet, in a great discussion of how discussions of the incarnation lead inevitably to the discussion and doctrine of the Trinity, Barth says that in God's revelation in the Son, "God is an irremovable subject that can never be confused with an object."[42] Thus, while we might apprehend God as an object, we know that God is precisely not an object like other objects. Barth goes on to explain that we cannot know God as an object, for that would be to know God as God exists in God's own self. Rather, we can know God as God knows God's self, or, in other words, as God has revealed God's self to us. Thus, we can know God through the incarnation. As such, in the revelation of the Son, "we become the subject of knowledge by faith and obedience."[43] And so, in the incarnation, humanity comes to realize that it is the beneficiary of the gift of divine knowability, or that it receives the ability to know God. In this way, humanity is gifted the role of subject, and accordingly God takes on the role of the object, though this relationship is not like any other subject-object relationship in that despite the gift of knowability, God is always shrouded in mystery. Barth is concerned that too much Protestant and especially Reformed theology has negated or avoided the mystery of God that is still present in God's revelation. And so on the one hand, Barth emphasizes that we cannot say that God is unknown

40. By this, I mean that Barth was perhaps the Reformation's truest son. When Barth uses the descriptive term "Reformed," he intends an ecumenical spirit or principle, not a religious "party" with a particular fixed agenda or platform to promote. For Barth, being Reformed was not about maintaining the "Reformed tradition," but was about the constant reform that is necessary if the Church universal is to faithfully follow her Lord.

41. Barth, *Göttingen Dogmatics*, 325.

42. Ibid., 327.

43. Ibid., 330.

or unknowable, and our language about God must be positive.[44] And yet on the other hand, Barth says that "our own knowledge, even and precisely our knowledge of Christ, is knowledge in a mystery, not direct knowledge. God's hiddenness, his alien work, meets us in Christ, and finally and supremely in the crucified Christ, for where is God so hidden as here, and where is the possibility of offense so great as here?"[45] Stating this more emphatically, Barth says, "the life of Jesus does not in itself impart the knowledge of God (John 14:8–9)."[46] God is a mystery for Barth, and thus any knowledge of God we have is necessarily the knowledge of a mystery.[47]

If God is a mystery for Barth, the logic of the revelation of this mystery is surely dialectic. In an important passage on this matter, Barth states that our knowledge of God is knowledge of a medium; it is indirect. This medium is the "third thing" that arises between the mystery of the transcendent God, on the one hand, and the limitations of human, creaturely knowledge, on the other. It is quite obvious that here Barth is utilizing dialectical language in hopes of explaining the unexplainable. His medium is not the mysterious God in God's self, but rather this medium is a puzzle: "Our knowledge has to do with a puzzle or part."[48] Barth even goes so far as to describe the puzzle that is revealed as *en ainigmati*, or a "dark saying," as Luther put it.[49] This medium, or dark saying, according to Barth, "fulfills its purpose, it becomes luminous, it unveils even as it veils, it causes to shine, it bears witness, it imparts."[50] And yet, in these moments of dialectic, and of the unknown God that is preferable in such a system, there is strong evidence that Barth was even then moving away from the typical construal of dialectic to something that is much more mysterious and much less characterized by tension and/or conflict. Likewise, though Barth seems to still be amiable toward the *Deus absconditus*, Barth's God is not the unknown God, but the unknown and yet fully revealed God. We are finite, created, and sinful creatures, says Barth, and

44. Ibid., 328.

45. Ibid., 335.

46. Ibid., 334.

47. This is not to say knowledge of the thing or object—i.e., God—but rather knowledge of the mystery itself, the mystery that shrouds God.

48. Barth, *Göttingen Dogmatics*, 333.

49. Ibid., 334. Surely this "dark saying" is very much at home with the *Deus absconditus*.

50. Ibid., 333.

thus our knowledge of the Creator will always be limited or partial. That being said, however, God has fully revealed God's self to us, in such a way that it can be said that through the gift of the capacity for knowability, humanity can, despite being finite, created, and sinful, know God as fully as is possible. Thus humanity can know God, *en total*, as far as God's relationship to creation goes, but that does not apply to how God is in God's own self. Human knowledge of God, or knowability, therefore is full and yet partial, total and yet incomplete, in that God is fully revealed and yet mysteriously so. Interestingly, Barth praises Roman Catholicism for dealing with this best, saying, "they see more clearly at this point."[51]

In concluding this brief look at the *Göttingen Dogmatics*, it can be said that humanity does not possess the ability to know God, but through grace, and specifically through the grace revealed on the cross, humanity is given the capability of the knowledge of God as God has revealed God's self. Barth calls the latter, knowability. Human knowledge of God is fully dependent upon revelation. It is not, therefore, a natural capacity. "Once the reality of revelation is presupposed," however, "we have to be taken seriously as those whose blind eyes and deaf ears are still eyes and ears that can be opened for revelation."[52] Barth clearly uses dialectical language to discuss human knowability, and yet he demonstrates throughout a penchant for something different than "traditional dialectic" and its fundamental agonism. Rather, Barth's way of conceiving of and articulating the problem of the human knowledge of God is fraught with the tension of allowing God to be both hidden and revealed, as well as allowing God and humanity to be completely separate, and yet extremely close. The revelation of God in Christ is that which holds these seeming opposites together, and even here in the *Göttingen Dogmatics*, Barth begins to articulate this complexity as paradox. When discussing how the temporal can know the eternal, or how the human can know the Divine, Barth appeals to paradox, saying, "what is this? Paradoxically enough, but very aptly, Paul calls it *aorata autou*, the ineffable things of God that one may perceive in his *poiëmata*, his eternal power and dignity."[53]

Likewise, Barth articulates the medium that emerges from the dialectical understanding of the human knowledge of God as a puzzle and utilizes language very similar to that of paradox in order to describe what

51. Ibid., 339.
52. Ibid., 341.
53. Ibid., 342.

he intended by the term "puzzle." Moreover, because of his use of and dependency upon dialectic in the *Göttingen Dogmatics*, and despite any appeals to his increasingly paradoxical logic, Barth's God looks much more like the *Deus absconditus* in this work than it will in later works.[54] In particular, Barth's appeal to Luther's *en ainigmati*, or dark saying, to articulate why the life of Jesus does not fully impart the knowledge of God shows the lingering presence of the *Deus absconditus*.

In short, though we are not permitted to delve any further into this important early work due to the constraints of this work, suffice it to say that in the *Göttingen Dogmatics*, one finds a whirlpool of Barth's old thoughts and theological habits, as well as his new convictions and his developing theological tastes. In the *Göttingen Dogmatics*, God is hidden and revealed; humanity is incapable of having knowledge of God, and yet humanity is capable of receiving the gift of knowability; dialectic is the preferred method of reasoning, and yet Barth's use of dialectic looks less and less like "traditional dialectics." Perhaps most important is Barth's keen desire not to be a Reformed theologian, but an evangelical one. Along with this is Barth's desire for dogmatics to be a completely biblical exercise, as opposed to one based upon a philosophical method or even one that attempts to follow a strictly "Reformed" method. Barth is not interested, ultimately, in being Reformed, but in being evangelical and catholic. As the editor Reiffen points out, despite being very Reformed himself, Barth clearly wants to uphold the ecumenical quality of his dogmatics. This is something that will only grow stronger in Barth's work in the years to come.

Having completed this brief look into the knowability of God in Barth's *Göttingen Dogmatics*, we will now turn to what is perhaps one of Barth's most important yet oft-ignored works, his book on Anselm.

Anselm: Fides Quaerens Intellectum (1931)

Much has been made of the importance of Barth's book on Anselm and the role it plays in relation to the rest of his theological writings. As we have already seen, some Barth scholars such as Hans Urs von Balthasar

54. Barth's repeated affirmation of Kant at the end of §15 offers further proof of Barth's indebtedness to "traditional dialectic" and the *Deus absconditus*. Gillespie's *Nihilism Before Nietzsche* offers strong support for a critique of both "traditional dialectic" and the *Deus absconditus* in Kant, as well as further support for the argument that the *Deus absconditus* leads to nihilism. (See ch. 2 of this work.)

offer the formidable contention that Barth's book on Anselm serves as the pivot point or hinge between Barth's older "dialectical" theology and his later "analogical" theology. Indeed, Barth himself, later in his life, insists that this thesis is accurate.[55] Despite this autobiographical claim, other scholars such as Bruce McCormack have disagreed, saying that Barth's theology always remained dialectical. While debating the validity of these claims is not central to my thesis, the issue is one that constantly swirls in and out of the topic at hand and therefore must be treated with the utmost seriousness. It is true that McCormack's understanding and articulation of Barth's life and work is enormous. The evidence found in Barth's own writings as well as his clearly demonstrated view on the matter of dialectic cannot be excused, however. I cannot agree, therefore, that Barth's theology remains firmly entrenched within the confines of dialectical theology. My contention is that Barth slowly progressed toward a somewhat different viewpoint, a different understanding of the Christian message that cannot easily be articulated within the logical confines of either analogy or dialectic. I call this different viewpoint "paradox," or "the absurd possibility of the absurd."[56] Likewise, this movement contains within it the movement away from anything close to the affirmation of the *Deus absconditus*, toward a more complexly understood revealed God.

Presently, the task is to examine Barth's understanding of the possibility of a natural knowledge of God. Analyzing his book on Anselm from this perspective, it should be very clear that the book is hugely important and definitely a sign of growth and of things to come. The fact is that for Barth, his book on Anselm was very important, and we do Barth a huge injustice if we fail to grasp this point. Regarding the book's importance, Barth said, "most of them [commentators] have completely failed to see that in this book on Anselm I am working with a vital key, if

55. In discussing the change or "deepening" that took place in his theology, Barth said, "The real document of this farewell is, in truth, not the much-read brochure *Nein!*, directed against Brunner in 1934, but rather the book about the evidence for God of Anselm of Canterbury which appeared in 1931. *Among all my books I regard this as the one written with the greatest satisfaction.* And yet in America it is doubtless not read at all and in Europe it certainly is the least read of any of my works." Barth, *How I Changed My Mind*, 43. Italics Mine.

56. Barth, *CD* IV.3.1, 178. Here Barth uses the phrases "impossible possibility" and "the absurd possibility of the absurd" to describe the paradox of evil. I take this to be a sufficiently helpful definition of the logic of paradox in Karl Barth, a logic that I believe is increasingly apparent in his later works.

not the key, to an understanding of that whole process of thought that has impressed me more and more in my *Church Dogmatics* as the only one proper to theology."[57] A proper understanding of this is hugely important to understanding Barth's corpus.

Barth says that the subject matter of his book on Anselm is perhaps "the key" to understanding all of what he intends to write about in his *Church Dogmatics*. As the subject matter at hand is Anselm's "proof" for the existence of God, which is essentially a discussion on the possibility of the knowledge of God and of the relationship between God and humanity, we will do well to heed Barth's words. As if this statement were not enough, Barth later states that while he began his theological work with a dialectical approach, he came, through his Anselm book, to hold that "God and humanity share a common narrative, God's own story."[58] With the understanding that Barth believed the book to be extremely important, let us now examine his *Anselm: Fides Quaerens Intellectum*, paying specific attention to his discussion of the human possibility of the knowledge of God.

Barth first published his book on Anselm in 1931, just prior to the publication of the first edition of volume one of his *Church Dogmatics*. In the introduction to a later reissue of this important text, Barth begins by stating his reasons for having written the book on Anselm. Barth said that his reasons were varied, but primarily the book is a result of a seminar he taught at Bonn in 1930, as well as the related reading, the student's questions, and a guest lecture by Heinrich Scholz.[59] Barth also confesses to have always liked Anselm, something that he will echo in *Church Dogmatics* I.1. Finally, he also points out that because of this appreciation of Anselm, he was later accused of both Catholicism and Schleiermacherism. Curiously, he adds in this introduction that the work on Anselm and his new introduction are not intended as a refutation of these accusations. Rather, Barth provides a hearty endorsement of Anselm and the need for contemporary scholars to explore his writings with more depth.

> I cannot deny that I deem Anselm's Proof of the Existence of God in the context of his theological scheme a model piece of good, penetrating and neat theology, which at every step I have

57. Barth, *Anselm*, 11. For further proof of Barth's clearly defined position on this, see also Barth, *How I Changed My Mind*.

58. Rumscheidt, *Way of Theology in Karl Barth*, 13.

59. Barth, *Anselm*, 7.

found instructive and edifying, though I would not and could not identify myself completely with the views of the author. Moreover, I believe that it is a piece of theology that has quite a lot to say to present-day theology, both Protestant and Roman Catholic, which, quite apart from its attitude to its particular form, present-day theology ought to heed.[60]

It is important at the beginning to point out that according to Barth, Anselm never set out to prove the existence of God. Rather, Barth firmly believed that Anselm's goal was always to be able to describe God as the supreme good.[61] It is during this attempt that he "proves" God and then the nature of God. For any theologian, and especially for one influenced by Barthian thinking, the very word *prove*, when used in relation to God, is an immediate red flag. Barth believes, however, that readers must understand what Anselm intends when he talks of proving or proof. First of all, Anselm himself does not even describe his work as a proof until one of his critics, Guanilo of Marmoutiers, uses the term to describe Anselm's work.[62] Anselm eventually gives in and adopts the term, but only in such a way that the substance of the proof, rather than the proof itself, is always the goal and outcome of his work. To develop the difference between the substance of the proof and the proof itself, Barth highlights Anselm's use of the Latin terms *probare, intelligere*, and *legere*. The first, says Barth, should be translated as "proof," as the end result of the project.[63] The second, *intelligere*, is actually the key to the whole project. *Intelligere*, according to Barth, should be understood as intellect or, more accurately, understanding.[64] Finally, Barth points out that Anselm will also use the term *legere*, which Barth says should be understood as reflection upon what has already been said in the Credo.[65] It is definitely the case, argues Barth, that *intelligere* is always the focus of Anselm's project. The goal is not to prove or to master, but to understand. "As *intelligere* is achieved," according to Barth, "it issues in joy."[66] Joy, or *delectatio*, is the goal of the entire project: joy in the Lord.

60. Ibid., 9.
61. Ibid., 13.
62. Ibid., 14.
63. Ibid.
64. Ibid.
65. Ibid., 40.
66. Barth, *Anselm*, 15.

If joy is the goal, then surely "prove" is used in a less than traditional way. To prove something is to know something, to stand above something as master. To prove a point, to prove the validity of a mathematical statement, is to master it, after which one usually moves on to something else. And yet here, to prove is so very different. Barth describes the proving accomplished by Anselm as simply the basis for the continual joy and delight in the mysteries of the Lord. Even in proof, there are further mysteries and a deeper love to experience and thus to enjoy. In this way, Anselm's proof is very much an internal argument or discussion. From the very beginning, the grounding assumption of Anselm's proof is not universal human reason, but rather faith. Anselm always assumes that a genuine Credo, or confession of faith, is the basis for his argument. For Anselm, and I would argue for Barth, Credo always precedes *intelligere*, or confession, and profession always precedes understanding.[67] Thus, and this cannot be stressed enough, Anselm's argument is not an outward argument.[68] Anselm's proof is not an apology, but rather an attempt to seek knowledge in and through faith. Barth recognizes this when he states, "Anselm wants 'proof' and 'joy' because he wants *intelligere* and he wants *intelligere* because he believes."[69]

Faith, for Anselm as well as for Barth, demands knowledge of God.[70] "Teach me to seek You, and reveal Yourself to me as I seek, because I can neither seek You if You do not teach me how, nor find You unless You reveal Yourself. Let me seek You in desiring You; let me desire You in seeking You; let me find You in loving You; let me love You in finding You."[71] Moreover, faith, as Barth observes in Anselm, summons a person to knowledge: *credo ut intelligam*. And so Barth shows that Anselm's whole project is one that is entirely perceived and conducted within the limits of faith, and in particular, faith in the revelation of God in Christ. For the most part, then, Anselm does not concern himself with the nonbeliever. His goal has nothing to do with making an argument toward God on behalf of some notion of universal human reason. But Anselm does believe that all humans are capable of having and receiving

67. Ibid., 24.

68. Ibid., 67.

69. Ibid., 16–17. I believe that this is the main point and argument of Barth's book on Anselm, and that it is perhaps the driving thought for his theological work thenceforth.

70. Ibid., 19.

71. Anselm, *Proslogion*, in *Major Works*, 86–87.

faith. This faith, though it may be only a small grain of hope or belief, is powerful and should not be ignored. The difference between a tentative knowledge of the God as Creator, however, and a knowledge of God in Jesus Christ—knowledge of salvation, that is—is great indeed. Anselm did believe, however, that this difference was anything but insurmountable, as even the tiniest inkling of faith is capable of summoning a person on the journey of discovering the knowledge of Jesus Christ as Lord and Savior, and therefore of the wondrous power of the Father, all of which is only made possible by the Holy Spirit. Essentially, Barth believed that Anselm thought that unbelievers were walking down the same path as believers—that is, the journey from belief to understanding. "If such is Anselm's interpretation of the quest of the 'unbeliever' then we can understand how he comes to engage in a discussion with him without either accepting the unbeliever's criterion, such as universal human reason, or stipulating that the unbeliever in order to become competent to discuss must first be converted into a believer."[72]

It is interesting that Barth positively notes not only Anselm's refusal to conduct his argument on the terms of universal human reason, but that he also refuses to assert that an unbeliever must first be converted in order to have an understanding of God's existence. All people, for Anselm, and arguably for Barth, have the possibility of the knowledge of God, in that they are capable of inquiring and believing.

Anselm believes that all people are capable of having faith and therefore knowledge because humans have the potential, the vestige of the Trinity, which distinguishes humans from other animals. "In faith," says Anselm, "this is actually actualized."[73] In faith, according to Anselm, human beings are made into the image of the Trinity. Anselm, therefore, has no trouble talking of humans having the potential or capacity for the knowledge of God. This potential or capacity is none other than the intellect or the understanding, what Anselm calls *intelligere*. "*Intelligere* is a potentiality for advancing in the direction of heavenly vision to a point that can be reached and that is worth trying to reach."[74] *Intelligere* is the basis and the potential for any and all knowledge of God, and we must recall that *intelligere* is made possible only by Credo, by a confession of faith, and faith itself is a gift from God. Thus, while it would seem that

72. Ibid., 66.

73. Ibid., 20.

74. Ibid., 21.

Anselm is arguing that all humans possess a natural knowledge of God, or at least the possibility of the natural knowledge of God, in actuality he is saying that all humans have been gifted with this possibility, which is not theirs by right, but is theirs nevertheless.

All humans have been gifted with this possibility, this tiny mustard seed of faith, according to Anselm. As a result, it is possible for humanity to come to a knowledge of God as "that than which nothing greater can be conceived." This is not, however, the goal of Anselm's work, for Anselm does not want to assert that "that than which nothing greater can be conceived" is the ultimate name for God. "That than which nothing greater can be conceived" is surely different and less desirable than names such as Creator, Redeemer, Messiah, or even Abba Father.[75] Anselm's proof is merely a way of describing the process of faith that seeks understanding, and that seeks to describe the God who is all of these things and so much more. While human reason, which we must not forget is a gift from God, might be capable of coming to the conclusion that there is a God who can be described as "that than which nothing greater can be conceived," we must not think that this is complete, decisive, and definitive of who God is. God is so much greater and more than "that than which nothing greater can be conceived."[76] To achieve, or attain to this type of knowledge, grace is essential. *Intelligere*, understanding, is always in search of this greater knowledge of God, but it can reach its goal only as a result of grace.[77] "Everything depends not only upon the fact that God grants him [the pious thinker—i.e., Anselm] grace to think correctly about Him, but also on the fact that God himself comes within His system as the object of this thinking, that he 'shows' Himself to be the thinker and in so doing modifies 'correct' thinking to an *intelligere ese in re*. Only thus does the grace of Christian knowledge become complete."[78]

It is a gift, the gift of faith, that allows a person to search for the knowledge of God, and it is a gift, the gift of grace, that allows a person to have the knowledge of anything more than that God is "that than which nothing greater can be conceived." In this way, it is seen that God provides the basis, terms, and possibility of any and all knowledge of God.

75. It might be that Anselm's "definition" of God is rooted in the Tetragrammaton of Exodus 3:14, but Anselm does not cite this. Rather, he seems to base his work in dialogue between the Psalms and human wisdom.

76. Anselm, *Proslogion*, 96.

77. Barth, *Anselm*, 40.

78. Ibid., 39.

Finally, it should be pointed out that Anselm's proof is shrouded in the mysteries of God. Standing over and above the *intelligere* that Anselm discusses is the reality that God does not exist as other things exist. Likewise, God is not a thing like other things. God is the integral element to existence itself. "No thing exists so necessarily that knowledge of it is indispensable because no thing has real, ultimate existence."[79] God is and defines existence itself, as God is ultimately the only one who really exists.[80] That is to say, God exists in such a way that defines and makes possible creaturely existence. "The reason why there is such a thing as existence is that God exists."[81] Only God constitutes God's own existence, whereas humans (like the rest of creation) owe their existence to their creator and cannot affect or change the terms of their existence. For this reason, all knowledge of God, all *intelligere,* is ultimately aimed at joy and praise. True knowledge of God forces us into the situation where we must confess that the real truth is that we cannot really know anything about God. In proclaiming this negatively construed affirmation, we come to the positive possibility of joy. For Anselm, therefore, and I would argue that the same is true for Barth, apophatic theology presupposes kataphatic theology.[82] This is the beauty of Anselm's proof. Anselm's proof is anything but neat and simple; it challenges us to reevaluate both knowledge and understanding. Even the most faithful and humble Christian must confess that her knowledge of God is always imperfect, introductory, and lacking. In so doing, her very confession, I believe, draws her nearer to God than she ever was before.

At its core, Anselm's proof was a radical statement first and foremost about God and God's existence, and only secondarily about the human possibility of the knowledge of God. It most certainly was not intended apologetically as a logical proof for the ontological existence of God. Instead, Anselm's proof was intended as an exercise in *fides*

79. Ibid., 100.

80. Ibid., 98. Clearly, here, though Barth is remaining within the realm of Christian orthodoxy, he is close to nominalism. I would argue that rather than read Barth as a nominalist in places such as this, one should instead see the impetus for the origins of nominalism in the first place. Much like Jaroslav Pelikan has argued regarding the majority of heresies, nominalism arose out of an attempt to do justice to the biblical teaching of the transcendent power and otherness of God. There are ways, however, to affirm this without buying into all that nominalism entails. Despite critics who might claim otherwise, I believe that Barth does this well.

81. Barth, *Anselm*, 154.

82. Ibid., 118.

quaerens intellectum, which was originally the intended title for Anselm's *Proslogion*. Anselm's proof is a prayer; it is a confession and exploration of God's goodness. Anselm's proof proves God's existence only in that it points human understanding toward the great unknowable mystery of God, amidst which we both know and are known. Anselm's proof is a devout internal quest into an ever-deeper understanding of God and God's nature. "But I do desire to understand Your truth a little, that truth that my heart believes and loves. For I do not seek to understand so that I may believe; but I believe so that I may understand. For I believe this also, that 'unless I believe, I shall not understand' [Isa. 7:9]."[83]

According to Anselm, all humans, Christians and non-Christians alike, have been gifted with the faith necessary to perceive the mere possibility of the existence of God. The potential or capacity for the knowledge of God results in anything but finality and true knowledge, but rather it allows for a person to begin the quest toward the true understanding of the God, which can only come by grace. In this way, Anselm's proof is not an example of the power of universal human reason, but rather it is an example of the universal scope of God's redemptive love for creation. With this in mind, Barth heartily endorsed Anselm's *Proslogion*: "He [Anselm] 'assumed' neither the Church's Credo nor his own *credere*, but he prayed and the Church's Credo and his own *credere* were assumed. On this foundation, comparable to no philosophical presupposition and inconceivable for all systematic theology, he has come to know and has proved the existence of God."[84]

After this brief examination of Barth's book on Anselm, the importance of this work should be clear. In his Anselm book, Barth shows that the knowledge of God as unknown or hidden is but a doxological beginning to the pursuit of the knowledge of the revealed God, which comes by grace. Anselm's theology provides a true way forward for Barth, in that it becomes evident how by faith, which comes through grace, humans are able to move from a faint knowledge of the hidden God, and therefore of God's wrath, toward God's unfathomable goodness and love, which is revealed in Christ Jesus. Anselm's thought, mixed with Barth's christological impulse, provides the necessary logic to move forward, and thus away from the *Deus absconditus*.

---

83. Anselm, *Proslogion*, 87.
84. Ibid., 170.

The fondness with which Barth affirms Anselm stands out as a wolf amongst sheep when compared with some of Barth's other writings concerning the knowledge of God. That Barth formally goes on record as affirming and not rejecting the vast majority of St. Anselm's works reveals much about Barth's theological growth and the direction in which he was headed. Does the Anselm book signal a break with dialectic in favor of analogy? I would have to say that it does. At the very least, the Anselm book marks a change or a significant development away from dialectic and nominalism toward something different. It is thus clear to me that with the Anselm book, Barth's theology begins to take on a very different shape, and while he may not have openly embraced a more analogical view of things, he does begin to openly reject and critique the use of dialectic in Christian theology. As Barth himself says, he does not agree with all the positions of the great saint, but he does believe that a reexamination and a reappropriation of his thought is vital to contemporary theology. What is more, Barth himself declares—and he does so in reflection, which I think makes the statement all the more powerful—that his book on Anselm is a, if not *the*, vital key to understanding the whole process of thought that slowly impressed itself upon him as the only way proper to Christian theology. This is the process of thought that he says is on full display in his *Church Dogmatics*, which is where we now turn our attention. Barth's Anselm book cannot be overlooked, and any attempt to argue that it should not be at the fore of Barth studies is based in complete disregard for the great theologian's own opinions regarding this work.

Church Dogmatics I.1 (1932)

When Barth published the first volume of his *magnum opus*, the *Church Dogmatics*, in 1932, there were six editions of *Der Römerbrief* in circulation. Furthermore, the first volume of the *Church Dogmatics* was released a decade after the conclusion of his infamous period of "re-education." Much like *Der Römerbrief*, Barth acknowledges that in the 1932 edition of the *Church Dogmatics*, volume one is actually a revision of an earlier version published some five years previous.[85] The earlier version was a stand-alone volume that was even smaller than the volume I.1 of 1932, which would be followed by volume I.2 in the coming years.

85. Barth, *CD* I.1, ix.

In the preface, Barth explains the impetus for producing a revision of volume one. In addition, he lays out the structure for the five volumes to come. Furthermore, Barth addresses the concerns of many of the critics of his work to this point, stating that he is not trying to put forth a "crypto-Catholicism."[86] It is in light of the accusations of being some sort of "closet Catholic" that Barth makes the previously mentioned comment about the *analogia entis*. Barth makes it clear that he is no longer afraid of scholasticism and is quite comfortable appealing to both Saints Anselm and Thomas for theological support.[87] The statement about the *analogia entis*, however, seems to be a pretty clear attempt to show that Barth does want to distance himself from Roman Catholicism on some points. The zealousness of his statement seems to be offset by his charitable comments. This reading might furthermore be plausible in light of the statement a few lines before the infamous rejection of the Catholic doctrine, where Barth says of the *analogia entis* that it is "legitimate only on the basis of a so-called natural knowledge of God in the sense of the *Vaticanum*."[88] Interestingly, Barth begins the previous sentence by saying that the doctrine or principle of the *analogia entis* has been exploited. This sets up the course that the *Church Dogmatics* is to run. On the one hand, Barth wants to avoid the often indulgent exploitations of the *analogia entis* characteristic of much of Roman Catholicism. On the other hand, Barth is trying to steer clear of the dangers of the Protestant liberalism of Schleiermacher, Ritschl, and Hermann, which, according to Barth, will most likely destroy Protestant theology and the Protestant church.[89] In addition, Barth laments that Protestants seem to be losing sight of the doctrines of the Trinity and the Virgin Birth, and especially of the sense of mystery in theology.[90] Finally, Barth states that he is not trying to advance his own system or theology, nor is he attempting to put forward a "dogmatics of dialectical theology."[91] I think that it is clear that Barth's intention is to essentially provide theological commentary on Scripture in line with the dogmatic teachings of the Church. His intention is not to write a systematic theology, as his primary aversion is to placing any

86. Ibid., xiii.

87. Ibid.

88. Ibid. Here Barth is referring to Vatican I, and its twofold order of knowledge.

89. Ibid.

90. Ibid., xiv.

91. Ibid., xv. As many have taken Barth to be doing precisely that, this quote cannot be overvalued.

type of system over and against Scripture. Barth's view is that any form of system necessarily serves as a Prolegomena and thus cripples and distorts Scripture. This is certainly the case for dialectics, and Barth is adamant that he is not advancing a "dogmatics of dialectical theology." His theology might have many similarities with dialectical theology at times, but it is most certainly not, and should not be categorized as, dialectical theology. Putting aside the very brief but rich preface, I turn to an examination of §6 of the *Church Dogmatics*, "The Knowability of the Word of God."

The title of §6 is essential to understanding the thrust of this section. Up to this point, we have discussed the knowledge of God. Indeed, knowledge of God is the traditional category in which to address the question of "what can humanity know about God." For Barth, however, to speak of knowledge of God, let alone the natural knowledge of God, is to make humanity a master, or a possessor of something that it cannot possess. Rather, Barth believes it prudent to speak of knowledge of God as knowability.[92] This argument is made on two fronts. First, and most simply, Barth believes that the Word of God is knowable; it can be both apprehended and comprehended. This is only possible, however, in that the Word of God provides the very conditions of possibility for its reception and comprehension.[93] Second, sinful humanity does not *possess* a knowledge of God, but rather is capable, as a dependent covenant partner with God, of *receiving* a knowledge of God. Humanity has the capacity to receive and then have faith. Faith, however, is not a natural capacity but rather a gift.[94] Hence, it could be said that humans *possess a knowabilty of God*. Of course, even to make this assertion risks making humanity capable of knowledge *on its own* by using the term *possess*. Yet, this is a danger that must be risked. The resolution of this tension lies in the covenantal aspect of creaturely existence. For Barth's theology it must always be remembered that God can exist without creation; creation, however, cannot exist apart from God. Thus all creatures, as created beings, possess—or are "determined," as Barth likes to say—by a dependency upon God for existence.[95] Creatures are determined by their dependence upon the Creator whether they acknowledge this fact or not.

92. Ibid., 227.

93. Ibid., 187.

94. Ibid., 238.

95. Ibid., 199. Barth points out that Schleiermacher's understanding of consciousness or self-consciousness is based upon the fundamental concept "being accepted." Barth says that this is actually quite similar to his "being determined."

The discussion of knowledge versus knowability leads Barth to the need to address again the *analogia entis,* and the almost synonymous subject of natural theology.[96] His point of contact for this discussion of the *analogia entis* and natural theology is theological anthropology and its tendency to grant the title "image of God" to humanity.[97] Similarly, he is hesitant to side with Anselm in seeing the image of the Trinity within humanity. For Barth, only Christ Jesus can be said to be the image of God. To ascribe this title to humanity is to make the image of God sinful (as opposed to the sinless Jesus). Staying true to the notion of humanity's being the image of God in Genesis, Barth affirms the traditional doctrine of original sin, saying that the image is "totally annihilated. What remains of the image of God even in sinful man is *recta natura,* to which as such a *rectitudo* cannot be ascribed even *potentialiter.* No matter how it may be with his humanity and personality, man has completely lost the capacity for God."[98] The ambiguity of these few sentences is alarming! Bracketed between two incredibly strong statements about the complete loss or annihilation of the image of God, Barth says that there is something that remains. This small remainder is but *recta natura,* or rule of nature, which I take to mean life or nature itself. In other words, there is life or nature that remains, but one that is no longer an image of God's life or nature. This life or nature is thus not a knowing-life or a knowing-nature. The knowledge aspect, which is closely related to the possession of the *imago Dei,* cannot be restored by humanity. Humans do not even retain the potential to restore the image and thus the knowledge of God. However, there is some sort of "capacity" that does clearly remain, though Barth would surely not like this term, in that a dependent creature cannot exist without its Creator. Barth says that through the gift of faith, Christ can restore the "point of contact" between God and humanity.[99] Barth describes this as "conformity to God."[100] Interestingly, Barth admits that this "conformity to God" by Christ through faith is quite similar to a proper notion of the *imago Dei* and the *analogia entis.* The proper notion of the *analogia entis* can be seen, according to Barth, in the Roman Catholic affirmation

96. While the two are not the same for Barth, you cannot have the former without the latter. This is not to say that the former necessarily results in the latter, but that natural theology is completely dependent upon an "exploitation" of the *analogia entis.*

97. Barth, *CD* I.1, 238–40.

98. Ibid., 238.

99. Ibid., 239.

100. Ibid.

that this analogy is characterized by "similarity in great dissimilarity."[101]
Proclaiming humanity's knowability will require the Christian to risk
the danger of being lumped in with both the Roman Catholic *analogia
entis* and Brunner's *imago Dei*. Barth writes, "As the Church provides the
ministry of proclamation and as we pursue dogmatics, we confess that we
believe this possibility [that of the knowability of the Word of God]. For
all the menacing proximity of the *analogia entis*, mysticism and identity
philosophy, and in spite of all the so-called dangers, we have every reason
to speak out clearly on this point."[102]

It should be pointed out that what Barth is truly worried about is Pelagianism, that is, the belief that human nature *on its own* can choose the
good and therefore even attain salvation, or the similar problem of saying
that grace is owed to nature solely due to its status as creation.[103] This
can be seen especially in the works of Schaedar and Wobbermin, whom
Barth critiques on numerous occasions.[104] Pure nature is the common
core of the exploitative use of the *analogia entis*, the non-christological
formulation of the *imago Dei* and the emphasis on the *ego* in Descartes'
philosophy.

By way of conclusion to this examination of the natural knowledge
of God as dealt with in *Church Dogmatics* I.1, Barth says,

> We have made a positive assertion, pronouncing a definite Yes
> to the knowability of the Word of God . . . others ought not so
> stubbornly to hear only the No in what has been said. To be
> sure, what has been said denies a connexion between God and
> man, that is, a knowledge of God's Word by man, and thus a
> knowability of God's Word by him, in the sense that a capability
> of man in abstraction from the Word of God can serve as the
> condition of this connexion. This condition, of course, cannot
> be met. The very man who knows the Word of God also knows

101. Ibid. It has recently been pointed out that this language is actually the result
of the teachings of Erich Pryzwara (with whom Barth shared a friendship) on the
analogia entis.

102. Barth, *CD* I.1, 242. Regarding mysticism, Barth believes that the doctrine of
the *imago Dei* can lead to a dangerous understanding of *theosis*. Identity philosophy,
for Barth, is essentially the Cartesian philosophy of the subject.

103. In addition to Barth's concerns about Pelagianism, I believe that the object of
some of his concerns here can best be categorized as "pure nature," though I have not
found him to use this phrase. I am hesitant to read into Barth the argument of pure nature—as articulated by de Lubac, for example—but it does seem very appropriate here.

104. Barth, *CD* I.1, 213.

that he can bring no capability of his own to this knowledge, but
has first to receive all capability.[105]

Thus for Barth, humanity cannot *have* or *possess* knowledge of God, but
humanity is capable of receiving knowledge of the revelation of God in
Christ and thus does possess, to a certain degree, an element of knowability. I have argued that the best way of understanding this knowability
is as the capacity for being gifted knowledge. Barth's typical theological
method is paradoxical, in that he gives while taking away, reveals while
concealing. The issue of humanity's knowledge of God or knowability is
no different. As with his positive appraisal of the *analogia entis*, Barth's
view of humanity's knowability of God is God's Yes encased in an even
greater No.[106] According to Barth, his modern critics just cannot accept
his qualifications, and thus they run too far with the divine Yes. For this
reason, Barth tends to overemphasize the No. Yet the Yes does remain,
standing in paradoxical tension with the No. This Yes is, ultimately more
so than the No, what humanity can know about God; it is God's deter-
minedness, and thus holds the possibility for humanity's conformity to
God.[107]

And so continuing on from his work on Anselm, *Church Dogmatics*
I.1 represents Barth's attempt to begin to answer the question of what
can we know about God in a positive manner. The No and the hiddenness remain but are not given the dominance they are in dialectical or
nominalist theology. Barth's arguments are subtle and confusing on these
points, which I believe points to the complexity with which the issue
of the knowledge of God is put forth in Scripture. As Barth attempts to
truly allow Scripture to speak in such a way that he is also dialoging with
Christian tradition, his positions do in fact shift and change, signifying
his increasing discomfort with dialectical theology, nominalism, and,
especially, the central position frequently given to the hiddenness of God.

Putting aside for now the *Church Dogmatics* I.1, I will turn to perhaps Barth's most famous denouncement of the natural knowledge of
God, "Nein! A Response to Emil Brunner."

105. Ibid., 196–97.

106. The fact that this No is actually a form of knowledge of God means that here
No is actually a form of or a participant in the Yes.

107. This discussion is one of the primary places where Brunner sees a "point of
contact" in Barth, though Barth himself does not use this term and vehemently rejects
its being attributed to him.

"Nein! A Response to Emil Brunner" (1934)

In 1934, Emil Brunner published an essay titled "Nature and Grace"[108] in which he attempted to clarify and critique the positions of Karl Barth on the issue of natural theology. In this section we will explore Barth's essay of response published in the same year, titled *"Nein!"* While Barth was definitely rejecting the content of Brunner's essay, it can be argued that Barth's essay results more from Brunner's insinuation that Barth is really in agreement with him, and that he (Brunner) is in line with Calvin's teachings about the natural knowledge of God. Thus, though Barth knew that he would look cruel for releasing such a stringent attack on his friend Brunner's theology, he felt as if he had to respond, saying that Brunner's essay was an "alarm signal."[109]

In his essay, Brunner put forward a number of theses that he said should be ascribed to Karl Barth. Barth strongly rejected this assertion, saying that the mere suggestion that this is the case showed that Brunner did not understand what Barth's theology was all about.[110] Barth was opposed to having any sort of philosophical system as the basis or prolegomena for theology. For Barth, only Christ Jesus could be the foundation upon which faithful theological reflection could be done. Brunner's failure to understand this crucial Barthian position can be seen in his 1929 articulation of the need for "the other task of theology" or the "point of contact."[111] Regarding the former, Barth is adamant that theology is to faithfully proclaim the revelation of God in Christ. The task of theology, then, is to recognize the revelation of God in Christ as the command of God to which humans are meant to be obedient.

As for the latter issue, the "point(s) of contact" are not so easily distinguished. We have already seen in the previous section how Barth himself advocated the knowledge of God, or knowability, as a "point of contact" of sorts. It is easy to see how Brunner would have thought that he could make the argument that he and Barth were really saying the same thing. Unfortunately for Brunner, Barth did not see it the same way. According to Barth, Brunner's "point of contact is 'the formal *imago Dei* which not even the sinner has lost, the fact that man is man, the

---

108. Barth, Brunner, and Fraenkel, *Natural Theology*, 15–64.

109. Ibid., 69.

110. Ibid., 74.

111. Ibid., 71.

humanitas.'"[112] This definition of Brunner's point of contact clearly illuminates his distinction between the formal and the material *imago Dei*. While the latter, for Brunner, had been obliterated by sin, the former remained. Barth's use of the "point of contact," on the other hand, is in no way possessed by creation. Rather, it is completely dependent upon the initiative of Christ by the power of the Spirit.

The dispute over the "point of contact" sheds light on Barth's fundamental critique, namely, that "he [Brunner] would always be addicted to an 'other' task of theology."[113] In this instance the "other task" is natural theology, to which, Brunner believed, his generation must return.[114] Barth defines this "natural theology" as "every (positive *or* negative) formulation of a system which claims to be theological, i.e., to interpret divine revelation, whose subject, however, differs fundamentally from the revelation in Jesus Christ and whose method therefore differs equally from the exposition of Holy Scripture."[115] Essentially, Barth believes that there are elements of natural theology in Scripture that will play a role in Christian faith, but a problem arises when natural theology is considered a legitimate end or pursuit on its own. Barth thought that this was the problem that had been plaguing Protestantism for about two hundred years. Brunner's theology was just another example, perhaps the best example, of *theologia naturalis* too easily slipping into *theologia naturalis vulgaris*.[116] "Natural theology is always the answer to a question which is false if it wishes to be 'decisive.'"[117] Rather than being one piece of the puzzle that is the Christian faith, natural theology falsely tries to be the subject and goal of its own pursuit of knowledge. This is the core of the argument between Barth and Brunner relating to the natural knowledge of God.

In conclusion, it is helpful to point out that in the section on Brunner and Calvin, Barth seeks to ground Calvin's statements about the knowledge of God in Scripture. Barth again asserts that Brunner has misinterpreted Calvin, this time in terms of the *duplex cognitioni Domini*. This twofold understanding of the Lord allows one to talk about the

112. Ibid., 88.

113. Ibid., 77.

114. Ibid., 70.

115. Barth, Brunner, and Fraenkel, *Natural Theology*, 74–75.

116. Ibid., 116.

117. Ibid., 128.

simultaneous knowledge of God as Creator and Redeemer, or from creation and Christ. Barth points out that Calvin grounds this in Scripture passages such as Romans 1:19ff. and 2:14ff., and Acts 14:15ff. and 17:24ff. Barth states that due to Calvin's fidelity to Scripture, he does not advocate for a natural capacity in humans that has been retained through sin that simply must be restored.[118] Rather, Barth spends several paragraphs arguing that it is only Jesus Christ as revealed in Holy Scripture that makes possible knowledge of God in a transformative manner. Thus, according to Barth, Calvin will allow for some degree of capacity or knowability, but one that is completely dependent upon the initial work of the Spirit which comes through the proclamation of Scripture, as a result of the faithfulness of Christ Jesus. It is safe to say that Barth would argue the same for himself.[119]

The polemical nature of "*Nein!*" is easily misunderstood. Though it might be easy to get lost in Barth's polemical splitting of hairs in this article, I believe that Barth's response to Brunner offers readers a clear warning and a guidepost of sorts in terms of the discussion of the knowledge or knowability of God. In "*Nein!*" Barth warns readers about just how delicate the topic of a natural knowledge of God can be. With Scripture, and even Calvin, as a guide, Barth insists that authentic, true knowledge of God comes only in and through the person of Jesus Christ. Negative knowledge, however it might be articulated, cannot move forward to positive knowledge of any type apart from Christ Jesus. In Barth's mind, Brunner was attempting to do just that. It should be increasingly clear just how important this investigation into the knowledge of God in Barth's theology is to the discussion of the *Deus absconditus*. Increasingly, Barth argued for a completely revealed God—revealed in none other than Christ Jesus. This privileging of a revealed God over a hidden one is certainly a distancing from any hint of Luther's *Deus absconditus*,

118. Ibid., 105.

119. Ibid., 115. Barth ends the essay as he begins, by stating that there are many things that he and Brunner would agree on. In discussing Brunner's theology of the natural knowledge of God, Barth says, "And who knows whether one could not find passages in the *Epistle to the Romans* in which I have said something of the sort myself." While I find Barth's points of departure with Brunner convincing—i.e., Brunner's articulation of the "point of contact," his imposition of a system "other" than theology, and his poor understanding of both Calvin and Roman Catholicism—I do think that I have shown that Barth, like Brunner, very much includes a type of natural knowledge of God, albeit in a negative fashion, in *Der Römerbrief*.

a theology that was surely much more compatible with Brunner's natural theology, for example, than with Barth's theology.[120]

Moreover, Barth rightly understood Brunner to be calling Reformed Protestants to entertain the possibility of allowing nature or creation to be an acceptable starting point on the journey toward the knowledge of God. Though Barth might concede that for some—namely, pagans who know nothing of Christ or of Christianity (or Judaism, for that matter)—this is conceptually feasible, it is inexcusable for those who already know about Jesus Christ. Moreover, it is certainly inexcusable and lazy for those who do know and believe in Christ to apply this mode of thinking to their non-Christian neighbors.[121] Christ must be proclaimed, and specifically as the way to know, exhaustively, God the Father. Even to have a discussion about any other starting point is to fail to grasp the very Gospel itself. For the very Pauline Barth, the goal for Christians is to proclaim Christ crucified, and the power of His resurrection.

The Knowledge of God and the Service of God— The Gifford Lectures (1937)

In 1935 Karl Barth was asked to give the world-renowned Gifford Lectures, which were to be delivered two years later at the University of Aberdeen. While the invitation came as a great honor to Barth, he felt nonetheless that he might not be the best person for the job. After all, he was "an avowed opponent of all natural theology."[122] Having been assured that he was a fit lecturer on this topic, Barth endeavored to put together a

120. The hidden God, revealed, albeit in cloaked fashion, through nature, is surely closely akin to the *Deus absconditus*. As such, the *Deus absconditus* serves as the dominant God for much, if not all, Protestant liberalism. In the next section, it is made clearer how natural theology, when thought of from a Protestant perspective, implies the *Deus absconditus*. Barth does not affirm this. Barth does think natural theology is a more appropriate posture to maintain within Roman Catholicism, however, and in such a way that it does not entail the *Deus absconditus*.

121. In this way, it could be said that Barth's understanding of the possibility of a negative knowledge of God, or the possibility of the knowledge of a creator, should both be understood within a missional context. It is, after all, just such a context that prompts the Apostle Paul to say, "For what can be known about God is plain to them, because God has shown it to them. Ever since the creation of the world his eternal power and divine nature, invisible though they are, have been understood and seen through the things he has made" (Rom 1:19–20).

122. Barth, *Knowledge of God and the Service of God*, 6. Hereafter cited as Gifford Lectures.

series of lectures that would faithfully convey his Reformation theology, giving particular emphasis to the Scottish Reformation and especially John Knox's *Confessio Scottica* of 1560. In addition, Barth took seriously the guidelines for the lectureship as detailed by Lord Gifford himself. According to Lord Gifford, the lectures were to have as their subject natural theology "in the widest sense of the term."[123] Barth described natural theology as "a science of God, of the relations in which the world stands to Him and of the human ethics and morality resulting from the knowledge of Him."[124] By examining a few of Barth's lectures, particularly lectures I, II, and VI, I hope to shed light on the position put forward by Barth in his Gifford Lectures concerning natural theology and, therefore, whether or not humanity possesses a natural knowledge of God.

After stating Lord Gifford's terms, terms that Barth says he will adhere to, Barth says,

> According to the presuppositions of "Natural Theology" as Lord Gifford understood the term—and he was perfectly correct in understanding it in this way—*there does exist a knowledge of God and His connection with the world and men, apart from any special and supernatural revelation.* . . . It is a knowledge of which man, since as man he still stands in an original relation to God, *indisputably possesses,* and it is therefore a knowledge which he only requires to discover, *as something which he himself possesses,* as he discovers the mathematical laws which lie at the basis of chemistry and astronomy, in order then to apply them to these sciences.[125]

Paradoxically, Barth continues by saying that this science, natural theology, does exist, though he says that he just does not see how this existence is possible. Surely, says Barth, this science "owes its existence to a radical error."[126] Barth expands his understanding of the existence of natural theology by saying that it only exists dependently. For Barth, true natural theology only exists within, and as antithesis to, Reformation theology.[127] This is because "true" natural theology emerged as a Tridentine reaction to the Reformation. Thus, there is a logic to natural theology that does "work" in some ways, so long as it is engulfed within

123. Ibid., 3.
124. Ibid.
125. Ibid., 3–4. Italics mine.
126. Ibid., 5.
127. Ibid., 6–8.

the broader Reformation–Counter-Reformation discussion, that is, the ongoing fruitful theological dialogue between the Roman Catholic and the Protestant churches. This definition of natural theology caused Stanley Hauerwas to argue in his own Gifford Lectures given at the University of St. Andrews that "Karl Barth is the great 'natural theologian' of the Gifford Lectures because he rightly understood that natural theology is impossible abstracted from a full doctrine of God."[128] That being said, Barth seeks to chart a course between Roman Catholicism and Protestant liberalism because neither of these traditions, according to Barth, stands in opposition to natural theology, and thus neither is able to truly do it justice. Like God and creation, so is Reformation theology and natural theology for Barth. The former does not need the latter in any way, but the latter exists in a completely dependent relationship with the former.

Barth concludes his first lecture by returning to John Knox's *Confessio Scottica*. Barth's lectures are organized as a commentary of sorts upon this *Confessio*. As prologue, Barth reminds his reader of the great beauty of Reformation teaching—that is, that the Reformation knows no law set over it other than the spiritual law of Scripture. With this in mind, "the *Confessio Scottica* wishes to be read and understood as a signpost pointing to Scripture."[129] It seems that this is a key to understanding not only Barth's Gifford Lectures but his own theology as well. For Barth, structure and method are important, but only as a guide or signpost. The purpose of such a signpost is simply to direct one toward Scripture, and thus Scripture is to stand as the constant critic of any and all previous methods or positions. Reformation theology, in that it claims to be Christian, is to stand in constant dialogue with and in subordination to Holy Scripture.

In Barth's second lecture, he argues that God is one and completely unaffected by creation. Thus, as was said in the first lecture, God does not need the world, but the world completely needs God. The curious thing about this "relationship" between God and creation is that humans are given freedom. As a result of this freedom, humanity can and has made itself the rule and measure of all things, and thus has begun to worship itself. By worshipping itself, humanity has placed itself above God.[130] This leads Barth to state, "The modern world has failed to hear the warning of the Reformed confession precisely at this point and has thought fit

128. Hauerwas, *With the Grain of the Universe*, 9–10.

129. Barth, Gifford Lectures, 12.

130. Ibid., 17.

to exchange the medieval conception of the world as geocentric for the much more naïve conception of the world as anthropocentric."[131] Interestingly for Barth, natural theology is not so much the worship of nature or the world, as the term might seem to indicate, but rather ontotheology, or the worship of the human [as] God. Barth's critique of Feuerbach must certainly be lurking in the background of Barth's concerns about natural theology. Given this insightful stance toward natural theology, it is clear why it is so important for Barth that natural theology not be thought of as an independent, or other, pursuit of theology. Standing on its own, natural theology becomes not a window into the heavens, but rather Feuerbach's mirror. According to Feuerbach, when humanity prays to God or contemplates the divine, the great irony is that humanity is simply elevating itself, for "man is the God of man."[132]

Returning to Barth's original statement about the role of natural theology in relation to Roman Catholicism, Protestant liberalism, and Reformed theology, it should now be clearer what exactly Barth meant. In both Roman Catholicism and Protestant liberalism, there is a certain degree of natural theology that can take place faithfully, in an albeit subservient and dependent manner. In Reformation theology, however, Barth believes that natural theology is strictly forbidden. Thus, it is not possible both to conduct true natural theology and to stand in the Reformation tradition for Barth. This means that any Reformed theologian who is advocating for a return to natural theology for any reason has chosen to pursue something other than the revelation of God in Christ as testified to in Holy Scripture. Accordingly, it would seem that while natural theology can serve as a window in both Roman Catholicism and Protestant liberalism, it will only serve as a mirror if one is attempting to stand in the Reformed tradition.[133]

Finally, in Barth's sixth lecture, he discusses God's revelation in Christ Jesus. In this lecture, Barth spells out just what makes natural theology so incompatible with the Reformation tradition. Essentially, it is

131. Ibid.

132. Feuerbach, *Essence of Christianity*, 83.

133. Since Barth is nothing but critical about Protestant liberalism, it seems safe to conclude that natural theology can be practiced in that context, because that context is thoroughly unfaithful already. In the context of Roman Catholicism, Barth's stance is more difficult to pin down. Given the earlier examinations in this volume, I would argue that a certain degree of faithful natural theology is faithful from within Roman Catholicism only as a result of the *analogia entis*, though this runs the risk of being exploited.

the statement "because God reveals Himself to Man in Jesus Christ" that prevents Reformation theology from holding a true natural theology.[134] For the Reformed theologian, God has exhaustively revealed God's self in the revelation of the Son. Thus, to speak faithfully at all about God is to begin with Jesus Christ. Any form of "natural theology," therefore, from within this particular tradition, would not be natural theology as it is commonly understood. The reason for this statement is that something remotely resembling natural theology from within the Reformed tradition would be a post-revelation or a post-faith statement wherein one sees further beauty of of the kind that has already been revealed in the person of Jesus of Nazareth. This positive statement could not be said about a nonbeliever. What the nonbeliever sees when examining nature (for this person, it would not be creation in the Christian sense) would not be the hidden God but rather herself as God. For Barth, this is not natural theology, but merely a form of ontotheology.

We see that in his Gifford Lectures, Barth, when assuming a very particular audience, is comfortable talking rather positively about the possibility of the knowledge of God and even natural theology. Here there is almost no trace of the *Deus absconditus*. The God conceived of as *Deus absconditus* is a God born of nominalism and thus one that is dialectically opposite to humanity and the rest of creation. For Barth, however, while God is transcendent and wholly other, God is at the same time, and perhaps to a greater degree, immanently present to humanity in the person of Jesus of Nazareth. Both are always true, though the latter provides meaning for the former and not the reverse. Thus, the classical analogical logic of Roman Catholicism allows for something like natural theology, though only when assumed within a much larger dogmatic structure. The logic of Protestantism, however, and the Reformation in particular, desired to emphasize God's radical otherness in a way that Roman Catholicism was not able to. What the nominalists lost sight of, however, and this is precisely Barth's genius, is just how immanent and relatable—by grace, of course—becomes this wholly other God when the paradoxical logic of the incarnation is applied. In the Gifford Lectures, Barth articulates the differences and the similarities between Roman Catholicism and Protestantism in a way that is invaluably helpful, primarily in light of the discussion of the possibility of the knowledge of God. The freedom he allows for Catholicism, for example, while maintaining that

134. Barth, Gifford Lectures, 57.

the Church continues to remain faithful to Christ, says much of Barth's true opinions of the knowledge of God and the role for something like natural theology within the Church.

Of course, there is much more wisdom to be gleaned from Barth's Gifford Lectures, but we will be unable to go any further just now. Having provided a cursory look at Barth's treatment of the natural knowledge of God in his Gifford Lectures, I turn now to a discussion of the *Church Dogmatics* II.1.

Church Dogmatics II.1 (1940)

In 1940 Karl Barth released part one of volume two of the *Church Dogmatics*. Having already discussed the doctrine of the Word of God in volume one, he turned in volume two to the Doctrine of God. The first sections of volume II.1 (§§25–27) pick up the theme of the knowledge of God. While the issue of the knowledge of God does come up again in later volumes of the *Church Dogmatics*, sections 25–27 mark the most sustained discussion of this topic. In this section, I will briefly examine each of these three paragraphs.

In §25, Barth discusses the fulfillment of the knowledge of God. In this section, Barth is definitely not concerned with a general theory of the knowledge of God. Rather, Barth is interested in true or fulfilled knowledge of God, which can be said to be only knowledge of faith.[135] Barth begins this section by saying that he has learned about the problem of the knowledge and existence of God from St. Anselm, and that his own book on St. Anselm should be kept in mind when reading this section.[136] Barth begins §25 by discussing the topic of "man before God," only to conclude that one cannot talk about "man before God" without first talking about "God before man." Thus, knowledge of God does not form an independent Prolegomena to the Doctrine of God.[137] According to Barth, God is always present and active prior to any involvement or participation on behalf of humanity. This fundamental priority creates the conditions for the possibility of the knowledge of God. This priority can be seen in that God creates in humanity possibility, capacity, or readiness to see God.[138]

135. Barth, *CD* II.1, 12.

136. See section D above.

137. Barth, *CD* II.1, 32.

138. Ibid., 33. Barth seems to be treating this "capacity" a little more loosely than in vol. I.1.

Thus for Barth, knowledge of God is only possible in that humanity as creature is completely dependent upon the Creator for all things. Fulfilled knowledge, moreover, is the moving from this vague dependent knowledge to the knowledge of faith as primed and made possible by the Spirit of God. Here, Barth says that it is necessary to restate the terms a bit, in that it is not simply that God stands before humanity prior to it standing before God, but that the triune God stands fundamentally prior to humanity. It must furthermore be said that as triune, God ultimately stands before God's own self. Creatures receive their origin in this divine self-sufficient love. It is by way of invitation that creatures come to participate in this relationship through revelation in an inconceivable way.[139]

In §26, Barth turns to a discussion of the knowability of God. This discussion focuses first on the readiness of God for this knowability, and then the readiness of humanity. I will primarily examine the former. Barth intends to discuss "the possibility on the basis of which God is known."[140] It is impossible, according to Barth, to talk about knowability apart from the revelation of God in Christ. While humanity does possess some sort of capacity for the knowabilty of God, it can only be activated or realized by God's revelation. This means that there is no "empty space" in humanity that can be filled up by a general doctrine of being and/or knowing.[141] This entire argument may seem quite circular, and indeed it is. Barth believes that the moment a person asks about the possibility of the knowability of God, the answer to the question becomes superfluous in that asking the question reveals that God's revelation has already allowed the person to ask.[142]

After a very complex argument for knowability's dependence upon the prior revelation of God in Christ, Barth affirms that "natural man" is capable of a certain type of natural knowledge of God. Barth says that this type of knowledge is a childish and dangerous game.[143] To prevent some of the danger, Barth briefly articulates the role of a *Christian* natural theology, as distinguished from a Christian *natural* theology. His main reason for making this distinction is to discuss the historic and sometimes positive uses of a Christian natural theology by missionaries

139. Ibid., 48–49.
140. Ibid., 63.
141. Ibid., 65.
142. Ibid., 68.
143. Ibid., 92–93.

to heathens.[144] Ultimately, however, Barth returns to his critical stance toward natural theology, saying that natural theology drops away like a superfluous object from any theology of the Word of God that properly understands itself.[145]

Finally, Barth ends his section on the readiness of God by dealing extensively with Scripture. I would like to focus, in particular, on his brief but important statement on Romans 1:19–21, as this is certainly a major part of the current work. To quote at length, Barth says, "If Rom. I.18–21 existed for us on its own, perhaps in the form of a fragment, as the work of a known or unknown secular author (one of the Stoics, say) of the age—and the possibility of an isolated consideration of this kind has been far too often presupposed in the exposition of this passage—we should hardly have any other choice than to acknowledge that it says that man in the cosmos in himself and as such is an independent witness of the truth of God."[146] Barth astutely points out that this passage does not exist in isolation, but has a very real context. Romans 1:18–21 exists within Paul's Epistle to the Romans—Paul's Gospel, as Barth often calls it. Specifically, Barth points out two contextual markers that serve to illuminate why Romans 1:18–21 does not endorse the type of bad natural theology, wherein humanity is capable of knowing and understanding God on its own, of which Barth is obviously a critic. First, Barth says that there is nothing in the prologue to Romans that would lead a reader to think that the apostle is assuming an autonomous humanity, in the cosmos or even in general.[147] On the contrary, Paul is assuming an audience of Jews and heathens. Yet these are not Jews and heathens as such. And thus Barth's second point is that these very same Jews and heathens have been and are confronted with the apocalypse or revelation of the righteousness of God. These are not innocent Jews and heathens. Having been confronted with the wrath and righteousness of God, they are without excuse. Paul's task, then, is to explain that which they can perceive but dimly. In identifying the recognition of God's wrath against creation, Paul's task is to proclaim God's redeeming righteousness as revealed once and for all in Christ Jesus.

144. Ibid., 97.
145. Ibid., 168.
146. Barth, *CD* II.1, 119.
147. Ibid.

In §27 Barth directly discusses the hiddenness of God as well as the veracity of humanity's knowledge of God, which fall under the heading "The Limits of the Knowledge of God." While Barth will talk about these issues periodically in later volumes of the *Church Dogmatics*, this section comprises the last formal piece of Barth's doctrine of humanity's knowledge of God. According to Barth, God can only be known by God alone. Despite this truth about God's knowledge of God's self, Barth firmly believes that God wants to be known by creation. In order to be known by sinful creation, however, God must create the ability within creation to again be able to know. Thus, "God's revelation is His knowability."[148] This means that God does not reveal what is already there within humanity, but rather reveals God's self as the bridge to God's very self. The only way humanity can understand this revelation, according to Barth, is to see it between the two limits of *terminus a quo*, beginning, and *terminus ad quem*, end.

The beginning of revelation is God's hiddenness. Recognizing that this term can easily be misunderstood, Barth says that this hiddenness is not the same as in Plato's or Kant's philosophy, nor is it the same as Luther's *Deus absconditus*, at least as Luther's position is traditionally understood. Since humanity is incapable of truly knowing or understanding God as it stands in sin, God clears the way for the revelation of God's own self. The hiddenness of God does precisely this in that it reveals God's knowability, which we have already seen is for Barth a way for and to the knowledge of God. This means that the hiddenness of God is not a negative statement about humanity or about God. It is rather a positive statement about God's desire to be known by creation and about God's ability to effect this knowledge. God does not desire to remain hidden from creation, or to be revealed only in wrath, which is why both of these are moments within the greater revelation of God's love for the world. Accordingly, it would make no sense for someone like Luther to remain constantly terrified by the *Deus absconditus* and the unknown will of this hidden God. And yet this is one of the overarching characteristics of Luther's theology. Barth, however, proclaims that the central tenet of Christian theology is that "Jesus Christ lives!"[149] Any claim to a *Deus absconditus* must, therefore, be subservient to positive revelation of God in Christ Jesus. Barth's is a theology of revelation, positive revelation, plain and simple.

148. Ibid., 179.
149. Barth, *CD* IV.3.1, 39.

The hiddenness of God, therefore, affirms that God and creatures are fully distinct, yet not completely so, in that God's hiddenness is revealed as a *way*. Thus, the relationship between God and creation is paradoxically analogous. For this reason, after a lengthy discussion of how best to talk about the relationship between God and creation, Barth argues that analogy and therefore the *analogia entis* must be maintained, but within the very specific context of God's revelation in Christ.[150] Neither analogy nor the infamous *analogia entis* are to be allowed the status of arbitrary philosophical principle.[151] Analogy simply becomes the way to describe the hiddenness of God that is revealed as a way across the infinite qualitative distinction between God and humanity.

150. Ibid., 232–33. This language sounds almost shocking coming from the pen of Karl Barth! This section is in fact riddled with similar language, the most astounding of which can be found in the lengthy section of small type found on pages 237–43. In this section, Barth discusses the German Lutheran theologian Johannes Andreas Quenstedt, and specifically how his dogmatic metaphysical theology relates to both Thomas Aquinas and Duns Scotus. In sum, Barth argues that both univocity and equivocity must be rejected in favor of the doctrine of analogy. With this affirmation in mind, Barth states that all of our arguments must stem from the Word of God as God's self-revelation. The ultimate issue in this discussion, for Barth, is the doctrine of justification. If any theology or philosophy claims to or even leaves the possibility open for justification that is not solely through the revelation of and faith in Christ Jesus, then it must be rejected. Too often, Barth sees analogy serving this way. This danger does not result, however, in the rejection of analogy. The other two options, univocity and equivocity, are much more dangerous than analogy ever could be. Thus, Christians must faithfully articulate, or rather incorporate, analogy—even the *analogia entis*—into a properly cruciform theology.

151. Barth is full of praise for his colleague Gottlieb Söhngen's articulation of the *analogia entis* as grounded in the *analogia fidei*. Barth provides a very lengthy explanation of Söhngen's teachings. He even goes so far as to say, "If this is the Roman Catholic doctrine of the *analogia entis*, then naturally I must withdraw my earlier statement that I regard the *analogia entis* as the 'invention of Antichrist.' And if this is what that doctrine has to say to our thesis, then we can only observe that there is every justification for the warning that participation in being is grounded in the grace of God and therefore in faith, and that substance and actuality must be brought into this right relationship." Barth, *CD* II.1, 81–82.

Barth concludes, however, by confessing that he is just not sure that it can be argued that Söhngen's doctrine is in fact the Roman Catholic Church's teaching on the *analogia entis*. Moreover, he wonders whether many in the wider circles of the Roman Church could even accept this version of the *analogia entis*. In response to his own question, Barth asserts that he will be forced to accept the "traditional" teaching on the *analogia entis* put forward by thinkers such as Feuling and Fehr, at least until it is proved that Söhngen's doctrine is widely accepted by the Roman Catholic Church.

The end of the revelation of God is the knowledge of God by humanity. Indeed, Barth says "the knowledge of God is the . . . goal of all Christian theology."[152] God would not reveal God's self unless God wanted to be known. This fact must be affirmed with the clarification and reminder from the first section of §27, that God is not an object of human cognition, but rather cognition is granted *vis-à-vis* revelation.[153] In Barth's discussion of the end of the revelation of God, we see that the knowledge of God is really faith in God. This faith-knowledge, for Barth, is to be characterized by joy, gratitude, and thankfulness, which are in fact the way to the knowledge of God by participation in the veracity of the revelation of God.[154]

This positive knowledge and faith moves Barth to remind the reader that the knowledge of God that comes through this whole process from hiddenness to veracity is "an event enclosed in the bosom of the divine Trinity."[155] The name Barth gives to this inner-Trinitarian event is the *circulus veritatis Dei*, or the circular truth of God. Humanity can never fully grasp God, for that would be to possess or control God. As a result, our knowledge of God is always circular; it is always new and exciting and frustrating. Barth's oft-used concepts of veiling and unveiling are the best way to characterize this circular truth of God. Yet somehow, despite the circularity of our knowledge of God, it is a knowledge that we do receive and possess in faith, and that does, by God's grace, move from the revelation of the hiddenness of God to the positive knowledge of God revealed in Christ. For this reason, Barth points out that the relationship between veiling and unveiling, which characterizes so much of his theology, are not equally balanced; they are not a true dialectic.[156] It is true that God always begins with veiling, but this is done always with the goal of unveiling. Thus, remaining in a state of veiling or hiddenness is not God's desired way to relate to humanity. We know this because of the once-for-all revelation of God in Christ Jesus. While the veiling is essential to unveiling, it is a preliminary step towards God's true goal, which is that humans might actually attain to the knowledge of God in Christ Jesus. This knowledge comes as a confusing gift, but in faith becomes an actual

---

152. Barth, *C.D.* II.1, 204.

153. Ibid., 205–6.

154. Ibid., 219.

155. Ibid., 205.

156. Ibid., 215.

and positive knowledge. In *Church Dogmatics* II.1, Barth continues the steady march away from Luther and Luther's anxiety over a hidden God in favor of the God revealed unilaterally in Christ Jesus—a God who, rather than being and remaining hidden, is closer to humanity than humanly imaginable.

A Shorter Commentary on Romans (1940–41)

Finally, let us briefly examine Barth's *Shorter Commentary on Romans.*[157] Barth states that this brief commentary stems from the manuscript for a seminar that he taught at Basel in 1940–41. Much of Barth's brief analysis of Romans 1:18–21 is simply a condensed repetition of what has already been examined from *Der Römerbrief.* For that reason, I will focus only on what seems to be new in this section.

In the preface he identifies Romans as Paul's interpretation of the Gospel with a definite concentration on the "proper interpretation of the Old Testament."[158] For Barth this means that Romans is truly meant to be good news. Yet in this good news of the revelation of God in Christ, there is contained both dark and light, wrath and love. Barth astutely notes that the dark or the wrath offends our modern tastes. Perhaps this is why, according to Barth, Paul begins with wrath.[159] As Barth begins his treatment of 1:18–21, he quotes at length the section from his *Church Dogmatics* II.1 in which he writes about how this passage would be regarded if it came to us in isolation from heathen philosophy.[160] Regardless of how most will interpret this passage, Barth reminds the reader that it comes in a particular narrative context, specifically verses 16–17, and from a particular apostle. What's more, Barth points out that if Paul did believe in a natural knowledge of God apart from Christ Jesus, then he would have proclaimed it in other places, as he also proclaims the cross. The lack of consistent attention, then, suggests that the natural knowledge of God apart from Christ Jesus is not a major motif in Paul's writings.

The most genuinely new element of Barth's brief treatment of Romans can be seen in his discussion of Paul's audience. Barth says that Paul is primarily speaking to Gentiles who are now confronted with the

157. Barth, *Shorter Commentary on Romans.*
158. Ibid., 11.
159. Ibid., 25.
160. See 128 below.

Gospel, whether they like it or not. They are without excuse. Paul tells the Gentiles that

> God has in fact for a long time, yea always, since the creation of the world been declaring and revealing himself to them. The world which has always been around them has always been God's work and as such God's witness to himself. Objectively the Gentiles have always had the opportunity of knowing God, his invisible being, his eternal power and godhead. *And again, objectively speaking, they have also always known him.* In all that they have known otherwise, God as the Creator of all things *has always been, objectively speaking, the proper and real object of their knowledge,* exactly in the same sense as undoubtedly the Jews in their Law were objectively dealing with God's revelation.[161]

For Barth, this powerful statement can only be made in light of the reflected fire that is God's wrath and grace in Christ Jesus. Because Jews and Gentiles come from God, they are in opposition to and therefore subject to God's wrath. This last statement is essential, for if this were not the case, the Gentiles could rightfully claim justification because they truly would have had no way of knowing.[162] Paul is not paying a great compliment to the Gentiles. Rather, he is declaring them to be guilty of being in flagrant opposition to God. As Romans 1:22 reads, "Claiming to be wise, they have become fools." What Paul is doing, then, is beginning with the Gentiles' wisdom, specifically their philosophy, and arguing that it is nothing but confusion. "If there is any position from which no bridge can possibly be built to the Gospel, to the knowledge of the living God, then this is it!"[163] As it currently stands, their philosophy is pure confusion, which is nothing other than idolatry. Paul declares this confused idolatry to be God's wrath. As we have seen, however, recognition of God's wrath, for both Paul and Barth, is the beginning of wisdom.

Conclusion

In this chapter, I have examined the eight main texts in which Karl Barth discusses the subject of humanity's natural knowledge of God. The eight

---

161. Barth, *Shorter Commentary on Romans*, 28. Italics mine.

162. Ibid., 29.

163. Ibid.

texts have been arranged in chronological order based upon the year in which each was published. To the best of my ability, I have attempted to examine each text on its own. The purpose of this type of examination was to see the consistency or inconsistency of Barth's argument on this topic, as well as how it developed over time. Under the title "natural knowledge of God" it has been necessary and helpful to include Barth's exegetical work on Romans 1:18–21, as well as examples of Barth's teachings on the Roman Catholic *analogia entis,* natural theology, and Anselm's "proof" of the existence of God.[164] While there are other passages of Scripture that can be said to put forward a natural knowledge of God, it was fitting to choose the Romans passage, as Barth has written extensively on it as the root of the tension over this issue. Moreover, both the *analogia entis* and natural theology have been shown to be very similar and dangerous results of the exegesis of passages such as Romans 1:18–21. Barth is both highly critical and surprisingly amiable toward both doctrines depending upon the context and the ends toward which they are employed. And finally, Barth's engagement of Anselm's work is a direct engagement with the issue of the possibility of human knowledge or knowability of God.

In what follows, I will conclude the present chapter by offering a synthetic reading of Karl Barth's teachings on the natural knowledge of God that takes seriously the complexities and context of his various arguments. I believe that Barth has been grossly misunderstood on this topic. This confusion has three essential sources. First, the sheer volume and complexity of Barth's theological writings must be taken into account. Barth's collected works are so vast that not many will be able to read all

164. I have attempted, for the most part, however, to remain clear of the argument over the *analogia entis* in Karl Barth's theology. Unless it has seemed impossible, I have left that particular topic aside for the sake of the larger argument about Barth's rejection of the *Deus absconditus.* Many excellent papers on this topic were presented at the Analogy of Being Symposium held at the Pope John Paul II Institute in Washington, DC, in Spring 2008. The papers from this conference have been published as *The Analogy of Being: Invention of Antichrist or Wisdom of God?.* Additionally, one might find the recent work by Keith L. Johnson helpful as a comprehensive examination of this topic, specifically in Karl Barth. See Johnson, *Karl Barth and the Analogia Entis.* Johnson's work is an excellent treatment of the subject and one that allows for a more generous reading of Barth on this issue than do most. Ultimately, however, I do not agree with Johnson's thesis that Barth's mature theology fulfilled rather than retreated from his early harsh critique of the *analogia entis* in *CD* I.1. The topic is one that is complex, and far from clear-cut in Barth, however, and thus the argument often becomes one based more on interpretation than on firsthand proof. For this reason, Johnson's work is still very helpful and deserving of examination.

his writings. For those who do read all or most of Barth's works, treating each with the delicacy that is necessary is a very consuming task. It is perfectly natural, amidst such a vast collection of writings, to look for synthetic documents that offer a summary of such a scattered and complex issue as the natural knowledge of God.

This necessarily leads to the second source of the confusion regarding Barth's teachings on the natural knowledge of God. Barth's polemical style, as seen especially in his infamous "*Nein!*" essay, lead many to assume that this work was his quintessential treatment of this issue. In fact, it was merely a small but complex piece of the argument. The polemical nature of Barth's theology often takes the form of dialectic, or more accurately, paradox.[165] This back-and-forth style of doing theology lends itself to confusion quite easily. This can be seen in two ways. On the one hand, many of Barth's readers are prone to simply dismiss everything as pure dialectic in a fideistic or nominalistic manner. On the other hand, many of Barth's readers fail to see the qualified nature with which Barth puts forward almost every single argument. This results in an oversimplified version of Barth's theology.[166] To properly do justice to Karl Barth's theological works, one must be willing to concede the qualified and confusing manner in which he often puts forth his arguments, while avoiding the temptation to simply negate the whole process by allowing the dialectical model to trump the positivity of the Gospel that Barth is proclaiming.

Finally, the third source of confusion over Barth's teachings on the natural knowledge of God is seen in the way he assumes a context or audience and worries about how that particular context or audience will interpret and make use of what he has said. For example, in "*Nein!*", Barth is very upset that along with Brunner's poor understanding of Aquinas and Calvin, he has also implicated Barth in his positive reading of natural theology. While Barth was a friend of Brunner's, he was not willing to be implicated—and thus responsible for how Brunner's call for a renewal of natural theology would play out. In this instance, because he is addressing a highly educated audience, his writing takes the form of an internal argument. Barth's Gifford Lectures serve in a very similar capacity, but

---

165. I would argue that there is increasingly less of the former and more of the latter. See ch. 4.

166. Barth shows in many places that he worries about the former, but this latter problem is especially problematic for him. Essentially, his entire problem with the natural knowledge of God stems from understandings of this teaching that are oversimplified accommodations.

almost as an antithesis to "*Nein!*". By this I do not mean that he is saying the opposite, but that he is trying to state his position in a more charitable, yet still quite firm, manner in the Scottish lectures. Likewise, in his two commentaries on Romans, Barth is writing in a way that will further biblical understanding and in a way that is completely guided by and subservient to the text itself. Thus, in these two sources, Barth says things that seem almost opposite to the statements in "*Nein!*," though with very good reasoning and support. In his book on Anselm, Barth writes a critical review of Anselm's argument or proof. His goal appears to be twofold in nature. First, he seems to want to encourage theologians to reengage Anselm, critically, in hopes of gaining new perspective on the great saint's theology. Second, Barth seems to be writing for himself. Rather than desiring to publish books, Barth seems to engage in his critical examination of St. Anselm's work for his own sake, in hopes of increasing his understanding. Finally, in the *Church Dogmatics*, Barth is assuming an educated pastoral audience, an audience with lifelong devotion and service to the Lord Jesus. Likewise, he is assuming an audience that regularly preaches and teaches about Scripture and tradition. Thus, in these documents, there is a good deal of wrestling and back-and-forth to his theology. Given this previous staging of Barth's argument about the natural knowledge of God, I argue that his argument should be synthesized in the following manner.

God can be truly known only by God. Desiring to be known by creation, God reveals God's self exhaustively in the person of Christ Jesus. The first word about this revelation is that this is the revelation of God's wrath. As such, Barth affirms that humans do not possess a capacity for the knowledge of God. In the revelation of God, however, God gifts humanity with a knowability that is actually a way of knowledge about God. This knowability leads to a knowledge of the No-God, which in Feuerbachian fashion is actually just the human herself gazing into a mirror of self-deception. This recognition inevitably leads to the true apprehension of God's wrath and thus allows for the statement that none is without excuse. The apprehension of God's wrath is the hiddenness of God, which for Barth is the *terminus a quo* or the beginning of our knowledge of God. It must be pointed out that this wrath as beginning is one aspect of the revelation of God in Christ, which is both wrath and love. Furthermore, this beginning is real and historical in that it is located in the person of Jesus of Nazareth. As such, hiddenness does not and cannot remain the primary way of knowing God, for clearly, God has been revealed. On this side of the incarnation, crucifixion, resurrection, and ascension, this must necessarily be affirmed.

With the recognition of God's wrath and thus of humanity's subjectivity, a positive knowledge of God begins. This knowledge might best be described as the positive knowledge that God is "that than which nothing greater can be conceived." It is within this positive knowledge of God, which is only the result of God's gratuitous gift of self-revelation in Christ Jesus, that analogy, even the *analogia entis*, becomes possible. It must emphatically be stated, however, that since this analogy is predicated upon God's free gift of love, the analogy is a partial analogy.[167] This analogy has a beginning: the cross of Christ Jesus. Moving toward the cross, knowability becomes faith, or more accurately, a sort of faith-knowledge.[168] Thus, for Barth, knowability becomes tempered by thankfulness, joy, and gratitude. These three qualities of positive knowability reveal that this knowability is not a possession by any means, but rather it is faith. And this faith rests in none other than Christ Jesus.

Having said all of this, human knowability of God moves toward an appropriate end, the *terminus ad quem,* that is the knowledge of God. For Barth, approaching this end, which God in fact desires for all creatures, reveals that this whole process is actually the *circulus veritatis Dei.* This circular knowledge of God, which takes place entirely within the divine self-love of the triune Godhead, is characterized by veiling and unveiling. This circular knowledge is not self-defeating knowledge, but rather God-affirming knowledge. The circularity allows Barth to talk about a real progression from knowledge of God's wrath to knowability and then finally to actual knowledge of God. This knowledge is circular in that humanity is instructed to be continually transformed through the reading of Scripture and the fellowship with God's people the Church. With this in mind, there is an ever-present reduction and excess to our knowledge and faith in God. Likewise, the knowledge of God is circular in that it cannot get moving on its own: God must initiate this knowledge. Given

167. It is here that I will point out the good work done on this subject by Hans Urs von Balthasar in his *Theology of Karl Barth*, 86–167. Essentially, von Balthasar states that Barth moved from critical dialectic thought to analogical thought in his theology. While I completely agree, I would qualify his statement to point out that analogy is not the shape of his argument, but a characteristic of his broader method. I would argue that this broader method is indeed one that begins in dialectics, but shifts towards paradox, within which analogy becomes a (or even the) critical element.

168. Of course, this knowledge actually began at the cross as well, though the human isn't initially cognizant of this fact.

that humanity is curved in upon itself in sin, in almost circular fashion, God must act from without to reveal that God is already more immanent than humanity is to itself.[169] The circularity of humanity's knowledge of God, characterized by veiling and unveiling, is perhaps the most often misunderstood piece of this issue. God begins in veiling, but always with the purpose of unveiling God's self. Humanity must be primed to be able to see and accept this unveiling, and thus the most loving thing that God can do is to begin with veiling. There is no ultimate dialectic between God's veiling and unveiling, however, as God ultimately desires complete disclosure of God's self.

For Barth, God is not the *Deus absconditus*; God is not veiled. For Barth, God is revealed once and for all, definitively, in Christ Jesus. And while it remains vital to maintain elements of hiddenness or veiling in the doctrine of God, for indeed Scripture does so, these elements are only initiatory. Hiddenness or veiling is only a way to begin the discussion of the knowledge of God, particularly in the context of pagans. The doctrine of God, however, for Barth, must never remain in hiddenness or veiling, because that would be inconsistent with the revelation of God in Christ. With this in mind, it is Barth's Christology, and specifically his mature theology of volume IV of the *Church Dogmatics*, to which we now turn. Paying specific attention to issues such as God's veiling and unveiling, as well as the related "Yes" and "No," I will continue to argue for Barth's rejection of a hidden God in favor of the hidden and yet always already revealed God, a tenuous position that is held together not by dialectic but by what I am calling the logic of paradox.

169. Here I am influenced by my good friend Matt Jenson's doctoral thesis. See Jenson, *Gravity of Sin*.

4

Barth's "Mature" Christology: The Absurd Possibility of the Absurd

For the message about the cross is foolishness to those who are perishing, but to us who are being saved it is the power of God. For it is written, "I will destroy the wisdom of the wise, and the discernment of the discerning I will thwart." Where is the one who is wise? Where is the scribe? Where is the debater of this age? Has not God made foolish the wisdom of the world? For since, in the wisdom of God, the world did not know God through wisdom, God decided, through the foolishness of our proclamation, to save those who believe. For Jews demand signs and Greeks desire wisdom, but we proclaim Christ crucified, a stumbling block to Jews and foolishness to Gentiles, but to those who are the called, both Jews and Greeks, Christ the power of God and the wisdom of God. For God's foolishness is wiser than human wisdom, and God's weakness is stronger than human strength. Consider your own call, brothers and sisters: not many of you were wise by human standards, not many were powerful, not many were of noble birth. But God chose what is foolish in the world to shame the wise; God chose what is weak in the world to shame the strong; God chose what is low and despised in the world, things that are not, to reduce to nothing things that are, so that no one might boast in the presence of God. He is the source of your life in Christ Jesus, who became for us wisdom from God, and righteousness and sanctification and redemption, in order that, as it is written, "Let the one who boasts, boast in the Lord."—1 Corinthians 1:18–31

They were greatly astounded and said to one another, "Then who can be saved?" Jesus looked at them and said, "For mortals it is impossible, but not for God; for God all things are possible."
—Mark 10: 26–27

Christians who regard themselves as big and strong and rich and even dear and good children of God, Christians who refuse to sit with their Master at the table of publicans and sinners, are not Christians at all, have still to become so, and need not be surprised if heaven is gray above them and their calling upon God sounds hollow and finds no hearing.[1] —Karl Barth

Introduction

IT HAS ALREADY BEEN shown that Bruce McCormack has declared that Karl Barth was a "critically realistic dialectical theologian" and that he remained so throughout his entire life.[2] McCormack's bold thesis is primarily a response to those who would claim that Barth's theology displays significant shifts—what McCormack has called the "periodization" of Barth's theology.[3] In particular, the periodization thesis that McCormack is so keen to denounce pertains to Barth's alleged shift from so-called dialectical theology to so-called analogical theology around the year 1931, with the publication of Barth's *Anselm: Fides Quaerens Intellectum*. McCormack primarily attributes the latter position to the great Roman Catholic theologian Hans Urs von Balthasar and his theological disciples. McCormack is the first to admit that such a simple description of the timing and of the argument is severely lacking, however. The issue is anything but simple, and McCormack's effort to combat the periodization thesis is laudable. In short, McCormack argues for a grounding of Barth's theology in Barth's own social context, his *sitz im leben*. McCormack believes that methodological concerns were far from Barth's attention or consideration and that he was primarily a Reformed pastor and professor who sought to do theology in the ever-present light of the revelation of God in Christ. McCormack thus elevates Barth's particular social context and his theological training over methodological concerns in his own exegesis of Barth's work. In this way,

1. Barth, *Christian Life*, 80.
2. McCormack, *Karl Barth's Critically Realistic Dialectical Theology*, vii.
3. Ibid., ix.

McCormack makes his case for the claim that Barth's theology was always both critically realistic and dialectical.[4]

For McCormack, Barth's "critically realistic dialectical theology" can be witnessed in any of Barth's works. Indeed, all of Barth's theological writings display this fundamental quality, according to McCormack. To best observe and understand this characterization, argues McCormack, one should look to what McCormack claims are the two central principles or concerns of Barth's theology, namely, "World remains world. But God is God,"[5] and the knowledge of God. Of the former, McCormack says that beginning with *Romans* I, "Barth's theological development from this point on represented a more-or-less continuous unfolding of a single theme: God is God."[6] Indeed, the claim that God is God and the world the world is central to Barth's theology. It is, after all, a fundamental claim of the very God whose self-declaration is "I AM" or "I AM That I AM," that is, YHWH.[7] God is, and God's quiddity provides reality and quiddity itself to creation. God is, therefore creation is. Thus, God is God, and as a result—and only as a result—the world is the world.

This truth, this central theological motif for Barth, is seen nowhere so clearly as in the eternal revelation of God in Christ. In Christ Jesus, the fullness of the Deity was pleased to dwell. In Christ Jesus, God—while remaining fully God—became human flesh and blood—and was fully human. In Christ Jesus, true and full divinity came to reside in perfect harmony with true and full humanity. Jesus of Nazareth—both fully divine and fully human—one person, two natures, without admixture or change. For Barth, theology is Christology, and the reason for this claim should be exceedingly clear: Christology, the study of the incarnation, life, death, resurrection, and ascension of Jesus Christ, is the fundamental way that we can know both God and humanity. In Christ Jesus, God is God and the world is world.

---

4. McCormack believes that a careful reading of Barth will produce such results and that this can be seen especially in German-language Barth scholarship.

5. McCormack claims that this is the central theme of Barth's first edition of his Romans commentary, and would continue to play a central role in Barth's theology throughout his life. See ch. 3 of McCormack, *Karl Barth's Critically Realistic Dialectical Theology*.

6. McCormack, *Karl Barth's Critically Realistic Dialectical Theology*, 134. Here McCormack cites Eberhard Busch, who developed this further in his "God Is God."

7. Exodus 3:14.

It is for this very same reason that the knowledge of God is so central to Barth. Barth is strongly opposed to any claim to a knowledge of God (especially a salvific knowledge of God) prior to or apart from the revelation of God in Christ. As I have argued in the previous chapter, true knowledge of God, for Barth, comes only in the person of Christ Jesus. This is so because in Jesus of Nazareth, God fully and definitively reveals God's own self to creation while at the same time revealing humanity, true humanity, to creation as well. All knowledge, according to Barth, is derivative to this fundamental revelation of God in Christ. Thus, in the same way that Barth's distinction, God is God and the world is the world, is ultimately a christological argument, so is the knowledge of God ultimately a christological argument for Barth. And so the only logical way to conclude this examination of Barth's theology, an examination in light of McCormack's potent and well-argued claims, is to examine Barth's Christology. "If I have a 'system,' it consists in that which Kierkegaard has called the 'infinite qualitative distinction' between time and eternity . . . 'God is in heaven and you are on the earth.' The relationship of *this* God to *this* human, the relationship of *this* human to *this* God is for me the theme of the Bible and the sum of philosophy in one. The philosophers call this crisis of human knowing the *Ursprung*. The Bible sees at the same crossroads Jesus Christ."[8]

Does Barth have a system, an intentional, overarching method used in his theological works? The answer to this question will surely best be discovered in a close observation of the man's own theological works, specifically his more christological works. McCormack believes that the fundamental distinction with which Barth works is that God is God and the world is world. An examination of Barth's Christology and of the New Testament cannot help yielding the answer that this fundamental distinction is revealed and thus understood in the ever-greater unity that is the person of Christ Jesus. I thus cannot help concurring with McCormack that the two issues he points out—that of God being God and the world being world, and the knowledge of God—are probably the two most important pillars of Barth's entire theological contribution. And again, with McCormack I must also conclude that these two bedrock issues for Barth point toward and are best identified and understood in his Christology.

But it is at this point that I must break ties with McCormack, for it is the ever-greater unity of the divine and the human in Christ Jesus that

8. Barth, *Der Römerbrief* (1922), 52. Quoted in McCormack, *Karl Barth's Critically Realistic Dialectical Theology*, 224.

I believe ultimately defines these issues for Barth. It is not distinction that ultimately defines the relationship between God and humanity, but unity. It is my hope that in this chapter it will become increasingly obvious just how far Barth distanced himself from dialectics in his later "mature" Christology. With this move away from dialectic came the movement away from the similar and connected *Deus absconditus*.

Barth was not preoccupied with methodology—this much McCormack and I can agree on. And yet, it is impossible for Barth not to employ some form of methodology, intentionally or not. Rather than a methodology of distinction, of dialectic, as McCormack has powerfully argued for, I believe that Barth's theology displays a method—a logic—of distinction amidst a greater unity. Distinction always remains, and Barth would want to push this distinction as far a possible. Yet as far as Barth pushes distinction—between God and humanity, and between human knowledge and divine knowledge—Barth, I believe, affirms even greater fundamental unity and compatibility between divinity and humanity. This is the fundamental truth of the person of Christ Jesus. Divinity, which is always greater than and other than humanity, exists fully in the person of Jesus of Nazareth who at the same time was fully human, and thus always less than and other than divinity. In Jesus of Nazareth, the fundamental difference between divinity and humanity, a difference in every way, is once and for all revealed to be a fundamental unity.

In Jesus of Nazareth, God journeyed into the far country to do that which humanity could not do—to bring reconciliation, to bring God's way to humanity and to make God's way the very way of humanity. This reality is, I would argue, nothing other than paradox. Distinction between God and humanity will always remain, and it will always characterize the divine-human relationship, but only in such a way that this same distinction is given its very meaning by the eternal unity that will forever characterize the divine-human relationship. This is the reality of the life, death, resurrection, and ascension of Christ Jesus, and it is the core of Barth's teaching in his doctrine of reconciliation. God is God and the world is the world: we can know and understand this distinction only in light of the ever-greater unity of the divine and the human in the person of Christ Jesus.

As I move to the central aim of this chapter, I must briefly explain the shape the chapter will take. Since I have argued, along with McCormack, that the central two tenets of Barth's theology are 1) God is God and the world is world, and 2) the knowledge of God; and since I have argued that these two ultimately point to and are best understood by Barth's Christology, this chapter will be a lengthy examination of Barth's christological writings. Though I will periodically engage with secondary sources, the overwhelming goal of this chapter, in similar fashion to the previous one, is to critically engage primary resources. As I want to avoid the periodization critique that McCormack wages, and since my intention is to examine Barth's Christology, I will focus my attention in this chapter on what I will call Barth's "mature" Christology, that is, his doctrine of reconciliation—*Church Dogmatics* IV. I am not concerned with arguing that Barth had an intentionally chosen methodology that he employed.[9] Rather, I am interested in examining the shape of Barth's theology—specifically his later theology. I believe that such a study will reveal that Barth's mature theology, and his Christology in particular, was undoubtedly not conceived in terms of the *Deus absconditus*. I believe this is most evident in his rejection of dialectic, in favor of something I will call the logic of paradox. The works examined in this chapter should be looked to as perhaps the finest examples of Barth's theology. In them, it should be clear just how far Barth moved in his later theology away from Luther and his hidden, unknown God, the *Deus absconditus*.

Church Dogmatics IV.1 (1956)

Having completed volumes in his *Church Dogmatics* covering the Word of God, the doctrine of God, and the doctrine of creation respectively, Karl Barth turned to his much-anticipated volume on the doctrine of reconciliation. Despite being unfinished, Barth's enormous volume IV stands at over twenty-five hundred pages—and almost three thousand if one counts the unfinished fragments of IV.4, *The Christian Life,* and the statements published as IV.4 regarding "Baptism with the Holy Spirit" and "Baptism with Water."[10] Had he been blessed with an even longer

9. Note: I must again state that I am not arguing that Barth employed a theological method known or characterized as paradox. I don't think that Barth ever intentionally employed a preconceived theological method—at least after his first few years of writing. Rather, I am simply arguing that it might be helpful, from a contemporary theological perspective, to conceive of Barth's very Reformed, and thus biblically driven, way of doing theology, and more importantly his way of conceiving of the revelation of God in Christ, in terms of paradox.

10. Barth spent several years working on IV.4. His intended topic was the ethics of reconciliation, and the volume was to be a companion, of sorts, to III.4. Unfortunately, Barth died on December 10, 1968, leaving IV.4 and his conclusion to the *Church*

life, or perhaps the fountain of youth, Barth intended to conclude his life's work with a fifth volume: *The Doctrine of Redemption*. It is beyond question that had Barth been able to publish this final volume, his impact upon both the Church and the academy would only have increased, and the scope and force of his highly christological theology would stand as completely and totally unrivaled today. While it is interesting and perhaps beneficial to venture a guess as to what Barth's doctrine of redemption would have looked like, I believe strongly that Barth was able to say what he needed to say in the works that he did publish. Barth's primary focus was the revelation of God and humanity in the person and work of Christ Jesus. This was the content of volume IV of his *Church Dogmatics*. It is arguably the case that all of Barth's life and theological writings were in service of his great goal of finally putting ink to his understanding of the revelation of God in Christ—indeed, that everything Barth wrote prior to *Church Dogmatics* IV was nothing but prolegomena to this great work. Barth's *Doctrine of Reconciliation* does in fact stand above all of his other works, even his great commentary on Romans, as Barth's most lengthy, thought-out, and definitive statement regarding Christology. For this reason, I think that it is reasonably safe to operate under the assumption that Barth would have his readers examine volume IV with care, treating it as his definitive statement on the doctrine of reconciliation and Christology as a whole. With this in mind, I will begin a lengthy examination of Barth's *Doctrine of Reconciliation* beginning with volume IV.1.

Barth first published the initial volume of his *Doctrine of Reconciliation* in 1956. In the foreword he states that the doctrine of reconciliation is "the centre of all Christian knowledge. To fail here is to fail everywhere. To be on the right track here makes it impossible to be completely

---

Dogmatics, a volume on redemption, unfinished. The statements on baptism with the Holy Spirit and with water were completed paragraphs that, at the time of his death, Barth intended to be included in IV.4. This fragment was published a year after Barth's death, in 1969, under the title *Church Dogmatics* IV.4: *The Foundation of the Christian Life* (fragment). Also published the same year, under a deceptively similar title, *The Christian Life, Church Dogmatics* IV.4 *Lecture Fragments*, was Barth's unfinished, unedited beginning to IV.4, collected from personal notes and lectures. I've chosen to include this text, while virtually ignoring the former, because in it I think readers get a chance to see straight into the last thoughts of Barth, to the way he was trying to conclude his great volume on reconciliation. In addition, the latter is more concerned with reconciliation and therefore Christology as such, whereas the former serves as an insight into Barth's continually developing understanding of baptism and its relationship to Christian ethics. The former is a valuable and important piece of Barth's great *magnum opus*, but simply won't factor too greatly into the present discussion.

mistaken in the whole."[11] Put simply, Barth believed that "reconciliation is the fulfillment of the covenant between God and man."[12] God, in God's ceaseless mercy and grace, made an unconditional covenant with all of creation through the people of Israel. The terms of this covenant, which was always intended to be for all the nations, stated that God would be Israel's God and they were to be God's people. God promised to love Israel and provide for her no matter what. And yet despite this unconditional love, Israel, like all of humanity, rebelled against God. Rebellion came to dominate the human side of the relationship long before the covenant was made, and would continue to be the chief descriptor of humanity's side of the covenant indefinitely. The omnipotent God knew this but made an unconditional covenant anyway. Thus, the fulfillment of covenant necessarily has the character of atonement, for humanity is not in—and tries to resist being in—harmony with God. It is in the fulfillment of covenant, therefore, that God realizes His eternal will with humanity, that is, reconciliation.[13]

Reconciliation is, therefore, the story of creation, the story of covenant, the story of Israel, and the person and work of Christ Jesus. Reconciliation, then, is the actuality of the atonement, to borrow a phrase from Barth. Reconciliation is, therefore, the story of the Church; indeed, reconciliation is necessarily our story. Reconciliation, from the very beginning, was God's plan. Reconciliation was God's intention. Despite humanity's continued acts of unfaithfulness, of idolatry and religious whoredom, God desired reconciliation to the extent that God indeed became reconciliation. This then means that God's nature, indeed the very character of God, is none other than reconciliation.

There is no conflict in God, only reconciliation. Reconciliation, then, is the paradoxical fabric of all things; it is the nature of the relationship between the eternal God and His temporal creation; it is the quality of divine love that spans the untraversable expanse between eternity and temporality, between divinity and humanity, between God and us. God is reconciliation and reconciliation is the paradoxical reality of the divine and the human.

11. Barth, *CD* IV.1, ix.

12. Ibid., 22.

13. Ibid., 67.

Emmanuel: Reconciliation Has a Name

When the angel of the Lord appears to Joseph in a dream at the beginning of Matthew's Gospel account, the angel says, "'Joseph, son of David, do not be afraid to take Mary as your wife, for the child conceived in her is from the Holy Spirit. She will bear a son, and you are to name him Jesus, for he will save his people from their sins.' All this took place to fulfill what had been spoken by the Lord through the prophet: 'Look, the virgin shall conceive and bear a son, and they shall name him Emmanuel,' which means, 'God is with us.'"[14] Quoting the words of the Prophet Isaiah, Matthew begins his Gospel narrative by declaring that in the child born of a virgin, God Himself has come to dwell in mortal flesh. Make no mistake, to a most likely Jewish audience, Matthew declares that Emmanuel, that Reconciliation Himself, has come. This Emmanuel, according to Matthew, is not just a sign that God is with us, but rather is God with us! In Jesus, Emmanuel, God is with us—that is, humanity as a whole!

Likewise, in Luke's Gospel account, Zechariah declares, "And you, child, will be called the prophet of the Most High; for you will go before the Lord to prepare his ways, to give knowledge of salvation to his people by the forgiveness of their sins. By the tender mercy of our God, the dawn from on high will break upon us, to give light to those who sit in darkness and in the shadow of death, to guide our feet into the way of peace."[15] Zechariah's words about his own son John revealed just what the expectations were for Emmanuel. In Emmanuel, God fulfills the covenant by forever reconciling Himself to His creation. In Emmanuel, the second person of the Trinity, the eternally begotten Son of God, becomes, in every way, human flesh and human blood. This was the good news, the Gospel, which rocked the foundation of Israel as well as the whole world. This is the good news that Christians have no choice but to declare today, for it is the very promise and the fulfillment of God's covenantal relationship with humanity. God with us is the core teaching and doctrinal statement of Christianity.[16] And as Barth emphatically states, God with us, Emmanuel, is primarily a theological rather than an anthropological statement. "[I]t is primarily a statement about God and only then and for that reason a statement about us men."[17] In Christ Jesus, God . . . , period.

14. Matthew 1:20–23.
15. Luke 1:76–79
16. Barth, *CD* IV.1, 4.
17. Ibid., 5.

This is what Barth is saying. Christ Jesus, as a human being, equals God, period. This is what Emmanuel means—that God with us is "God Himself in this act of His."[18]

Everything about the biblical story, the relationship between God and creation, hangs in the balance of Emmanuel. It is in Jesus of Nazareth, Emmanuel, that all things are drawn together and given reason, purpose, and fulfillment. In Jesus as Emmanuel, we affirm that God dwells with—and in fact takes upon God's very self—humanity, even sin itself. God's entire economy centers on the Christ event, on the proclamation of Jesus as Emmanuel. And this man, this Jesus, is not characterized by inner personal turmoil or cosmic tension. No, in Jesus of Nazareth, we learn that the union of divinity and humanity does not mean the crossing of two polar opposites, that uniting divinity and humanity does not result in cosmic destruction or the utter annihilation of humanity, but rather that divinity lends itself to humanity in such a way as to redeem, heal, and transform humanity to the covenant partner we were always intended to be. Emmanuel is the title of the unthinkable. Emmanuel is the name given to the perplexingly harmonious relationship between God and creation in the person Jesus. Emmanuel is the core teaching of the Christian faith. Emmanuel is the opposite of the *Deus absconditus*. Emmanuel is the basis for centuries of wrestling with the logic of the incarnation, and the basis for the Christian affirmation of the Trinity and for the Chalcedonian Confession. Emmanuel is the logic of the hypostatic union. The affirmation of Emmanuel makes no sense according to human reason. Emmanuel is, in short, the paradoxical logic of the incarnation, of the Gospel. Emmanuel is the encounter between human reason and the divine, and the result is pure, unfathomably clear paradox.

In Emmanuel, God is with us, and yet God remains who God is in God's own self.

> He is both in His life in eternity in Himself, and also in His life as Creator in the time of the world created by Him: by and in Himself, and also above and in this world, and therefore according to the heart of the Christian message with us men. How can we know God if His being is unknown or obscure or indifferent? But how can we know God if we do not find the truth and power of His being in His life, and of His life in His act? We know about God only if we are witnesses—however distantly and modestly—of His act. And we speak about God only as we

18. Ibid., 6.

can do so—however deficiently—as those who proclaim His act.
"God with us" as it occurs at the heart of the Christian message
is the attestation and report of the life and act of God as the One
who is.[19]

This is, as Barth so emphatically declares, the starting point for the Christian message—for the Christian faith itself. God is God and humanity is humanity. These two are different. And yet, God is not unknown, obscure, or indifferent. In Emmanuel, God is revealed, visible, and actively involved in creation.

God and humanity are so different as not to warrant even being considered together as things, for God is not a thing in the same way that humans are things. God is not a being as humans are beings. There is no univocal ground or substance uniting God and humanity. In short, the difference between God and humanity is total. In affirming the difference between God and humanity, we affirm an unfathomable difference, one that arguably results in nothing but apophatic doxology. God is different in such a way that creaturely existence is derivative upon, and ultimately unable to truly speak about, God. As Kierkegaard has said, and Barth has concurred, there is an "infinite qualitative distinction" between God and the world. And yet . . . In my appraisal, Barth's entire corpus displays a sense of wrestling with this "and yet."

"And yet" is the definition of paradox; it is the substance of the foolish stumbling block that Christians proclaim. And yet Jesus! God is completely and totally other than humanity, and we can only know anything about this God because God became flesh and dwelt among God's creation. God need not have anything to do with God's creation, and yet God's eternal plan is to dwell in covenantal relationality with God's creation. "To put it in this simplest way, what unites God and us men is that He does not will to be God without us, that He creates us rather to share with us and therefore with our being and life and act His own incomparable being and life and act, that *He does not allow His history to be His and ours ours, but causes them to take place as a common history.* That is the special truth which the Christian message has to proclaim at its very heart."[20] God is different than humanity—totally different. And yet this difference, though it remains eternally, is defined by the revelation of God in Christ, in the proclamation of Jesus as Emmanuel, God

19. Barth, *CD* IV.1, 6–7.
20. Ibid., 7. Italics mine.

with us. Difference remains, but only in light of and derivative of the fundamental unity between divinity and humanity revealed once and for all in Christ Jesus. This is what Barth calls "the insoluble mystery of the Grace of God."[21]

That Jesus is Emmanuel is the core teaching of the Christian faith. As Barth declares time and again, everything we can know about God we know in and through Christ Jesus. Jesus is the starting point and the goal for all theology that would call itself Christian. At the heart of this declaration is the paradoxical "and yet" of Emmanuel. The tension created by the claim that Jesus is Emmanuel is the arena in which all Christian theology is to be done, and it is certainly the arena in which Barth lives and moves and has his being. Jesus is Emmanuel, God with us. This means that the most fundamental truth we know about God and therefore about God's relationship to sinful humanity is that God became human, that divinity is a noninvasive element in creation, that conflict does not mediate the interplay of God and humanity.

In Jesus as Emmanuel, God reveals that God's ways can be our ways and that our ways can be God's ways. In Jesus as Emmanuel, we hear a clear and resounding "Yes" proclaimed to all of humanity, though we might do our best to misunderstand that "Yes" for a "No."[22] The difference we know to exist between God and humanity is a difference that is subject to a deeper and more fundamental unity. This difference enhances and makes more beautiful the unity between God and humanity, in that we learn that it need not be so.

> The Lord became a servant but does not cease to be the Lord. On the contrary, as a servant He is truly the Lord in His very Godhead. He is the omnipresent, the eternal, the almighty, the only wise and righteous and holy. He is not, therefore, untrue to Himself but true. He does not give Himself away or give Himself up, but offers Himself in His divine Lordship, and as such maintains Himself. This is what God does in Jesus Christ. And He does not do it in the chance of a caprice or variation of His divine being, or under the compulsion of any inward or outward necessity, but in the determination of His free love on the basis of His eternal election, in fulfillment of the eternal decree of His mercy. The God who is great enough to be obedient and humble and small, and therefore truly great, wills to be and is

21. Ibid., 83.

22. Ibid., 41. This is an oft-repeated concept for Barth.

this. This is what He does in Jesus Christ. And He does it for our sake, for us, to take us to Himself, to reconcile us with Him, to convert us to Him, to save us, to restore His covenant with us, to be our God, that we may live under and with Him in His kingdom. God elected us when in His Son He elected to offer Himself, to condescend, to humble Himself, to set up His lordship in that divine obedience and therefore in that humility. We are His intention and goal. It is for our sake (*pro nobis*) that God determined and came to this action which cuts right across all human belief and surmise and thought about God, this action in which His Word becomes flesh. And if it is not in vain that He does what He does, then it is right and proper that we should turn from His action to ours, that we should ask concerning the correspondence of our actions to His action, concerning our own form as reflected in what God does, and does for us. And we describe this reflection exactly when we say that it is the picture of human pride as the sin in which we do despite to Him, thus making ourselves impossible and plunging into the abyss of our corruption. It is in view of our pride and to overcome it that God wills to be our God, our Helper and Redeemer, as He is in Jesus Christ.[23]

This is effectively a summary of all of volume IV.1, and perhaps of Barth's entire doctrine of reconciliation. God remains God and humans remain humans, and there is complete difference—and yet God, acting out of nothing but sheer, boundless, unsolicited love, does the unthinkable and becomes human *pro nobis*. This unthinkable action proves to be the very heart of God's own self, as Jesus, the unthinkable unity between the divine and the human, reveals all that we need ever know about God. God does this for us, for the entire world, for all of creation, in order that all of creation might be reconciled to God. In Jesus as Emmanuel, God crosses the infinite qualitative abyss of difference that separates God from humanity, by filling up that very abyss with God's ceaseless and boundless love. This love is Jesus, who encounters human pride not irresistibly, but with total and complete grace, transforming and mysterious.

The Christian understanding of humanity, then, is that humans exist as always already confronted by God's grace, in the person of Jesus. Despite God's redeeming love, despite Emmanuel, despite God's "and yet," humanity persists in its pride. Barth calls this reality the "terrible

23. Barth, *CD* IV.1, 417–18.

paradox" of human pride and divine reconciling mercy.[24] We could never contemplate and discuss the paradox of Emmanuel enough, and considering the paradoxical logic of Emmanuel only forces us into another, even more maddening paradox—that of human pride in the face of the reality of Jesus, and especially his death and resurrection. Christians, like all humans for Barth, live in the terrible paradox of human pride and divine mercy. After confessing the good news of Emmanuel, then, the primary goal of the Christian message is to accept the mediating and atoning work of Jesus. Only in accepting this reality can sense be made of the terrible paradox of human existence.

The God-Human: Jesus the Mediator

Cur Deus homo? To fulfill the covenant between God and humanity. When St. Cyril of Alexandria discusses the incarnation, he literally says, "in-manment" to describe the Son's gracious act.[25] Cyril chooses this tricky statement in order to reject two heresies. On the one hand, Cyril did not want to agree with the likes of Arius in saying that Jesus was adopted, that his divinity was a gift given to a good human, and thus not the same as the divinity of the Father. On the other hand, Cyril also wanted to reject the idea that the two natures did not really unite in the person of Jesus of Nazareth, something that was espoused in various ways by people like Nestorius. Contrary to these false options, Cyril, following Athanasius, taught that Jesus of Nazareth was truly one person with two natures, divine and human. Cyril affirmed that Jesus was truly both divine and human, and also truly one. Cyril preferred the latter over the former. As this one, Jesus is the true Mediator, the intersection of divinity and humanity in a completely perfect and unique way. Jesus was not a man who was adopted into divinity; neither was Jesus an alien-like

24. Ibid., 418.

25. One could, of course, state this inclusively as "in-humanment." In other words, in Jesus of Nazareth, the eternally begotten Word of God is in-fleshed or in-humaned. "He did not change himself into flesh; he did not endure any mixture or blending, or anything else of this kind. But he submitted himself to being emptied and 'for the sake of the honor that was set before him he counted the shame as nothing' (Heb. 12:2) and did not disdain the poverty of human nature. As God he wished to make that flesh which was held in the grip of sin and death evidently superior to sin and death. He made it his very own, and not soulless as some have said, but rather animated with a rational soul, and thus he restored flesh to what it was in the beginning." Cyril of Alexandria, *On the Unity of Christ*, 54–55.

hybrid of two completely distinct natures: Jesus was and is one, and thus He is the true Mediator between God and humanity, the fulfillment of the covenant.[26]

I believe that Barth is very heavily indebted to this Alexandrian Christology, primarily through Athanasius, but therefore through Cyril as well. The unity of the two natures is always Barth's operating assumption; it is always the bedrock of his theological endeavors. Be that as it may, however, Barth also believes in the importance of maintaining the integrity of the two natures in relationship to one another inside their overarching unity.[27] As Emmanuel, as the great Mediator between divinity and humanity, Christ Jesus is the complete and total revelation of God to humanity. Likewise, Christ Jesus is the complete and total revelation of true humanity to fallen and sinful humanity. Attention to the divine revelation in Christ Jesus teaches us, and allows us to experience, all that we can know about God. Attention to the human revelation in Christ Jesus teaches us, and allows us to experience, that which humanity was intended to be by the Loving Creator God. And finally, attention to the unity of the two natures calls humanity to return to God and embrace the covenantal relationship that we have forsaken. Attention to the unity of

---

26. Surely only a Nestorian Christology could lend itself perfectly to a truly dialectical theology.

27. A good example of this is the way that Barth will spend countless pages devoted to the discussion of Jesus' divinity and the impact of this upon humanity and then later spend countless pages discussing the humanity of Jesus and the impact of this upon humanity. For example, §59 of the *Church Dogmatics*, all two hundred pages, is devoted to a discussion of the obedience of the Son of God. Here, Jesus is described as the Son of God, traveling into the far country to find and redeem humanity, reconciling us with God. In addition to this two-hundred-page emphasis on Jesus as the Son of God, it is arguably the case that the rest of IV.1, over four hundred pages, stands in light of this emphasis on Jesus' divine nature. Then, in §64 (the first paragraph of IV.2), Barth spends over 250 pages discussing Jesus as the Son of Man, emphasizing his human nature. As was the case with the paragraphs following §59, it is again arguably the case that the entire rest of IV.2, almost six hundred pages, stands in light of this emphasis on Jesus' human nature. The point is, Barth believes it to be very plausible and helpful to tease out the importance of both the divine and human natures of Jesus and how these relate to humanity. But readers must always keep in mind that these extremely lengthy discussions of the two natures, focused and isolated as they may be, exist always within the greater and even lengthier framework of Jesus as the Mediator, as the unique and paradoxical God-human. In short, paragraphs 59–63 and paragraphs 64–68 are bracketed, intentionally, by paragraphs 57–58 and §69. Jesus Christ, Emmanuel, God with us, is the Mediator between humanity and divinity. Christ Jesus is fully God and fully human, one person with two natures, for Barth, in very Alexandrian fashion. This is always the case for Barth.

the two natures calls and requires humans to live lives of obedience and worship.[28]

It is appropriate, then, that Barth begins his enormous volume on the doctrine of reconciliation with a discussion of Jesus Christ as Emmanuel (§57) and then moves directly to a discussion of Jesus Christ as Mediator (§58). To discuss reconciliation, Barth begins with a discussion of God who loves the world, and thus from God downwards, and then moves to a discussion of the world that is loved by God, and thus from the world upwards.[29] Barth conducts these discussions simply to illustrate the situation and to move to the one thing that unites these two seemingly opposite directions: the person of Jesus Christ. As this one thing, as Mediator, Jesus is both Emmanuel and the Paschal Lamb; He is the atonement and the fulfillment of the covenant. Jesus is the event of reconciliation between God and humanity, and as such Jesus provides meaning to both God and the world.

> The atonement as the fulfillment of the covenant is neither grace in itself as the being of the gracious God, nor is it the work of grace in itself and as such the being of the man to whom God is gracious. Nor is it the sum of the two nor their mutual relationship. It is rather the middle point, the one thing from which neither the God who turns to man nor man converted to God can be abstracted, in which and by which both are what they are, in which and to which they stand in that mutual relationship. It is only from this middle point that we have been able to look upwards and downwards, and as we tried always to find and name something concrete we had all the more necessarily to come back to it again and again. But that one thing in the middle is one person, Jesus Christ. He is the atonement as the fulfillment of covenant. In Him that turning of God to man and conversion of man to God is actuality in the appointed order of the mutual inter-relationship, and therefore in such a way that the former aims at the latter and the latter is grounded in the former. In Him both are in this order the one whole of the event of reconciliation. Our third task—in our present order of thinking—is obviously to understand Him as this one whole.[30]

28. I take this to be one of the central points of §57, section 2, "The Covenant as the Presupposition of Reconciliation." The christological basis of the covenant *is* the call to Christian ethics. "χαρισ always demands the answer of ευχαριστια." Barth, *CD* IV.1, 41.

29. Barth, *CD* IV.1, 122.

30. Ibid.

Jesus Christ is this one whole. Neither God nor humanity can be abstracted from this one whole. There can be no abstract doctrine of God, and no abstract anthropology that stands separate from, or outside of, Christology. The difference between God and humanity, therefore, is always encompassed within and defined by the unity of this one whole, Jesus. Jesus, then, as the middle point between the two previously described movements, encompasses the whole and gives meaning to the whole by bringing together the two as one.[31]

And yet, as this middle point, as this one whole, Jesus the Mediator is not something different than the other two movements. Avoiding the error of Nestorius, this one whole is not the sum of the addition of divinity and humanity resulting in a third or new thing. Jesus is not a *tertium quid*. In the unity of the person of Christ Jesus, one plus one equals one. According to an utterly unique, perplexing, and indeed paradoxical logic, this one whole is truly one in such a way that its uniqueness, its oneness, is not predicated upon, but rather lends meaning to, the previous two moments of the equation.[32] Divinity and humanity need not and must not conflict in order for Jesus, the God-human, to exist. Rather, Jesus as Mediator exists as the one whole in such a way that the integrity of divinity and humanity is not only affirmed, but both are given their very meaning. The one whole, Jesus, exists within the nonviolent tension and also provides the very terms for the existence of both divinity and humanity. Jesus is one, both God and human, in a way that is utterly unique and yet not alien; He is not a *tertium quid*. Jesus Christ is the definitive, solitary one that provides the possibility of and the understanding of all else. Christ Jesus teaches perfectly about both God and humanity by being none other than Himself.

In this way Jesus is the Mediator, the perfect middle between divinity and humanity. In this way Jesus fulfills the covenant, by enabling humanity to fully participate in the covenantal relationship with God. "Jesus Christ is not what He is—very God, very man, very God-man—in order as such to mean and do and accomplish something else which is atonement. But His being as God and man and God-man consists in

---

31. Ibid., 123.

32. This is very similar to Maurice Blondel's very non-modern and perplexing use of dialectic. I believe this is better called paradox. I will address this more in the final chapter.

the completed act of the reconciliation of man with God."[33] Jesus as Emmanuel, as Mediator, is Himself Reconciliation.

Jesus as Mediator is a way for Barth to talk about atonement. At its core, Barth believes that the atonement is reconciliation. This reconciliation is the reconciliation of all things; most especially it is the reconciliation of God with humanity. This reconciliation is not an act or a decision, but rather it is a person, an event. The atonement is the actuality or the proof of the paradoxical logic of the covenant, of Emmanuel. Jesus is this reconciliation in that He is this atonement. Jesus unites two things that are usually thought to be distinct and shows that they are more closely related than we could ever imagine. Jesus Christ is very God. Jesus Christ is very human. And yet, Jesus Christ is one. Christ Jesus is the self-emptying of God and the raising up of humanity.

> In Him humanity is exalted humanity, just as Godhead is humiliated Godhead. And humanity is exalted in Him by the humiliation of Godhead. We cannot regard the human being of Jesus Christ, we cannot—without denying or weakening them—interpret His predicates of liability to sin and suffering and death, in any other way than in the light of the liberation and exaltation accomplished in His unity with God. It is in its impotence that His being as man is omnipotent, in its temporality that it is eternal, in its shame that it is glorious, in its corruptibility that it is incorruptible, in its servitude that it is that of the Lord. In this way, therefore, it is His true being as man—true humanity.[34]

Jesus is the lowering, the *kenosis*, of God, and yet, simultaneously, the raising up of humanity. This movement downwards coupled with this movement upwards is only discovered and understood in its location in Jesus of Nazareth.

Thus the logic of Jesus as the Mediator is the logic of the coming together of two allegedly distinct realities in the atoning work of Jesus Christ. And this is, again, where the paradoxical logic of the Christian message can be witnessed in Barth. In Christ Jesus, the eternal becomes temporal, Spirit becomes flesh, and the Impassible suffers. In Christ Jesus, sin and death are conquered, flesh is redeemed, and the suffering are vindicated. Christ Jesus encompasses all of these and more. In Christ Jesus, the eternal, omnipotent God comes to humanity in all its pride and vanity and lowers Himself, forever connecting the ways of God with

33. Barth, *CD* IV.1, 127.

34. Ibid., 131–32.

the ways of humanity.[35] In Christ Jesus as Mediator, we are witness to the incontrovertible fact that God rejects God's own self, in favor of the sinful and broken ways of humanity, that in doing so, humanity might be restored to its status as covenant partner. There is no conflict within God on this point, for God has forever acted once and for all to redeem and reconcile humanity with God's self in Christ Jesus. This is the paradox of grace revealed in the affirmation of Jesus as Mediator. It is heard most clearly in the cry of dereliction uttered by Jesus on the cross: "My God, my God, why have you forsaken me?" Here, Barth says, Jesus, the one whole mediator,

> Although He was the Son of God, died as very man, was dead and buried and lay in the tomb—and all apparently in the most marvelous contradiction, but really in the most wonderful unity, the eternal and living and almighty God thrown back in the person of this man upon the free grace of God the Father, upon His unmerited justification, upon His undeserved mercy, upon the gift of His creative power believed in hope against hope (Rom. 4:18) . . . He had nothing but nothingness under and behind and beside Him, and nothing but God before and above Him—nothingness in all its unsearchableness and power, and God as the One into whose Hands He was delivered up without reservation and without claim—He the man who was Himself also the Son of God. He did this for us. This is—in its sharpest form—the humility of the act of God which took place for us in Jesus Christ.[36]

Jesus Christ was the marvelous contradiction: the judge who was judged, the God who was humbled, the man who was redeemed. Jesus Christ was and is and always will be the Mediator between God and humanity, the one whole who paradoxically contains both perfectly within Himself.

In IV.1, Barth's language and method moved away from dialectic to something I am calling paradox. Barth employs this strange type of logic in order to account for the relationship between God's radical otherness and God's simultaneously close immanence. This relationship was held in balance and defined by the fundamental unity of Jesus of Nazareth, the Messiah, who is Emmanuel and Mediator.

35. Ibid., 143.
36. Ibid., 458.

Finally, there is one other instance of Barth's paradoxical logic in IV.1 worth pointing out. While some argue that Barth often eschews analogical language, here Barth makes a different move. After discussing his Roman Catholic colleagues, especially his "French friends," Barth says that faith necessarily forces upon us the "concept of analogy."[37] Faith, says Barth, is a "free act of man."[38] Though Barth is often quick to state that there is no analogy between God and humanity, here he declares that in faith, we become *analogans* to Christ Jesus.[39] Thus, there is no analogy, and yet there is analogy. Barth—who we have seen affirms an infinite qualitative distinction between God and the world, between eternity and time—says this distinction is swallowed up or vanquished in Christ Jesus. In words that I can't help finding ironic and paradoxical given his own theological work, Barth says, "It is a poor theology that persists in the inequality between me and Jesus Christ—a pious cushion which is content to maintain the distinction from Him."[40] In many ways Barth's theology is this pious cushion. And yet, if Barth's radical unilateral understanding of the reconciliation that has taken place once and for all in the atonement is taken into consideration, Barth's theology becomes radically analogical—something that I think displays the increasingly paradoxical way he thinks about the Christian message.

Having shown the paradoxical way in which Barth develops his understanding of Emmanuel, and having explained what it is to say that Jesus is the Mediator—the two core principles of the doctrine of reconciliation—I turn now to an examination of volume IV.2.

Church Dogmatics IV.2 (1958)

Barth began his doctrine of reconciliation by laying out reconciliation in terms of Jesus as Emmanuel (§57) and Jesus as the Mediator between God and the world (§58). Having completed this lengthy and important "introduction," Barth turned to a discussion of the obedience the Son of God (§59), a theme that I believe brackets the remaining paragraphs of volume IV.1. Introductory work aside, Barth begins volume IV.2 in an equal and opposite fashion, by discussing the exaltation of the Son of

37. *CD* IV.1, 768–69.
38. Ibid., 769.
39. Ibid., 770.
40. Ibid., 771.

Man (§64). As I have previously mentioned, Barth begins by discussing Jesus as the Son of God in terms of God lowering God's self in obedience, and then Barth moves to discussing Jesus as the Son of Man in terms of raising humanity up to God, again through the obedient faithfulness of Christ Jesus. The former cannot stand without the latter, and likewise the latter cannot stand without the former. Both large sections, including the paragraphs that follow, are mutually dependent upon one another and thus can only be understood as a whole. This whole is bookended, on both sides, by Christ the Mediator, who provides the arena for understanding this most important and perplexing issue: reconciliation.

In examining volume IV.2, I will focus on the paradoxical logic with which Barth talks about the human Jesus and His effect upon those he encountered both during his ministry as well as today. Barth will begin by briefly reexamining the two-natures talk and then focus a significant amount of writing on how the human Jesus was encountered by his contemporaries. This discussion will lead Barth to one of his favorite topics, the "Yes" and "No" of God spoken to the world in Christ Jesus. Here, I believe, Barth makes it very clear that there is no dialectical relationship between the "Yes" and the "No." In fact, not only does Barth continue to utilize the logic of paradox in volume IV.2, he becomes increasingly vocal about his disdain for and rejection of dialectical language and logic, especially in terms of the relationship between God and humanity. Finally, I will briefly examine Barth's discussion of the suffering and death of Jesus on the cross. Here Barth will employ a phrase, the "logic of the cross," that I take as foundational for much of my argument regarding paradox.

Two Natures

As we have already seen, Barth heartily agrees with the classic affirmation of Christ Jesus as one person with two natures. This statement alone is one of the most abundant and wealthy in the Christian faith. Barth utilizes two-natures talk to explore both who God is and who humanity is. It is Christ Jesus, after all, who once and for all perfectly reveals both, according to Barth. This is the core of Christology for Barth—that Jesus Christ reveals both God and humanity. Thus he says, "Every sound christological discussion will necessarily start not only with an explanation of the *vere Deus* which declares the equality of Jesus Christ with God, but with an explanation of the *vere homo* which declares His equality with us."[41] God is who we know in Christ Jesus, and humanity is who we know in Christ Jesus.[42] This is so because Jesus is fully God and fully human, always both and yet, in an even greater way, always one.[43] Barth explains the union of the two natures in Jesus this way:

41. Barth, *CD* IV.2, 25–26.

42. This is different than saying God is what God does, which is a claim that Bruce McCormack has championed recently. McCormack, "Christology and Metaphysics in Paul Tillich and Karl Barth." This article, which I heard delivered a the 2009 annual meeting of the Wesleyan Theological Society, is a summary, in many ways, of Mc-Cormack's work in his latest book, *Orthodox and Modern: Studies in the Theology of Karl Barth*. In particular, McCormack develops this theme in section 3, a section titled "Karl Barth's Theological Ontology." Here, McCormack praises Barth's understanding of election as his chief gift to the theological world. While I too agree with the importance of Barth's understanding of election, and his Christology that serves as the basis for such an understanding, I worry that McCormack's "mantra" is less helpful than he would hope it to be. McCormack's position is a logical progression from Barth's staunch rejection of any prolegomena or starting point to theology other than Christ, as well as his assertion that there is no hidden reserve within God. While I agree, I worry that this "what you see is what you get" theology makes it increasingly difficult to talk about God as triune, for example. In particular, this makes pneumatology a particularly tenuous topic to pursue. In short, I believe this position is one that can be put forth as the logical progression of Barth's work, but I do not believe this is a helpful pursuit—in fact it is, ultimately, harmful.

43. Barth provides a very helpful discussion of the *communcatio idiomatum* in CD IV.2, 51–60. Here he rejects Hegel's "absolute Spirit" which develops into a synthesis only in terms of thesis-antithesis, etc. Barth describes the perplexing *communicatio idiomatum* as "the work of the mercy of God turning in inconceivable condescension to very dissimilar man." In this section, Barth makes it clear that understanding the *communicatio idiomatum* in terms of dialectic is not helpful, and yet he clearly wants to make distinctions between the two natures, all the while holding them in unity. In doing so, he makes reference to Athanasius as the primary influence upon Calvin's understanding of this issue. This connection is made in order to justify the latter and not the former. Athanasius' complex theology of the incarnation is clearly preferred by Barth above all others. Barth states that he prefers to use the Reformed language of the *communicatio operationum*, which focused the two natures onto the person of Jesus of Nazareth, as opposed to the Lutherans, who in Barth's opinion kept the discussion too much in the abstract. Barth, *CD* IV.2, 104–5. As a helpful aside to this discussion, a further distinction can be made within the *communicatio idiomatum*, that of *in abstracto* and *in concreto*. The former, being an example of Alexandrian Christology, conceives of the two natures within an "incarnational center," according to which the two natures are abstracted from the unity of Christ, thus moving from one to two. The latter, on the other hand, as representative of much of Antiochene Christology, keeps the two natures separate, in that the two natures are concretized in Jesus, thus moving from two to one. The term "incarnational center" has been borrowed from George Kalantzis, whose work on this subject is outstanding. See Kalantzis, "Sovereignty of God and Divine Transcendence," 35–39. I believe the *in concreto* is in line with Barth's

> By divine and human essence (the equivalent of divine and hu-
> man "nature," or quite simply divinity and humanity) we mean
> on the one hand that which Jesus Christ has in common with
> the Father and the Holy Spirit as the Son of God, that which
> distinguishes His being and its nature from the being and na-
> ture of man, and of all other reality distinct from God, with an
> absolute (and infinitely qualitative) distinction; and on the other
> hand that which (even in His exaltation) He has in common
> with all other human creatures as the Son of Man, that which
> marks off His being and its nature from the being and nature of
> God in His eternal modes of existence as Father, Son and Holy
> Spirit, and in His position and function as Creator and Lord of
> all things, with what is again an absolute (and infinitely qualita-
> tive) distinction. . . . The statement that Jesus Christ is the One
> who is of divine and human essence dares to unite that which by
> definition cannot be united.[44]

Jesus Christ is the paradox of all paradoxes. He is the uniting of that
which by definition cannot be united. Jesus Christ is always this paradoxically bound unity of two distinct natures: never one and then the other.[45]
Christ Jesus is two-in-one, and therefore He is completely unique in such
a way that is not foreign or invasive, not overpowering or destructive, but
in such a way that both divinity and humanity, both Creator and creature,
come to exist with one another as God had always intended. God does
not cease to be God, but God at the very same time became human flesh
and human blood in Jesus of Nazareth.[46]

God is God and the world is the world. Divinity is completely
separate and distinct in every way from humanity. There is no ground
or substance that links the Creator with creation. And yet, Christ Jesus,
paradoxically, eradicates the difference by becoming Himself that very
difference. Jesus overcomes the distance between God and humanity by
Himself becoming that very distance. Christ Jesus is the making of all
things new, He is utterly unique, and thus provides meaning to all else:
divine and human.

It is important to point out that just as Barth wants to emphasize
the difference between the divine and the human, just as he pushes the

---

attempt to distance himself from the Lutheran position, which looks a lot like the *in
abstracto*.

44. Barth, *CD* IV.2, 60–61.

45. Ibid., 81.

46. Ibid., 38.

distinction between Jesus as the Son of God and Jesus as the Son of Man, he always emphasizes the overwhelming unity of these two. This unique unity, for Barth, is absolutely essential. In fact, despite his fondness for two-natures talk, Barth worries that it can be quite dangerous. His fear is that with talk of the two natures in Jesus, we assume previously defined categories of divinity and humanity, both of which can be seen in Christ, rather than Christ Jesus being the foundation and definition of divinity and humanity.[47] Barth wants to avoid the twofold danger of a generalized Deism and a general anthropology. This means, for Barth, that any discussion of the two natures, of either divinity or humanity, must necessarily be rooted solely in the person of Jesus of Nazareth, the Son of God and Son of Man. As such, the God revealed in Jesus Christ is most assuredly not the *Deus absconditus*.

To put it simply, Barth believes that if we are to affirm the hypostatic union, and he believes that we should, then we must move from one to two (and then back to one again), and not from two to one. Faithful Christian theology, for Barth, is Christology, in that theology must begin nowhere else but with Christ Jesus, Emmanuel, the Mediator between God and humanity. The order of this statement reveals Barth's concern. Christians must begin with Jesus of Nazareth. As Emmanuel, He fully reveals both God and humanity, and in light of this, the importance of the unity that He Himself is between the two must necessarily come into focus.

Having again discussed the two natures of Christ, and the overarching unity of the two, Barth sets out to discuss the human nature of Jesus as the Son of Man. Barth affirms that in Jesus of Nazareth the Word became flesh, not just a man. He was more than just a man, according to Barth; he was the bearer of the human essence.[48] The essence of humanity, all that it means to be human: this is what Jesus was. In encountering Jesus of Nazareth, therefore, humanity encountered its very essence, its goal and possibility. In encountering Jesus, humanity encountered the eschatological possibility and foundation of the kingdom of God on Earth.[49] In Jesus, as Barth has said, humanity encountered the actuality of the end of its past and the reality of the beginning of its future. And yet, having said

47. Ibid., 26.

48. Ibid., 92. On the whole, Barth is not, unfortunately, a very inclusive writer or thinker in terms of gender or sex. This point, however, is pregnant with inclusive possibility.

49. Ibid., 161.

all of this, this Jesus was an ordinary, simple, and poor peasant from the humble town of Nazareth.

Despite the lofty prophecies and predictions spoken of Jesus, the fact remains that he was anything but lofty. Jesus was not a great political leader, a mighty warrior, or even a reputable public speaker. Jesus was, rather, a simple man with an anything-but-simple message. Jesus was not the Messiah that Israel expected, but He was the Messiah that Israel was promised. As Barth reminds his readers, we do not really know Jesus, at least the Jesus of the New Testament, unless we know Him as this poor, revolutionary friend of the forgotten and of the sufferer.[50] Jesus was a surprising, unexpected, and straightforward leader. Jesus was a paradox. Jesus' actions were highly paradoxical, in that he refused to acknowledge and play by the rules of society.[51] Jesus was a poor dinner guest, he pursued friendship with the wrong sort of people, and he would upset the powerful and elite by making them wait as he helped the poor and insignificant. "In the acts of Jesus an alien will and unknown power invaded the general course of things in what the majority of men accepted as its self-evident and inflexible normality."[52] Jesus took people to the edge of what they could understand and then beyond, in that he claimed that there was a different way of living, a different definition of power, a different way of being human. This different way that Jesus walked and proclaimed was completely antithetical to all that was deemed rational and sane. In this way, Jesus' actions were paradoxical in that they inverted the so-called ways of the world.

Likewise, Jesus' teachings were paradoxical. Jesus taught people to live as He did—to live in a way that was counter to everything that made sense according to society's norms and values. This is nowhere more on display than in Matthew's account of Jesus' so-called Sermon on the Mount, and especially His beatitudes.

> Blessed are the poor in spirit, for theirs is the kingdom of heaven. Blessed are those who mourn, for they will be comforted. Blessed are the meek, for they will inherit the earth. Blessed are those who hunger and thirst for righteousness, for they will be filled. Blessed are the merciful, for they will receive mercy. Blessed are the pure in heart, for they will see God. Blessed are the peacemakers, for they will be called children of God. Blessed

50. *CD* IV.2, 180.

51. Ibid., 211.

52. Ibid.

are those who are persecuted for righteousness' sake, for theirs is the kingdom of heaven. Blessed are you when people revile you and persecute you and utter all kinds of evil against you falsely on my account. Rejoice and be glad, for your reward is great in heaven, for in the same way they persecuted the prophets who were before you.[53]

Taken at face value, these familiar words seem to be nonsensical. And yet Jesus, in His very body and blood, as the fulfillment of covenant and also as the suffering servant, shows these words to be not only true, but to be the very fabric of the universe. For the first time, Jesus declares the way things really are to the world of sin and death, a world that stands in stark opposition to the truth of the Beatitudes. Jesus' words in the Beatitudes are

the proclamation in human words of a divine judgement. Their content is a paradox—obviously so in many ways, and totally at bottom. It stands at an angle of 180 degrees to current ideas of happiness and good fortune. Strictly speaking, no one can ever come to the point of calling himself (or others) blessed in the way in which it is done here. . . . It can be said only by the royal man who Himself brings and is this new thing; who is the Head, the σωτηρ, the true Shepherd, who is for them as the world of God's revelation. . . . It is he alone who can pronounce this human Word, for He *is* this Word.[54]

Jesus' words are true, His pronunciations of blessing are true, because He is true, and He is divine blessing.

This is the same Jesus who in Luke's Gospel narrative proclaims this same paradoxical truth in regard to His mission. Using Isaiah's words, Jesus declares, "The Spirit of the Lord is upon me, because he has anointed me to bring good news to the poor. He has sent me to proclaim release to the captives and recovery of sight to the blind, to let the oppressed go free, to proclaim the year of the Lord's favor."[55] Jesus' actions and teachings are sheer paradox, "obviously so in many ways, and totally at bottom." Jesus is the paradoxical reality he proclaims. Jesus, therefore, proclaims good news to the poor because He is good news to poor, sinful humanity. Jesus proclaims release to captives because He is release to all humanity in its captivity. Jesus proclaims recovery of sight to the blind,

53. Matthew 5:3–12.
54. Barth, *CD* IV.2, 188.
55. Luke 4:18–19.

because He Himself is the beatific vision that humanity must be trained to see by grace alone. Jesus lets the oppressed go free because only He is able to offer pardon to humanity, visiting humanity in its jail cell and accepting incarceration in its place. In doing so, Jesus explodes the confines of the prison cell and transforms the bars and walls into luscious green fields of hope and possibility. And finally, Jesus declares the year of the Lord's favor, the Jubilee Year, because He Himself is the perfect jubilee. Jesus erases all debts, restores lost property, and equips humanity to live as it should: in justice, equality, and peace.

And yet, despite all of this, sin continues. Despite Jesus' actions and His teachings, and even despite His death and resurrection, suffering and poverty continue to hold so many in its grip. Healing, release, and transformation abound, but paradoxically alongside of suffering, captivity, and decay. This was how Jesus appeared to his followers, and to the powerful of the world. This is the same way He appears to us today. Barth refers to this as the "riddle of the existence of Jesus Christ."[56] All of these things happen in Christ Jesus, and yet their opposites still remain. Christ Jesus showed He was the King of the Universe, the Lord of all things, and then continued to allow humanity to play the role of King. Jesus did not come and reign in coercion, but rather in love and in peace. The actions of Jesus, His teachings, and his very presence are paradoxical. Their logic is not the logic of humanity. This paradoxical logic is not in conflict with human logic, nor is it overpowering; rather, it is transforming; it is an instructive and healing logic. The paradoxical logic of Christ Jesus, the God-human, must be believed and seen as the reality of the life, death, resurrection, and ascension of the Son of God as the Son of Man.

But Barth warns his readers that paradox cannot be the final word. In fact, Barth goes so far as to say that "all Christian errors" stem from our confrontation with this paradoxical logic and our false belief that we must choose one side of the antithesis or the other.[57] "Paradox," according to Barth, "cannot be our final word in relation to Jesus Christ. Even as it is presented in the New Testament this paradox is not in any sense in conflict with the *doxa* of God. Therefore, although we have not to seek its removal, we have certainly to seek its basis in the *doxa* of God, which

56. Barth, *CD* IV.2, 353.

57. Ibid., 348. Here, Barth's description of paradox is definitely laid out as dialectic. The paradox he is describing is the either-or logic of human dialectical thought. Personally, I agree with Barth's sentiment here, but not with his word or categorical choice.

means again in the Trinitarian life of God."[58] Paradox, *if it is understood in terms of conflict*—which, I would argue, is not paradox but rather dialectic—is not the ultimate word about Jesus Christ. Rather, *doxa*—glory and praise—is the ultimate reality of Jesus Christ. Here Barth is again talking about the two natures, about the divine and the human in one person of Jesus of Nazareth. These two are not in conflict whatsoever. Just because there are two, there need not be struggle or conflict of any sort. Recall that for Barth, the two are two only in the glorious unity of the one person Jesus, who perfectly reveals both God and humanity. The two remain, and thus, as Barth says, we are not to seek the removal of the tension between the two. We are, however, to seek the basis for the tension, the basis for the distinction between the divine and human in the one person of Christ as pure doxology. Barth goes even further in saying that this *doxa*, this glory and praise that characterize the overarching unity of the two natures, is the very Trinitarian life of God being made manifest in Christ Jesus. The tension, and therefore the paradox, remains, and it must remain—but it remains not as conflict, but rather as the doxological gift of difference between God and humanity amidst an ever-greater unity of the two.

Jesus: God's "Yes," "No," "Yes and No" or Something Else?

Another aspect to the reception of Jesus of Nazareth by those he encountered during his ministry, as well as his reception today, is as God's judgment: God's "Yes" and/or "No" spoken to humanity. This is a topic of discussion in Barth's *Der Römerbrief*, and has already been covered briefly in the previous chapter. Barth does pick up this topic in volume IV.2, however, and he does so in a way that I believe lends further support to my argument for the increasing paradoxical logic employed by Barth in his "mature" Christology. Barth's usage of "Yes" and "No" language can be somewhat confusing. My belief is that it is used in almost the exact same way as Barth uses the language of veiling and unveiling. Recall that for Barth there is no dialectic whatsoever between God's veiling and unveiling, but rather God's veiling is always a part of, and in service of, God's unveiling. Unveiling is always the goal. God desires to disclose, to unveil God's self to creation as a gracious covenant partner. Where veiling is witnessed, it is simply the result of human sinfulness and

58. Ibid.

misunderstanding, and not the reality of God's reconciling act. God does not hide; the Christian God is no *Deus absconditus*; the Christian God is *Deus revelatus*.[59] Barth writes, "As His self-revelation, His resurrection and ascension were simply a lifting of the veil. They were a step out of the hiddenness of His perfect being as Son of God and Son of Man, as Mediator and Reconciler, into the publicity of the world for the sake of those for whose reconciliation He was who He was and is who He is."[60] In short, humans perceive veiling because they are not yet open to, and therefore capable of seeing, the unveiling of God's own self. I believe the same can be said of Barth's view of the relationship between God's "Yes" and "No" in Jesus Christ.

In a previously examined passage in which Barth discusses the paradoxical form of Jesus as a poor revolutionary, Barth explains what this means for humanity in terms of judgment. Barth says that through Jesus, who assumed the paradoxical form of a poor servant, humanity learns decisively that God is not against humanity, but rather God is for humanity.[61] The royal man Jesus, Barth says, "is the image and the reflection of the divine Yes to man and his cosmos."[62] He goes on to call this a "critical Yes" and says that it corresponds to the Yes that is spoken to the existence and actions of the man Jesus. Barth says that this is a Yes and not a No, "even though it includes and is accompanied by a powerful No."[63] In Christ Jesus, God speaks a loud, audible, transforming Yes to humanity. God affirms humanity as God's covenant partner, despite human unfaithfulness and idolatry. God's affirmation of this relationship is thus surely a one-sided affirmation. As such, there is rebuke and chas-

---

59. Barth addresses this issue in many places. One such instance comes in IV.3.1, where Barth is addressing the issue of whether or not there can be a "third side" to God, that is, a hidden side that is superior to the Father and the Son that have been revealed. He says, "Such a third side could only be a word of God different from that spoken in Him and superior or at least equivalent in value and force: the word, perhaps of a *Deus absconditus* not identical with the *Deus revelatus*, or identical only in irreconcilable contradiction. Now we have no cause to reckon with such an alien word, such a self-contradiction, on the part of God. But we have every cause to keep to the fact that He is faithful, and that in Jesus Christ we have His total and unique and therefore authentic revelation, the Word in which He does full justice both to Himself and to us." Barth, *CD* IV.3.1, 100.

60. Barth, *CD* IV.2, 133.

61. Ibid., 180.

62. Ibid.

63. Ibid.

tisement contained within this affirmation, but only in such a way that the affirmation is all the more powerful and effective. As such, God's affirmation of humanity as God's covenant partner is unaccompanied by an equal or even a substantially lesser rebuke. No, God affirms; God speaks a Yes to humanity and not a No. "The only No which has power as such, let alone the power of a secret Yes, is the No which is spoken in and with a superior, genuine Yes."[64]

With all Barth's talk of the Yes of God, it is clear that a No is spoken. Somehow, in some way, a No is spoken toward humanity, and it is experienced as wrath. This is surely the No that was spoken to the Son on the cross. It is this No that caused the crucified Jesus to cry out, "My God, my God, why have you forsaken me?" It is to Christ Jesus on the cross that God speaks No to humanity, loud and clear. It is on the cross that God pours out God's wrath upon humanity, in the person of Jesus of Nazareth. On the cross, where God is most humiliated and humanity most exalted, God the Father rebukes humanity and thus rebukes God's own self as well. God says No to the wickedness, idolatry, and whoredom of God's people. And yet the sheer fact that this No was spoken to, and this punishment executed against, the eternally begotten Son of God means that this No is not and cannot be the end of the story. In Christ Jesus, God was pleased to reconcile the world unto God's own self, and thus the definitive No spoken against humanity is seen to be anything but definitive. And so it is that Barth continues his discussion of God's judgment by moving to this No spoken on the cross. He says, "It is not merely that the Yes is spoken in and under the powerful No of the cross, and has to be received and repeated in defiance of it. The fact is that in and under the No of the cross a powerful Yes is also spoken: 'Christ is risen,' and that this powerful Yes may also be received and repeated."[65] God speaks a No toward humanity on the cross of Calvary. This No is a rebuke for the repeated and bold forsaking of God's covenant faithfulness. God has warned humanity time and again that there is a price to pay for unfaithfulness. While God has promised to remain forever faithful to God's people, God has also promised to judge and rebuke them. It should therefore have come as no surprise to Israel, and in fact to the whole world, that a time would come when God would say, "Enough. No more." There is ample evidence

64. Ibid., 285.
65. Ibid., 355.

for the coming wrath of God, the No that would be spoken to and even against God's own people.

And yet when it came time for God to speak this No, God acted in such a way as to provide the ultimate, definitive example of God's boundless love toward humanity, which encompassed and triumphed over that selfsame No. It must be clearly stated—God spoke a loud, terrible No to humanity on the cross. And yet, the very fact that this No was spoken to God the Son, who in the ultimate act of kenotic debasement had become perfectly and fully human, revealed the even greater Yes being spoken by God to humanity. God spoke No and became that No so that humanity would hear and live the Yes of God's love. And thus God's judgment, God's wrath upon the cross, must be seen as Gods' ultimate, definitive, and eternal Yes spoken toward creation. God does not, therefore, speak a No and then a Yes. God does not even speak a No alongside a Yes. Rather, God speaks a Yes, and we know that in some paradoxical way, a No was included within the Yes in a powerful and yet diminutive way. The mystery of this Yes that includes a No is located solely in the person of Christ Jesus, and it is made known most definitively on the cross. This mystery, this paradox, is the very existence of Christ Jesus as both the Son of God and the Son of Man for the sake of the world.

> The existence of Jesus Christ attests this living divine act. It does this in the very fact that it is so puzzling. But, deriving from the dynamic and teleology of its basis in God, it does not attest any of our own foolish paradoxes. It does not attest a No alongside a Yes. It does not attest a Yes that may revert to a No. It attests a No which is spoken for the sake of the ensuing Yes, and which is powerful and necessary and unforgettable in this order. And it attests Yes which is a valid and definitive Yes—a Yea and Amen (2 Cor. 1:20)—as it comes from this No. Its witness does not, therefore, destroy the fact that it is so puzzling, but transcends it by causing the work and wisdom of God to be known in it.[66]

The logic of the very existence of Jesus Christ—of what it means for God and humanity to be perfectly joined, with each completely maintaining its own integrity amidst a deeper and more fundamental unity—is foolishness; it is a paradox of human reason. And yet this is what we have in the person and work of Jesus of Nazareth. This is not our reasoning, it is not in accord with human logic, but rather this is the very heart of the mystery of divine logic. This is not and cannot be, according to Barth, a

66. *CD* IV.2, 359.

simple paradox of human reasoning, however. No, this paradoxical relationship of Yes and No, as we have already seen, is divine reasoning, and
it is meant to drive us to *doxa*, to praise. In encountering a traditional
paradox, the temptation is simply to view the perplexing intermingling
of two seeming opposites with curiosity and bewilderment and to leave
it at that. The paradox of the existence of Christ, however, which is the
paradox of God's Yes and No spoken to humanity, is meant to call us on
toward a level of understanding that is puzzling and strange, yes, but that
is also glorious and logical given the revelation of God's very self in the
person of Jesus of Nazareth. Barth says that this paradox is puzzling and
that we cannot deny or escape this fact. We also, however, cannot avoid
the fact that through this bewildering paradox God's love shines forth as
a glorious and overwhelming Yes revealing the paradoxical wisdom of
God, which is counter to and yet capable of transforming human wisdom
by its own logic of self-giving.

Barth's theology is a theology of the cross. With Paul, Barth's primary theological concern is nothing more than "Jesus Christ and Him
crucified."[67] Of course, for Barth, as is the case with any good theologian, the cross cannot be separated from the incarnation, Jesus' teachings, the resurrection, or Jesus' ascension. In short, Barth's theology is a
christological theology. While all aspects of the life, death, resurrection,
and ascension of Christ Jesus must be developed in mutual dependence
upon one another, the cross necessarily takes on a central role, as it is the
ultimate mediation between God and humanity. The cross is the place
where the Yes/No is spoken, where God completely unveils God's own
self in love—and thus the cross is, above all, the place where we must
look to learn of both God and humanity. The cross serves as a focal point
for Barth; it is the mediating point for all that humanity ever can or will
know about itself and about God. The cross, in short, is the center of
knowledge. In volume IV.2 of his *Doctrine of Reconciliation*, Barth has
shown that this logic of the cross is the heart of divine logic. As such, the
logic of the cross encounters humanity as the most perplexing of paradoxes. Barth says that what the disciples saw when they looked upon the
cross "was either nothing at all or only the frightful paradox of a radical
contradiction and destruction of the Son of Man, the overwhelming of
the new actuality which He had introduced by the old."[68] The disciples

67. 1 Corinthians 2:2
68. Barth, *CD* IV.2, 254.

did not see logic when they looked at the cross; they did not see understanding or wisdom. What they saw, according to Barth, was radical contradiction—frightful paradox. And yet by the power of God's Holy Spirit, the teachings of the Crucified One began to penetrate the dark, mysterious recesses of the frightful paradox upon which they gazed. What the disciples saw very clearly as terror and hopelessness soon became joy and hope. What the disciples thought to be foolishness and contradiction, they soon understood to be wisdom and knowledge. What they saw, and what Barth saw, was the paradoxical logic of the cross. This paradoxical logic dominates Barth's *Doctrine of Reconciliation* because it is the core of the Christian confession of Christ Jesus as the Messiah, as Emmanuel, as the Mediator, and as the crucified and resurrected Lord.

Church Dogmatics IV.3.1 (1961)

Barth states that he grudgingly acquiesced to the division of volume IV.3 into two parts because "the total bulk of the volume has exceeded that which was seriously deplored by so many in the case of I, 2."[69] As has already been mentioned, Barth begins volume IV.3 by providing a bookend to his teaching about Christ Jesus as the Mediator between God and humanity. Barth provides this bookend in the 300-plus page §69, titled "The Glory of the Mediator." Here Barth expounds upon the wonder of the Christian proclamation that Jesus Christ lives![70]

Barth begins §69 by revisiting his continually developing theme of God's Yes and No spoken to humanity in Christ Jesus. He reiterates that the doctrine of reconciliation is about the triumph of God's superior Yes over the No.[71] This triumphal Yes is important, as it is the key to the life of the Christian community, in obedience to God. This Yes stands over and against the falsehood of humanity (which Barth discusses in §70) and is the basis for not only the life of the community of believers, which will be discussed in the rest of volumes IV.3.1–2, but also for the *Doctrine of Redemption*, which was to be the finale of Barth's *magnum opus*. For Barth,

69. Barth, *CD* IV.3.1, xi. Barth did not understand the fuss and lamented about the length of the great tomes of the seventeenth century compared to his more "bearable" works!

70. An affirmation that, in my opinion, reveals Barth's continued use of paradoxical reasoning. As such, this I believe this central affirmation in IV.3 stands as yet another example of Barth's continued rejection of the *Deus absconditus*.

71. Barth, *CD* IV.3.1, 3.

God's Yes is really a Yes—reconciliation really occurred, and redemption is not just a possibility, but a reality. This is what life in the Spirit is all about for Barth, and this life is made possible only by the revelation of God in Christ. Barth believes that in Christ we are witness to the fact that "God moves towards man in spite of his No, cancelling this No and pronouncing His own Yes; in which He justifies and sanctifies sinful man; in which He addresses him as His own child and claims him for His service."[72] God does not declare a Yes and a No to humanity, "but an unequivocal because intrinsically certain, reliable and valid Yes."[73] This Yes, this exaltation of humanity, is real and certain and reliable because Jesus Christ lives!

Jesus Christ lives! "This is at once the simplest and most difficult christological statement."[74] Barth is correct in saying that "Jesus Christ lives" is such a simple and yet profound statement. How often is this phrase uttered without taking into account the sheer audacity, the blind faith, the paradoxical logic that allows for such a statement. To say Jesus Christ, is first and foremost to affirm that Jesus of Nazareth was and is, in fact, Emmanuel. We have already seen just how important this affirmation is for Barth. As Emmanuel, Jesus is God dwelling among creatures, as a human. As Emmanuel, moreover, Jesus is God dwelling with us and for us, *pro nobis!* To speak the name of Jesus is first to say that God and humanity are bound and live together. "This is the epitome of the whole order of creation."[75] This much we have already seen.

But to say not just the name Jesus Christ, but to affirm that He lives, is to affirm that there is life after and amidst death. To say Jesus Christ lives is to challenge the finality of death and to affirm the reality of bodily resurrection. To say Jesus Christ lives is to say that He is the very life and possibility of the new age, of the age of His Spirit. To say that Jesus Christ lives, therefore, is to say that it is in Him that we live and move and have our being.[76] "Hence the fact that Jesus lives means concretely that He exists in the manner of the God whose divine transcendence does not find it incongruous but supremely congruous to exist also in the limited manner of the human creature; and conversely that He exists

72. Ibid., 42.
73. Ibid., 12.
74. Ibid., 39.
75. Ibid., 43.
76. Acts 17:28.

in the manner of the man to whom there is given by God that which He cannot take to Himself, namely, to exist also in the sovereign manner of God. It is thus that Jesus Christ lives. It is thus that He exists."[77] To affirm that Jesus Christ lives, therefore, is to affirm that paradoxical logic of the God-human Jesus, that he is both the "Lion of the tribe of Judah" and the "Lamb that was slain from the foundation of the world," that He has conquered death, and therefore that He exists in the perfect tense of the word.[78]

To say that Jesus Christ lives is to say that there is now something different about reality than before the Word became flesh and dwelled among us. "Jesus Christ lives" is an eschatological statement that is powerful, effective, and true, both now and forevermore. To say that Jesus Christ lives is to say and believe that Jesus Christ changed things forever. This claim, and its premise that Jesus really changed the very grain of the universe, is key, in my opinion, to why Barth is not, or was no longer, a dialectical theologian.[79]

In the Old Testament, prior to the incarnation, dialectic was a perfectly justifiable position to maintain in regard to the relationship between God and the world. In the Old Testament, despite God's loving relationship with Israel, God always remained God and the world always remained the world.[80] The difference between God and the world was absolute; the expanse was infinite. God was wholly transcendent in every way. Barth highlights this well in a brief discussion of the difference between the Old Testament prophets and Jesus.[81] Barth rightly points out that the Old Testament prophets were elected and called to prophecy; that they spoke almost exclusively to the people of Israel; that they spoke on the basis of the covenant that was then unfulfilled; and, finally, that they were not mediators between God and humanity. This last point is true in that the prophets sought to bring people closer to God, but they did not bring God to humanity. Dialectical theology is therefore compatible

77. Barth, *CD* IV.3.1, 39.

78. Ibid., 5. Great discussion of the early and medieval Church's understanding of the *munus duplex* of Christ, and how Christ is always both.

79. Perhaps it would be more appropriate to say that Jesus brought humanity in line with the grain of the universe.

80. One of the many functions of the covenant, though, was to avoid making God completely unknown.

81. Barth, *CD* IV.3.1, 49–52.

with the Old Testament understanding of God.[82] Though God was loving and chose to enter into a covenant relationship with humanity, the ever-greater distinction between God and humanity always remained. In this way, a theology that held YHWH on one side and Israel (indeed, all of creation) on the other was perfectly justifiable. And yet, while dialectical theology might be affirmed prior to the Christ event, the affirmation that Jesus Christ lives, voids the very rules and basis for dialectics.

That Christ Jesus makes a dialectical understanding of the relationship between God and humanity impossible can be seen again in the difference between Jesus and the Old Testament prophets. Barth shows that Jesus is not the opposite but rather the fulfillment of the Old Testament prophets. Unlike the prophets, who were elected and called to proclaim the prophetic will of God, Christ Jesus is the very prophetic will of God. As such, Jesus, in his very existence, is the fulfillment of the message of the prophets. Jesus is the reconciling, prophetic truth that he proclaims. "His exercise of the apostolate is identical with His calling to it, and both may be equated with His life as such as the life of the Revealer."[83]

Second, rather than speaking exclusively to Israel, Jesus addresses all of humanity. Barth points out that though a prophet of Israel speaking primarily to a Jewish audience, Jesus was "delivered up by His own people to the nations and the world, and who speaks to the nations and the world as such."[84] This second point is very interesting. Barth affirms that Jesus came to preach to the lost sheep of Israel. Jesus came to Israel, God's unfaithful covenant partner, as the fulfillment of the covenant, as God dwelling with humanity. Had Israel accepted Jesus as their Messiah, then their destiny of being a blessing to all the nations would have been fulfilled by their learning to truly welcome the nations as brothers and sisters in Christ. Unfortunately, while some Jews did accept Jesus as the Messiah, most did not. And the Passion Narrative depicts the Jews, both peasants and elites, handing Jesus over to the Gentile authorities to be tried and executed. When Jesus was betrayed and handed over to the Gentiles, the covenant was fulfilled, Barth says, in that what was once interior or secret to the people of Israel was made exterior or public.

---

82. Though again, even this is difficult to affirm in light of God's covenant with Israel.

83. Barth, *CD* IV.3.1, 49.

84. Ibid., 49–50.

Jesus' betrayal made it possible for Gentiles to witness and believe in the revelation of God in Christ Jesus.[85]

In the third instance, Jesus spoke from the vantage point of "enacted reconciliation, of the present reality of the kingdom of God."[86] Jesus did not promise that one day reconciliation would come, that one day the covenant with God would be fulfilled. Instead, Jesus was living proof of the immanence of the kingdom of God. In the speech and actions of Jesus, the longing of Israel was fulfilled: "The kingdom of God on earth, which is the goal of the covenant, is no longer an indicated future. It is the present in and from which he speaks."[87] Jesus was the substance of the Old Testament prophecies in immanent, tangible form—in flesh.

Finally, Christ Jesus is the mediator between God and humanity, something that none of the earlier prophets can claim. This is certainly true with all the Old Testament prophets. The very prophetic messages of the Old Testament prophets were one-way directives given by God to wayward humanity. "Their prophecy, which is an alien 'burden' laid upon them, can consist only in opposing to the contradiction of Israel the superior contradiction of its God, and therefore in revealing unmistakably the opposition as such, no less in the word of promise than that of judgment. None of them can remove the opposition. None of them has bridged, let alone filled up that abyss."[88]

The message of the prophets, according to Barth, was always that of opposition, of contradiction. This is not to say that the Old Testament prophecies are not loving and gracious, nor that the God of the Old Testament is different from the God of the New Testament; rather, this is simply a statement about the insurmountable difference and distance that separates God from humanity.[89] Assuredly, it can be seen here

85. Ibid., 53ff.

86. Ibid., 50. This is another bold example of Barth's paradoxically realized eschatology.

87. Ibid., 51.

88. Ibid., 51.

89. It is not uncommon for biblical exegetes and theologians alike to claim that the God of the New Testament and the God of the Old Testament are different. This distinction is usually made in terms of the "God of grace" versus the "God of the law" or perhaps the "God of love" versus the "God of wrath." A common passage that draws out such alleged distinctions is Jesus' commandments to love enemies and pray for persecutors (Matt 5:44), and his connected teaching about turning one's cheek and not resisting one's enemy (Matt 5:38–42). It is commonplace for scholars and beginning Bible readers alike to claim that these teachings, especially the love of enemies, are not

that the God of the Old Testament alone, in abstraction from the New Testament, can be depicted as the *Deus absconditus*. Because of this distance, any message given to humanity via the Old Testament prophets is a one-sided gift given to both Israel and the prophet himself. This is definitely not the case when it comes to Christ Jesus, as Jesus Himself has removed the opposition between God and humanity. Jesus Himself has bridged and, what is more, filled up the abyss.[90] Jesus is the paradoxical point of intersection for two parallel and completely different realities. At this last point, the difference between Jesus and the Old Testament prophets is seen to be complete. The fundamental presupposition of the very possibility for prophecy before Christ Jesus was dialectic. God and the world were and had always been different. The difference between the two provided the very meaning for prophecy itself. For this reason, dialectical reasoning was justified and in fact unavoidable prior to the incarnation of the Word of God. In Jesus of Nazareth, however, this fundamental presupposition was evacuated. The infinite qualitative distinction between God and humanity was qualified, and even filled up, by Jesus Himself. Thus, according to Barth, dialectical reasoning gave way to and was trumped by the logic of the Mediator, the logic of the incarnation, the logic, that is, of the cross.

Faithful Christian theology, then, would be wise to heed this new logic and eschew all continuing traces of dialectic in favor of the paradoxical reality of Christ Jesus. Barth says this most succinctly when he says, "it is better to abandon the term 'dialectic' and to replace it quite simply by that of history."[91] The historical event of Christ Jesus negates the possibility of dialectic by providing its own paradoxical reasoning. This is true because in Christ Jesus, the *Deus absconditus* is shown to be a false way of understanding God and God's relationship with creation. The

---

present in the Old Testament and are not in accord with the Old Testament depiction of God. To this issue, Barth lends an amazingly simple and yet profound insight in §59 of IV.1. Barth says that turning one's cheek and enemy forgiveness do not reveal a different God or a contradictory teaching to that of the Old Testament. This is because the entire Old Testament, for Barth, is proof that God loves God's enemies and allows them to continually cause God undue harm. "The God of the Old Testament rules amongst His enemies. He is already on the way into the far country to the extent that it is an unfaithful people to whom He gives and maintains His faithfulness" (Barth, *CD* IV.1, 171). In my opinion, this is an amazingly powerful and important reading of the Old Testament, one which to the best of my knowledge has yet to be really grasped.

90. Barth, *CD* IV.3.1, 51.

91. Ibid., 195.

reconciliation of God and humanity has been forever accomplished by Jesus in history. As a result, Christian theology is to avoid the philosophical vagary of dialectical reasoning and its resulting ontology of conflict.

So much for the first half of volume IV.3. I will now proceed to the latter half in hopes of discovering further examples of paradoxical thought in Barth's mature Christology.

Church Dogmatics IV.3.2 (1961)

It has already been stated that the division of volume IV.3 into two parts was purely an editorial decision, one that Barth was not exactly happy with. Given this, Barth does not begin IV.3.2 with the customary preface but instead jumps directly into paragraph 71. Having already provided a bookend of sorts to his christologically focused doctrine of reconciliation in IV.3.1, here Barth sets out to discuss the effect of the doctrine of reconciliation on humanity, and specifically on the Church. Barth focuses on the human predicament and the Church, and how these are shaped and changed by Christ and the Holy Spirit.[92] Barth's contention is that reconciliation is real and its effects powerful and transformative.

In terms of the topic of this work, volume IV.3.2 has less to do with divine revelation than the rest of volume IV, and this is perhaps the weakest example of Barth's rejection of the *Deus absconditus* and of his increasingly paradoxical theology.[93] Still, there are several instances in volume IV.3.2 where Barth's increasingly paradoxical theology is quite evident, which I find pertinent and helpful to the discussion of Barth's Christology. All the instances of Barth's use of and comfort with paradox in IV.3.2 are echoes of points that Barth has already made, but in my opinion these discussions are nonetheless valuable. And so volume IV.3.2 will receive the least attention of any of the parts of volume IV.

The first instance of Barth's paradoxical Christology in volume IV.3.2 is again in regard to the issue of universal election. Barth picks up

92. By "human predicament" I mean the existence of humanity. This specifically entails the present situation humanity finds itself in, given the paradoxical relationship between the old age and the new, between sin and grace, and between the cross, resurrection, and ascension, on the one hand, and the *parousia*, on the other.

93. This is not to say that he changed his argument. Rather, the content of Barth's writing in IV.3.2 lends itself less readily to the project at hand than does the rest of volume IV.

the issue of election in his discussion of the "vocation of man."[94] Barth firmly believes that all human beings, and especially Christians, have been elected by the free, sacrificial, and atoning work of Christ. Barth believes that Christ Jesus' death was once and for all and universal. Christ died for all, and He bore the sins of all. As a result, all human beings who ever have been, and even all those who will be but are not yet, have been and are elected by God in Jesus Christ. Barth does not believe in any form of double predestination, at least according to how it had been defined and developed by theologians before him.[95] No one is born, according to Barth, destined for damnation. "Not in and of himself, but in Jesus Christ as the eternal beginning of all God's ways and works, no man is rejected, but all are elected in Him to their justification, their sanctification and also their vocation."[96]

Barth moves forward with this point and states that it is because the eschaton is both here and now and also not-yet that we speak of biblical universal election. By eschaton, Barth means the end or goal for which all Christians long—indeed, all of creation. The eschaton is the coming kingdom of God, the *parousia*, the return of Christ and the completion of the work that God began in creation. The eschaton is both now and not-yet simultaneously. When we add to this the fact that Christ died for all, made atonement for all, and as such truly is the Mediator for all, we see the biblical foundation for universal election, according to Barth.

> What "will be" there and then in the *eschaton* is in visibility that which really is here and now in virtue of the reconciling action of God, which constitutes the controlling sense of temporal history. That which comes finally is not a second reality distinct from a supposed first reality here and now, and therefore necessarily exposed to the suspicion of being merely ideal and therefore unreal. On the contrary, it is already the one reality which

94. Barth, *CD* IV.3.2, 481–97.

95. Barth concedes that there are biblical exceptions to this position, though they are few and problematic. The overwhelming teaching, according to Barth, is universal election in Christ Jesus. One such exception is Jesus' statement given at a wedding feast: "many are called, but few are chosen." His opinion is that this passage is a foreign saying, perhaps intended to refer to the tragically few good and noble men among those who are called. Barth feels comfortable viewing the passage in this way, as he believes it stands in stark contrast to the entire rest of the New Testament, especially the Pauline writings. Barth engages in this fascinating discussion of Matthew 22:14, a passage that he calls a paradox, in *CD* IV.3.2, 484–86.

96. Barth, *CD* IV.3.2, 484.

here and now still encounters us in concealment but there and
then will make itself known, and will be knowable and known,
without concealment. Hence we shall misunderstand the uni-
versalism of the Bible if we take its statements eschatalogically
and therefore (provisionally at least) unrealistically instead of
supremely realistically and therefore eschatalogically.[97]

In this way the eschaton, and the universal election which results from it,
is yet another example of the impossible possibility which is so prevalent
in Barth's theology.

Another instance of the logic of Barth's paradoxical Christology
comes in his discussion of the people of God, the Church, as they exist
in the world. Because of Barth's exceeding emphasis upon the actuality of
the atonement and the resulting immanent breakthrough of the kingdom
of God, Barth believed that the faithful can and should live obedient,
faithful lives. Yet, be that as it may, Barth also believed in the endurance
of evil and of the age of sin and death and the continual problem of human pride and idolatry. This caused Barth to say of the Church as it exists in the world, "we may speak quite confidently of the strength of the
Christian community, we must also speak quite openly of its weakness."[98]
The Church is, for Barth, both mighty, strong, and one, and also weak,
powerless, and divided. Moreover, the Church is both the continuing
presence of Christ in the world—and testimony, therefore, of Christ's
unparalleled power—and also a great whore who shames the name of
Jesus and testifies rather to the power of human pride and vanity. The
Church is both victorious and yet defeated. It is strong and yet simultaneously weak. "Strength means ability. Weakness means inability. Of the
Christian community in world-occurrence we have to say both that it
can do nothing and that it can do all things."[99] Surely this is yet another
example of Barth's comfort with the logic of the impossible possibility, or
the absurd possibility of the absurd.

This paradoxical description of the Church is real, says Barth, and
it is visible. There is no such thing as the invisible Church, according to
Barth.[100] The paradox of the Church is so precisely because it is visibly
so. The Church is always both victorious and defeated, mighty and weak,
faithful and unfaithful. To pretend as if the unfaithful of the Church

97. Ibid., 489.
98. Ibid., 742.
99. Ibid., 742.
100. Ibid., 783–84.

are not really a part of the true Church is to operate under a false understanding both of the human predicament and of the presence of the Church in the world.[101] There can be no distinction between the faithful and unfaithful, the qualified and the unqualified, as the visible and the invisible Church. Both must stand together, and in fact it must be the case that all are shown to be, in reality, both at the same time. "There is no cleavage of the community into qualified and unqualified members. We are all qualified and all unqualified."[102] This is the true reality of the Church as both sinner and saint. The paradoxical reality of the Church is fitting, as it is the image or body of Christ, the very heart of that which is impossibly possible. The Church, much like its savior, is a paradox.

The Christian Message Is Not Dialectic; It Is Something Else. Paradox?

In addition to these two minor and yet helpful examples of Barth's increasingly paradoxical theology, it is worth noting that there is somewhat of a theme running through IV.3.2, which is a critique of Hegelian dialectic in favor of paradox. This theme is powerful—and in my opinion decisive. It is the triumph of a third way over and yet not against the two seeming opposites of God and the world.[103] Barth shows that the Christian message is not a matter of thesis, antithesis, synthesis, but rather it is something more like thesis, antithesis, Jesus. The former, according to Barth, is characterized by conflict, with one always winning and destroying the other, whereas with the latter, the first two moments (thesis and antithesis) can only be properly understood and allowed their respective roles in light of the new thing, which is Jesus. This third thing is not a result of a combination of or a conflict between the first two in any way. Rather, this third and new thing provides the conditions for the possibility of the very existence of the first two, all the while maintaining the freedom and integrity of both in relation to each other. Jesus Himself is this third thing, in that as Emmanuel, Mediator and Victor, He is the paradoxical unity of divinity and humanity. In addition, Jesus reveals God and humanity perfectly in such a way as to allow each to remain itself, in

101. Not only this, but such a view of the Church would effectively rule out virtually all professing Christians from membership in the "true Church."

102. Barth, CD IV.3.2, 784.

103. This third way, in my estimation, is not something other than God: it is Jesus.

complete freedom, as defined by an even greater and more fundamental unity, of which He is the reality.

In discussing the people of God in the world, Barth points out the "old song of tension or dialectic of the two principles or kingdoms and of the attitude to be desired on the part of man."[104] In particular here, Barth is discussing the providence of God and the foolishness of men, in the same vein as the old familiar dialectic of God and the world, as well as the new age with the old age. As McCormack has rightly pointed out, the issue here is that God is God, and the world is the world. These two points are typically placed as opposites or antitheses, desperately in need of synthesis. The tempting thing to do, at this point, is to simply allow the two to do battle until one conquers the other. As a result, one is elevated above the other, which is degraded. In this case Barth discusses the providence of God and the foolishness of humanity. If we carried this "traditional" dialectical logic out, then either God's providence is elevated—and as a result, we underemphasize the foolishness of humanity—or we do the exact opposite and elevate human foolishness, which then trivializes God's providence. This is necessarily so, according to Barth. One side must ultimately triumph over the other, and the result is an imbalance of the two issues, so that both are not allowed the freedom and integrity they are due. Barth demands great caution here: "Why is caution demanded at this point? What we have said concerning the *providentia Dei* and then the *confusio hominum* might so easily be regarded as Hegelian thesis and antithesis, and the third and superior view or decisive word which is to be sought at this point might then be envisaged or understood as the Hegelian synthesis which takes the contradiction into itself, integrates the two sides and thus overcomes it."[105] Keeping with the present example, Barth believes that the providence of God must be absolutely affirmed, whereas the foolishness of humanity must be absolutely confessed and detested.[106] Both must absolutely remain, with neither giving way to the other. The temptation is, according to Barth, to affirm the providence of God—and therefore God's providence is the basis for human foolishness, which in turns justifies human foolishness, in reality, to a place where it is acceptable and permissible. Giving in to this temptation, though it might seem as if it is faithful to the two distinct realities, in fact elevates

104. Barth, *CD* IV.3.2, 702.
105. Ibid., 703.
106. Ibid., 704.

humanity above God, as it is human wisdom that conceives of this higher, synthetic plane. This is so, in that humanity forgets that it is trapped in its predicament of foolishness and thus cannot claim to transcend to some lofty plane where the wisdom of God reigns supreme over and against the foolishness of humanity. The very thought of this transcendental possibility is the core of the problem.

> If the attempt to go beyond that twofold view, even while recognizing its inevitability, and the elements of truth in it, is not to end so fatally by leading back, as Christian confusion, to the confusion of man, then we must start in a very different way from that adopted at the beginning of the path indicated. If we are really to attain to the overarching view of world-occurrence which is both requisite and permissible for the Christian community, we must not begin by thinking that any of us can go beyond that twofold view in his own strength or by his own choice, finding and fixing a supposedly superior point in the void, ostensibly establishing himself there by a bold resolve, and then looking back on the contradiction and antithesis and seeing it as a unity. . . . And if he begins with this attempt at mastery, the usual result is not a real overcoming of the antithesis but a regression to the affirmation of the human confusion which competes with divine providence.[107]

In short, what we think is synthesis is really no synthesis at all. Rather, it is the epitome of human arrogance and pride, and therefore this impulse towards dialectic must be jettisoned.[108]

Though the argument is confusing, Barth's point is clear: dialectical thinking is a temptation that Christians must avoid at all costs. How is it, then, that we are to move forward? How can we ultimately talk about the relationship between God's providence and human foolishness? The answer, according to Barth, is very simple: Jesus. Barth says, "Jesus Christ is the third word which the Christian community is both required and authorized to consider and attest beyond and in integration of the first two as it turns its gaze on world-occurrence."[109] Jesus Christ is not a synthesis of God and humanity, nor a higher plane that humanity can climb to through the use of reason; rather, Jesus Christ is the living reality of the

---

107. Ibid., 705.

108. It seems to me that in this way, dialectical thinking is shown to be dangerously close to Feuerbach's ontotheology.

109. Barth, *CD* IV.3.2, 706.

eternal God of providence as well as the living reality of true humanity. Jesus Christ is not an answer to a problem or a riddle, and He is not the victory of one over the other. Jesus Christ is the God-human, Emmanuel, the Mediator and Victor.

> Jesus Christ is not a concept which man can think out for himself, which he can define with more or less precision, and with the help of which he can then display his mastery over all kinds of lesser problems and therefore over the problem of this antithesis too. On the contrary, Jesus Christ is a living human person who comes and speaks and acts with the claim and authority of God, and in relation to whom there can be no question whatever of controlling and using Him to grasp or master this or that even in the sphere of thought.[110]

Jesus Christ is something completely new and unique and yet not alien and foreign. He is not the result of cosmic conflict or violence but is the eternal love of the Father poured out for all of creation through the weakness of flesh even to the point of the cross. Jesus Christ is *the* impossible possibility. Jesus stands at the center of all human thought and knowledge about humanity and about God; He stands at the center of the very universe itself and provides the deepest level of meaning and understanding. This Jesus is the supreme paradox, not according to human rules of paradox, but according to the logic of the absurd possibility of the absurd.

It is perfectly in line with much of human experience and reasoning, as well as the testimony of the Old Testament, to discuss God and humanity as two distinct opposites, separated by an abyss of more than just time and space, but even of reality. It is understandable, thus, to articulate a worldview of diastasis, of conflict and violence. This, says Barth, is the riddle of the occurrence and existence of humanity.[111] Left to itself, this is the best logic that humanity can devise, and indeed it is quite appealing. And yet, this view of reality as ultimately defined by conflict or diastasis, which is dialectic, is rendered completely impossible by the eternal revelation of God in Christ Jesus. Because of the reality of Christ, dialectical opposition cannot constitute reality. As I have already said, there remains a fundamental difference between God and reality, and this difference is complete. And yet, in Jesus, this difference is given its very meaning and

110. Ibid.
111. Ibid., 708.

identity within the ever-greater unity that He does not merely represent but in fact *is*. As such, God and humanity, though different in every way, are set not in opposition to one another, as is the case with dialectical reasoning, but rather are set alongside one another, united forever and yet remaining distinct in the person and work of Jesus Christ.[112] It is only God's grace that allows this to be so. Only God's grace, which we know in the person of Christ Jesus, reveals that God and humanity, despite complete juxtaposition and difference, are forever characterized by an even greater unity and harmony. This unity does not eradicate one or the other, nor does it prevent the fullness of one for the sake of the other. Instead, the unity of Christ Jesus allows for God to be truly God and humanity to be truly humanity in such a way that the impossible unity between these two impossibly separate realities is shown to be quite possible indeed. "What opposes that antithesis and contradiction, preventing the disruption of the cosmos and shining over the abyss as the promise of peace, is the grace of God."[113] Jesus Christ is the grace of God that shines over the abyss of difference between God and humanity; He is the love that fills up the abyss, and He is the Son who travels into the far country, bringing the ways of God to humanity, that creature and Creator might be forever bound, according to His divine self-giving love.

Church Dogmatics IV.4 *(Fragment): Baptism as the Foundation of the Christian Life* (1969)

Deciding what to do with *Church Dogmatics* IV.4 is something of a problem. In fact, it is difficult even to place what exists as volume IV.4 alongside the rest of I.1–IV.3. The truth is, Barth passed away on December 10, 1968, leaving volume IV.4 largely unfinished. As a result, what remains are fragments, and they are incredibly short compared to the rest

112. Ibid., 520. The foundation for this statement comes at the end of a discussion of the christological foundation for the vocation of humanity. Barth here is describing the seeming conflict between the inner and outer vocations of humanity. He says that these cannot be set in opposition to one another, but rather must be placed alongside one another. In my opinion, this adds a bit of depth to Barth's way of understanding and articulating paradox. As such, two things, though completely different, are not in conflict and thus set in opposition to one another. Rather, these same two distinct things are set alongside one another, and they are given meaning and allowed their integrity by the unique, non-synthetic third thing. In this particular case, the inner and outer vocation are given meaning by Jesus' unique embodiment of both.

113. Barth, *CD* IV.3.2, 709.

of the *Church Dogmatics* and Barth' stated goals for IV.4. Most complete sets of the *Church Dogmatics* contain a volume IV.4, which is a finished essay on "The Foundation of the Christian Life."[114] In this work, Barth primarily discusses the topic of baptism, focusing first on baptism with the Holy Spirit and second on baptism with water. In the present work, we will not be examining the body of this essay. There does exist, however, another portion of volume IV.4, which is titled *The Christian Life: Church Dogmatics IV.4 Lecture Fragments*. *The Christian Life* is essentially Barth's unfinished start to IV.4, which was published posthumously in its unedited state in 1981.[115] As a result, *The Christian Life* is a raw glimpse into Barth's attempt to finish volume IV. As such, it is essentially the final example, or at least one of the final examples, of the "late Barth's" theological concerns.[116] I believe that as *The Christian Life* is a raw and basically unedited sample of some of Barth's final work, it is very much a glimpse into how his mind functioned, and it is an important example of the shape of his mature theology. For the reasons I have mentioned, and because the points of discussion in *The Christian Life* are more closely related to the present work than that of the essay on "The Foundation of the Christian Life," we will be examining the former.

Before moving to *The Christian Life* fragments, however, a quick examination of the preface to IV.4, which is to be found in the essay on "the Christian Life," is quite helpful in examining the confusing relationship between the two IV.4 fragments. The preface also reveals some of Barth's final concerns and opinions. Most importantly, Barth states his goal for IV.4 and provides a rough outline, and he explains why he was unable to finish.

First, in regard to the shape IV.4 was to take, Barth states that it was to include a chapter on special ethics, "this time from the standpoint of the reconciliation of the world with God effected in Jesus Christ," which would be a parallel of sorts to the chapter on special ethics in volume III.4.[117] Volume IV.4 was to begin with §74, which Barth says he had already written but not revised. This chapter was to lay the groundwork

---

114. Barth, *CD* IV.4 (*Fragment*).

115. It is noted in the work that minor editorial work was done, but only in terms of spelling, grammar, etc. It was not subjected to "official" editing, which was then approved by the author.

116. Barth wittily refers to himself as "late Barth" in the preface to the essay on "The Foundation of the Christian Life," viii.

117. Barth, *CD* IV.4, x.

for the presentation of Christian ethics as "the free and active answer of man to the divine work and word of grace (IV, I–3)."[118] Section 74 was to be followed by a paragraph on the doctrine of baptism, part of which is the essay on "The Foundation of the Christian Life." Barth summed up his efforts in IV.4 by saying that "at every point, then, the volume was to deal with Christian (human) work as this corresponds to, and thus has its own place in respect of, the divine work of reconciliation outlined in IV, I–3."[119] Unfortunately, Barth says that long before he reached even the middle, his efforts came to a halt. And thus ended Barth's great *magnum opus*, which he jokingly referred to as his *opus imperfectum*, due to its incomplete nature.[120]

During the years between the publication of IV.3 and his death, Barth said that he faced almost constant questioning about when the rest of the *Church Dogmatics* would be finished. Barth often had tongue-in-cheek responses ready for his questioners.[121] But the fact remained that as Barth's life came to a close, he knew that he had a contracted period of time in which to convey his thoughts. Rather than to try to finish IV.4, something which he had decided was impossible, Barth decided that he would instead publish a portion of his writing from IV.4. This portion, which is the essay on "The Foundation of the Christian Life," was intended as a formal correction to Barth's thoughts on a topic that he had addressed quite differently in a previous publication. That topic was baptism. After about twenty years of further study, and in particular after reading and digesting the work of his son Markus on the sacraments, Barth decided to amend his teaching on baptism.[122] Thus, as Barth came to grips with his inability to finish his great work, he decided that it was important to publish at least a small portion of one of the paragraphs, which would enable him to decisively and controversially correct his previous position on baptism. Barth believed that this new position, this *aggiornamento*, would most likely be criticized and that he would lose the support of many of his followers and friends. Barth believed that the

118. Ibid., ix.

119. Ibid.

120. Ibid., vii.

121. My favorite of which is the response to such interrogators with the counter-question regarding "whether, to what degree, and with what attention they have read and studied the material already at hand!" Ibid., vii.

122. Interestingly, Barth describes his new position, or his reorientation, as *aggiornamento*, explicitly borrowing this term from Vatican II. Ibid., x.

rest of what he would say in IV.4 and even volume V could be inferred, for the most part, from a close reading of volumes I.1–IV.3. On baptism, however, Barth did not think that his readers would be able to infer his true thoughts, and so he revised and published this small section of his work in progress.[123] Because of this, it has been deemed important to include the essay on "The Foundation of the Christian Life" in the larger *Church Dogmatics* as a fragment of IV.4.

Finally, in the preface to the IV.4 fragment, Barth explains the reason for the incomplete status of his great work. First, Barth says that his transition from a teaching professor to a professor emeritus ended much of the impulse behind the *Church Dogmatics*.[124] He also says that he spent a good amount of time touring North America, giving lectures and sightseeing; got sick and had a stroke; concerned himself with the Second Vatican Council, even traveling to Rome to observe; and finally, that his longtime assistant, Charlotte von Kirschbaum, suffered a very serious illness that would end her ability to assist Barth in his work.[125] To put it simply, Barth says that he "gradually began to lose the physical energy and mental drive necessary to continue and to complete the work which I had started."[126] It is as a result of these and other factors that Barth was forced to put down his work on volume IV.4, work that he says had a very "promising beginning."[127]

Since we do not have a completed volume IV.4 to analyze, I think that it is logical to briefly examine that which Barth did leave, partial and unedited though it may be. This brief look at *The Christian Life* fragment, then, will merely examine the places in which Barth's logic is paradoxical, either implicitly or outright, in hopes that it might add to the thesis being developed in this work. It is my hope that this final, brief example of Barth's work will reveal the same comfort with and use of paradox, and likewise the complete abandonment of all traces of the *Deus absconditus*, as is evident in the rest of volume IV.

---

123. Barth's position on baptism, though interesting to say the least, is not important for the present work. Suffice it to say that Barth believed that Jesus was the only true Sacrament, and that while the Sacraments that are often spoken of, namely baptism and the Eucharist, are important acts, they are not to be understood as anything other than human acts in service to and in praise of God.

124. *CD* IV.4, vii–viii.

125. Ibid., viii.

126. Ibid., vii.

127. Ibid.

The Christian Life: Church Dogmatics IV.4
Lecture Fragments (1981)

In *The Christian Life,* Barth again revisits the issue of God's Yes and No revealed to humanity in Christ Jesus. As we have seen in other places, Barth affirms that there is not both a Yes and a No in Jesus, but only a Yes.[128] There is definitely a No spoken, as Barth has previously stated, but this No is dependent upon and indeed a part of the Yes. There is not both, only Yes. The logic of this argument continually bespeaks the logic of the impossible possibility that Barth is so apt to fall back on in his later theology. Now, the discussion of God's Yes and No is a discussion of God's judgment. Barth's stance is that God's judgment against humanity, and indeed against the world as a whole, was carried out in Jesus of Nazareth. In electing Jesus, God elected all people and revealed that God's judgment was not against but rather for humanity. Any hint of the opposite is the result of human reason and perception, and not the reality of God's free gift of grace. Thus what we think is a dialectical relationship between God's Yes and No is really not dialectic at all. There is not dialectic, for there is only, in reality, a Yes spoken once and for all by God in Jesus. Barth says, "His powerful action is the great and active Yes of His free and gracious address to the world created by Him and to man who is at the heart of it."[129] God loves the world, and this love is affirming, transforming, and full of grace. This is the heart of the covenant, of the Gospel, and of God in God's own self. "There are riches in God," says Barth, "but no antithesis, contradiction, or dialectic."[130] The power of this last statement is seen in its straightforward nature. There are many things in God— wonderful things, according to Barth—but antithesis, contradiction, and dialectic are not among those things. If he has not done so already, Barth has truly broken free from the shackles of the dialectical theology that held him for so long.

Having affirmed that there is no dialectic in God and, therefore, that dialectic does not constitute the relationship between God and humanity, Barth revisits the issue of the knowledge of God. Barth believes that God has fully revealed God's self in Christ Jesus, and so it is possible for all people to know God. Contrary to what many have claimed, Barth says that God is not hidden, nor is He an unknown quantity; rather, He

128. Barth, *The Christian Life,* 19.

129. Ibid., 15.

130. Ibid., 18.

is revealed and made known as "the one Jesus Christ: God and man, if not in their essence, at least in their work and therefore in their manner; God and man accessible to human apprehension, if not expressible in human words, at least describable and attestable."[131] Mysteriously—and, I would argue, paradoxically—God remains both known and unknown, and this is the paradoxical predicament that all humanity finds itself in.[132] And yet, as we saw in the previous chapter, the very statement that God is unknown means that God is known. For how could one claim that something is unknown, after all, unless one knows for a fact that it is unknown, and therefore knows the thing itself, in some strange, paradoxical way? Barth argues this point when he discusses Kutter and the Social Democrats and their belief that pagans had a knowledge of God. Barth says, "These impressions should not be generalized and systematized along the lines of natural theology, but when they lay hold of us with serious force, they cannot be denied."[133] Barth admits that it cannot really be refuted that God is known to the world as Creator. This is weak knowledge, however, for Barth, not the perfect knowledge that much of natural theology would like to claim.

As a general rule, therefore, Barth does not sympathize with the arguments of natural theology. That being said, however, Barth fully admits that a knowledge of God as Creator is very possible for all of humanity. That this is true is the result of nothing less than the revelation of God in Jesus Christ, which has made all capable of the knowledge of God.[134] This is incredibly paradoxical: Jesus Christ makes it possible for people to know God as Creator apart from Himself, but only in Himself! Despite all of Barth's years of argument on this matter, he believes this is unarguably so. Jesus Christ renders all capable of knowing God as Creator, even apart from Himself. For creation to be able to know God as its Creator is an incredible gift indeed, one that is undeserved. And yet, the life and works of Jesus testify to a higher and truer knowledge of God than is possible. Not only is it possible for creation to know God as its Creator, but in Christ Jesus we learn the paradoxical truth that we can and should call and know the Creator as Father.[135] That this is true can only be grace.

131. Ibid., 5.

132. Ibid., 115. Barth develops three ways God is both known and unknown on the following page. This is a very helpful discussion of this matter.

133. Ibid., 122.

134. Ibid., 125.

135. *CD* IV.4, 70.

Everything about the paradoxical logic of Jesus as Messiah, Mediator, and Victor, everything about the paradoxical logic of the human possibility of the knowledge of God, is grace. It is this grace, according to Barth, that is the logic of God, and that is ultimately made the logic of humanity as a result of God's paradoxical self-giving. "Grace is the factual overcoming of the distinction between God and man, Creator and creature, heaven and earth—something that cannot be grasped in any theory or brought about by any technique of human practice."[136]

Grace is not the way of the world. Grace stands in complete contradiction to the principle of just retribution. Grace contradicts all rules of discipline and punishment. Grace explodes the principles of karma. Grace is the giving of the undeserved to the undeserving in such a way that it sets the undeserving on equal footing with the giver. Grace is absurd. Grace is illogical. And yet grace is, and God is grace. Grace is completely incompatible with any philosophy or methodology that would allow contradiction and/or conflict a central role. Grace is nondialectical; it transcends the very categories of dialectics with a higher way, a third way, that can allow for difference without needing conflict, contradiction, or victory. Grace stands alone; it has no competitor.[137] Grace is the absurd possibility of the absurd.

Conclusion

Grace is the name for the paradoxical logic of Jesus as Messiah, Mediator, and Victor, and grace is the name for the paradoxical logic of the cross. It is my belief that this grace was always at the fore of Barth's thoughts, guiding and inspiring his perpetual wrestling with Scripture. This grace, in my opinion, slowly converted his logic into the logic of paradox. As I have already stated, Barth did not set out to write this or any other of his more mature works under any pretense of a methodology. The fact is that Barth was incredibly allergic to such a pursuit. Barth violently eschewed all starting points other than Christ Jesus. In fact, for Barth there

136. Ibid., 72.

137. Barth makes a fascinating statement about darkness, saying that it wants to be understood theologically in a dialectical synthesis with light. Darkness wants desperately to be considered as an opposite, as a yang to the yin of light. But this is precisely what is so different about Christianity: there is not dualism and no dialectic. At the heart of reality is grace, which, like light, is completely other than darkness and thus not really threatened by it. Ibid., 146.

is no starting point fit for theology (and perhaps for any other pursuit) other than Christ Jesus, the God-human, the perfect revelation of God and the author of grace. Barth held to this staunch opinion because he read Scripture. Perhaps more than any other, Barth was truly Reformed. He attempted to subject every thought, desire, and opinion to Scripture. Barth's goal was to expound the truth and reality of the Gospel, a truth that is made manifest by the power of the Spirit. For this reason, Barth's theological positions and arguments often shift or even change completely. Never happy with his work, Barth attempted to increasingly allow Scripture to trump his previous positions and his concerns. This is especially evident in his wide and various discussions on the possibility of the human knowledge of God.

The ultimate reason for these shifts was Barth's Christology. Theology is Christology for Karl Barth. Everything that we can and will ever know about both God and humanity has been forever revealed in the person of Jesus of Nazareth. It is Christology and nothing else that shapes and drives Barth's theology. Thus, any attempt to split up his work according to a periodization thesis is doomed to fail. Barth's theology does not change because the times change, nor does it change because he decides that he prefers one methodology to another; no, Barth's theology shifts and grows and even changes because his understanding of the person and work of Christ constantly shifts, changes, and grows as he continually wrestles with Scripture. This is unequivocally true.[138] This continual wrestling with Scripture, and especially with the narrative accounts of Jesus and the Pauline Epistles, caused Barth to stare straight into the maddeningly beautiful paradox of the Gospel. Over time, and I believe this is especially true by the time of Barth's *Doctrine of Reconciliation*, Barth saw the error of the dialectical way of looking at things. Yes, God was God and the world was the world, and the two are different, but in Jesus, this was shown to not be definitively conflictual, nor was a suitable synthesis between the two achieved in Jesus. Instead, Jesus was something completely different, something completely and radically contrary to all the rules of human understanding and logic. Jesus Christ,

138. Of course Barth does change with the times, and his social situation plays a huge role in his work and his concerns. McCormack has perhaps offered some of the best evidence of this argument. Hunsinger's work also gives testimony to this. Yet these things are not intentional, and as both concur, Barth did not intentionally advocate or subject himself to any sort of philosophical approach or methodology. Scripture alone was Barth's method.

the God-human—as Emmanuel, as Mediator, and as Victor on the cross, and through His resurrection—revealed a deeper paradoxical logic that beckons to humanity, promising to transform human understanding and reason into the reason and understanding of God. Christ Jesus is the impossible possibility, the absurd possibility of the absurd. This absurd possibility of the absurd is the core and basis for everything that Karl Barth writes and teaches. The absurd possibility of the absurd, which is, as we have seen, none other than grace, is completely incompatible with the rules of dialectical reasoning. Barth's thought, therefore, though it most definitely was heavily influenced by dialectical reasoning early on, gave way not only to analogy, but to something completely other, something completely different, something not ultimately defined by conflict and/or contradiction. Barth increasingly saw the relationship between God and the world, and the possibility of the human knowledge of God, as a purely christological discussion. This discussion, as we have seen, did not settle for the rules of conflict and its resulting synthesis, but rather saw the paradoxical distinction amidst the ever-greater unity of the two natures of Christ as the key to everything. Barth did not embrace this as method, but he did embrace the logic of the impossible possibility as truth. In conclusion, when examining Barth's mature Christology, it is clear that at the heart of Barth's understanding of the Gospel—of the Christian message, that is—was not dialectic but rather paradox. It is my contention that a contemporary reading of Karl Barth's theology, especially his later theology, will benefit from understanding and interpreting his christological theology in this way.

5

Ethics, Ecclesiology, and Ecumenicism
in the Works of Karl Barth

A most extraordinary development is the fact that a young man
from Lucerne, for seven years thoroughly trained in Rome and
having become a doctor of theology in Paris, has presented in
a book razor-sharp arguments for the thesis that between the
Reformation teaching as now interpreted and presented by myself and the rightly understood doctrine of the Roman Catholic
Church there is precisely on the central point of justification
by grace no essential difference! So far this book has not been
repudiated by Catholic officialdom, but to the contrary has been
openly lauded by various prominent representatives of that
church. What is one to say to that? Has the millennium broken
in, or is it waiting around the next corner? How one would like
to believe it![1]—Karl Barth

Introduction

AFTER THE TWO PRECEDING chapters, it should be resoundingly
clear that Bruce McCormack is correct to say that the two greatest
characteristics of Barth's theology are indeed (1) that God is God and the
world is the world, and (2) the knowledge of God. I have further agreed
with McCormack and many others in demonstrating that both of these
characteristics are ultimately christological categories for Barth, in that

1. Barth, *How I Changed My Mind*, 69–70.

Christ Jesus is the very living definition of what both God and world are, as well as the goal and guarantor of the knowledge or knowability that we can, as creatures, have of the Creator God. And so, we have come to see that Barth's God, as eternally revealed in the Son, is not hidden but revealed. Indeed, Barth has no room for the concept of the *Deus absconditus*, an understanding of God that has haunted and continues to haunt modernity. Rather, Barth's entire programme is consumed with the affirmation that Jesus Christ lives, that His atonement is real and efficacious for the sins of all of humanity, and that, defying all human logic, God can be known, fully, in the flesh, in the man Jesus of Nazareth.

In chapter two, I argued that Luther's *Deus absconditus*, which he very much inherited from the likes of Scotus and Ockham, et al., became the dominant theological framework for modernity.[2] For the most part, I would argue that this framework is operative for the vast majority of modern Protestant theologians and philosophers. When Barth stepped on the scene, therefore, and became disenchanted with his early instruction, he truly changed the theological world. Barth's was still a God of power and might, of distance and difference, and yet Barth's God was also present to humanity in all the beautiful awkwardness of mortal flesh and blood. Barth's incredible theology of transcendence resulted in a simultaneous and equally powerful theology of immanence. Barth is singularly unique in this aspect and, indeed, he sparked a theological revolution that is still gaining force and momentum to this day. And while there are many aspects of Karl Barth's theology that remain in need of examination, in this final chapter I will briefly treat Barth's views on ethics and ecclesiology. I believe that Barth's theology, as extensively praised and critiqued as it is, still has much to offer to those willing to spend the time needed to adequately examine his works. I would argue that Barth's ethics and ecclesiology are at the top of the list of that which Barth still has to offer, or at least has much more to say in regard to. Barth's theology, as intellectual and dogmatic as it might be, is always focused on the ethical, on the command of God given to each particular man and woman. Furthermore, Barth knows that the command of God is not entrusted to isolated individuals, but rather to a group of people, i.e., the Church.

---

2. It should come as no surprise that atheism has become such a dominant metaphysical stance in modernity, for surely where God cannot fully be known, or even trusted, skepticism and doubt and eventually disbelief will spread.

After all, "the call to be a Christian and the call to be a part of a Church is necessarily connected."[3]

In the space that remains, I will examine these two aspects of Barth's theology—ethics and ecclesiology—with the hope of further illuminating the important role each plays in Barth's theology. I will begin by examining Barth's views on theological ethics, an area that will reveal Barth's unwavering rejection of nominalism. Subsequently I will turn to a brief discussion of Barth's ecclesiology, wherein I will examine the position of Reinhard Hütter, with whom I both agree and disagree. In hopes of exposing Barth's extremely radical stance on this position, I will turn to an excursus on Barth's view of the relationship between Israel and the Church. It is my contention that the relationship between the two is the very key to Barth's ecclesiology and will provide insight into his theology as a whole.

It has been my goal, up until now, to document just how different Karl Barth's theology is from most modern (especially Protestant) theology. I believe this is a severely underappreciated point, due in large measure to the preoccupation with or personal loyalty to certain methods and categories such as dialectic on the part of so many Barth scholars. If this is even remotely true, then it is time to reengage the theology of Karl Barth from a new perspective. For this reason, much of this final chapter is intended as suggestions for a way forward. Here I offer a constructive appeal to Barth scholarship in particular to reconsider "the old man from Basel" and his lasting effect on the Church. It is my belief that with the rejection of the *Deus absconditus*, as well as the rejection of the principles and method of dialectic, Karl Barth's theology is ripe for new exploration and especially ecumenical dialogue with perhaps the most unlikely partners: Roman Catholics. And so, finally, and constructively, I will conclude this chapter and work with a look at Barth and the Roman Catholic Church. Having thoroughly examined Barth's texts, it is my opinion that his continued preoccupation with Rome and with Roman Catholic scholars can go ignored no longer. Returning to the excursus from chapter two on Roman Catholicism's very different experience of modernity, I will argue that Barth scholarship, as well as all Protestant scholarship, need be much more concerned with Rome than it has been previously, and that perhaps Barth's best theological allies would have been (and are today) Roman Catholics and not Protestants. If successful,

3. Barth, *CD* III.2, 681.

I hope not to make a critical statement about current Barth scholarship, but rather to offer a faithful nudge in the direction in which I think Barth was logically moving.

Ethics

For Karl Barth, theology is ethics—or perhaps more accurately, "implicitly, dogmatics must always be ethical as well."[4] Theology is not done in a vacuum; it is not pontification done from an ivory tower. Barth understood the revelation of God in Christ as "the command of God." A command, logically, requires a response. Either one acknowledges and obeys a command or one does not. It is really as simple as that. The revelation of God in Christ, as Barth understands it, is not a passive proposition on the part of God the Father that one is free to deliberate over. No, for Barth there is no neutral ground in this exchange. The revelation of God in Christ is universal—it takes place once and for all, and is thus instantaneously and decisively effective for all of humanity.[5] This means, for Barth, that Christ elected all of humanity for salvation while simultaneously and universally electing to take upon Himself the punishment and suffering of all of humanity on the cross.[6] All of humanity, as a result, stands in either acceptance or rejection of God's unilateral revelation of God's self in the Son Jesus Christ. In this way, Barth rejects and transforms one of Calvin's primary theological positions: double predestination. Double predestination, when understood this way, leaves a very large place for the faithful response of finite human beings through the power of the Holy Spirit. This response *is theological ethics* in that the response proceeds from dogmatics. "[T]he ethical question—at least, if it is intended and understood in a way which is meaningful from the Christian and theological standpoint—cannot rightly be asked and answered except

4. Barth, *CD* III.4, 32.

5. This is because Christ Jesus is both the electing God and the elected human, and he is this completely. This is election for Karl Barth. Barth, *CD* II.2, 145.

6. Ibid., 145–94. In Christ the sole author and guarantor of election are located. Likewise, Christ is both the means and the end of election. Here it must be recalled that Christ Jesus is both God in all of God's perfection and power and true humanity as well, sharing in everything with humanity, except sin. In election, however, God in Christ elects to take upon God's self all of humanity's sinfulness, once and for all, electing God's own self for rejection while simultaneously and completely electing humanity for forgiveness and divine favor, thus unilaterally enacting reconciliation.

within the framework, or at any rate the material context, of dogmatics."[7] For Barth, dogmatics answers the question, how do we know what to do? We know what to do—or more accurately, we know how to act—because we have been told by God through Christ Jesus. This task that we know as theological ethics is to seek continually to understand what we have been told by Christ through Scripture, and then to do it. The call of Jesus to His disciples ("Come, follow me")—the call to discipleship, that is—is the call to the singular task of both dogmatic reflection and instruction as well as theological ethics.[8]

So, how do we know what to do? We follow Jesus. Thus, "The task of theological ethics is to understand the Word of God as the command of God."[9] Barth is not concerned with doing situation ethics, nor is he attempting to construct a system for ethical deliberation wherein all situations are already neatly addressed beforehand. "We must not have the effrontery secretly or openly to try to write in advance the text which ethics has to read, understand and expound."[10] Life is complex, and it is so in

7. Barth, *CD* III.4, 3.

8. Barth, *CD* IV.2, 533.

9. Barth, *CD* III.4, 4. The Word of God, Christ Jesus, is the command of God; he is the call to Christian ethics. As such He provides the shape and scope for Christian ethics.

It is helpful to mention also Barth's discussion of the horizontal and the vertical within the command of God. The vertical is virtually a given: God speaks to humanity definitively in the Son, Jesus of Nazareth. But as almost all human beings have never encountered Jesus in the flesh, the matter of how one comes to understand and follow the command of God is crucial. This he calls the horizontal. Many conceive of this horizontal revelation or command in the form of nature, creation, or society. Barth lists Brunner's "orders" along with Luther's "estates" within this group, which Barth of course rejects. Barth offers his readers the example of Bonhoeffer's "mandates" as a preferable option to the aforementioned ways of conceiving of the horizontal. The reason for Barth's choice of Bonhoeffer's "mandates" is their christological basis. Bonhoeffer's "mandates," which he lists as work, marriage (the family), authorities, Church, and culture, are relationships that exist as referents to the relationship of the world to Christ. Thus it is not the relationship, or the thing itself, but rather that Christ is its master that validates these "mandates" as proper horizontals. Barth states that these "mandates" provide us with "formed references" to the vertical command of God. Ibid., 19–23.

10. Barth, *CD* III.4, 27. This type of thinking causes some to see nominalism in Barth's theological ethics. But remember that nominalism is predicated upon a truly unknown God, one who might save you or might damn you, for example. Still, the critique may be raised due to his lack of concreteness in his theological ethics. This sense of openness, or perhaps a lack of concreteness, in the ethical arena prompts many to make this claim. Though it can be problematic, I believe that Barth's theological ethics

different ways for each and every individual. And so, while Barth clearly advocates for many ethical norms, he also leaves room for God to work in and through particular events and experiences. Bruce McCormack, praising the work of John Webster, puts it best when he writes, "It has often been noted that Barth is more concerned with ethos than with an evaluation of ethical options, but that is to put the matter much too blandly. What he is concerned with, as Webster convincingly demonstrates, is a comprehensive description 'of the "space" which agents occupy' (p. 2), the 'moral field' within whose boundaries alone an act is qualified (or, more strongly, 'determined') to be either good or evil."[11] Barth's ethics is discipleship. It is about learning to follow and thus imitate the crucified and risen Lord Jesus.[12] Ethics is thus about submitting to the ethos of discipleship, the ethos of obedience, i.e., to the command of God. This is important, because as Barth pointed out in *Church Dogmatics* III.4, Jesus does not address many modern issues such as abortion, the use of nuclear weapons, and workers' rights in an industrial or post-industrial society, to name just a few. One must develop a certain sensitivity to the character or ethos Jesus in order to be faithful in these types of situations.[13] Further, it is not always possible to prescribe how one should act in a given situation, according to Barth. His refusal to claim hard-and-fast "answers" to some ethical situations causes many to see in Barth a great similarity to Luther and his often unknown God, and while this is certainly a valid critique, I would argue that the issue is the difficulty of human understanding and the complexities of the modern world, and not the

is consistent with the rest of his work, and that he avoids nominalism there, as in the rest of his work. I believe that Barth's theological ethics might actually best lend itself to a kind of virtue ethics understanding. Moreover, I believe that Barth's theological ethics portrays a deeply evangelical trust in God and the ongoing help of the Holy Spirit in situations that are not easily addressed.

11. McCormack, review of *Barth's Ethics of Reconciliation*, 273

12. The choice of the word *imitate* is mine, as this term tends to worry Barth.

13. Surely Barth was no virtue ethicist. That being said, Barth was likewise a critique of the natural law "tradition" and its inherent casuistry. The latter for Barth has much too high a view of human reason, and thus remains far too subjective. I would argue that Barth's position is, therefore, much closer to virtue ethics. For Barth, we must learn to hear the command of God and to heed it. Moreover, we cannot claim to know God's definitive will in many ethical situations. It is based upon how well one hears and heeds the command of God—something that must be learned and experienced—that one will know how to act in certain ethical situations. Though Barth does not use the language, and can in fact be said to be slightly critical of it in principle, this places Barth much closer to virtue ethics than it might seem.

command of God. Barth's statements on contemporary ethical dilemmas reveal a certain tension between the human and the divine, according to which, Barth wants to avoid the claims of exclusive knowledge of God's commands and directives at all times regardless of context. Life is simply more complex than this, argues Barth, and so is both the command of God and our response to it.

A perfect example of this tension can be found in Barth's discussion of legitimate or illegitimate killing in self-defense in the section on the protection of life in *Church Dogmatics* III.4. Throughout this section, Barth makes it very clear that Scripture, especially the Gospel accounts and the writings of Paul, supports a nonviolent stance toward one's oppressors. And while (and I would agree with this claim) the New Testament does make this abundantly clear, Barth is quick to suggest that this is never revealed to be a command of God—something that seemingly receives strict, unwavering adherence. Barth instead describes nonviolence as a direction for service.

> Tolstoy, Gandhi and others who share their understanding of this direction for service are certainly right in wishing it to be accepted and taken more seriously in its literal form than has usually been the case even in Christian circles which are supposed to be loyal to the Bible. But they are wrong in understanding it as a law rather than a direction for service, and in thus refusing to leave room for the living God to give man direct instructions as well, in the same sense and with the same intention as the direction, but not necessarily in the precise verbal form. To be sure, one can know the spirit of God's command only from the scriptural letter. Hence in matters of the order and direction of what God wills or does not will as regards self-defense we should undoubtedly keep up what we are shown in the New Testament. Nevertheless, we are not to apply the letter in such a way as to stifle the spirit, but rather in order that we may seek from it the Spirit who is the freely commanding Spirit of the Lord. It is as we do this that the exception arises.[14]

It is here, in the discussion between the command of God and the direction for service, that Barth might be susceptible to the charge of nominalism.[15] While I am certainly uncomfortable with Barth's argument

14. Barth, *CD* III.4, 433.

15. Again, as I mentioned earlier, personal experience prompts this note. In many of the classes I've taken throughout my career as a student where Barth was the primary subject, or at least examined in length, a common concern was that Barth's ethics

and wish that he would be a bit firmer about nonviolence, I must likewise acknowledge that this argument is not based on a hidden, unknown God such as the God of Luther and the nominalists. Rather, this position is based upon the revelation of God in Jesus of Nazareth, and upon the sheer knowability of God that is possible in Christ Jesus. Barth's argument is based upon a sense of fidelity to Scripture and to an understanding that neither the Father nor the Son provides us with an exclusive command about the protection of life. Jesus' life and teachings certainly point those who would follow Jesus toward a life of forgiveness and nonviolence, and yet Jesus does not provide his followers with a definitive and universal command on this matter (such as is given by God in the form of the Ten Commandments, for example).[16] Thus, the direction is made clear, but discerning how best to live into that direction requires a great deal of discernment and creativity. Living into the direction for service, furthermore, requires a strong sensitivity to the Spirit of God's ongoing work.[17]

---

were nominalist ethics. This is a position argued not only by students; I had several professors who saw in Barth's ethics the roots of nominalism as well. Additionally, it could be said that this is perhaps one of the biggest concerns raised by many of those with the Radical Orthodoxy sensibility, such as Conor Cunningham and John Milbank. As I have shown previously, both dismiss Barth rather quickly, and both are extremely opposed to nominalism. The two surely are connected. This of course cannot be said for Graham Ward and D. Stephen Long, if indeed the latter should be grouped with the Radical Orthodoxy "camp."

16. Of course, it could be argued that it is hard to get more straightforward than "You shall not kill." But even here, there is the debate over killing as opposed to murdering. The point is that the Ten Commandments are often looked upon as being clear and direct commands from God.

17. In my opinion the so-called Yale School gets it right here, as they rely heavily upon Barth, while advancing a reading of Scripture and thus a view of the Christian life based as it is upon much of narrative theory and the tradition of virtue ethics. As I mentioned earlier, Barth is not, strictly speaking, a virtue ethicist. At the same time, though, he is most certainly not a proponent of casuistry, or the natural law tradition. The language of "direction of service," as best I can tell, lends itself very well to a character- or virtue-based ethical system. John Howard Yoder and Stanley Hauerwas are possibly the best examples of such a merger of Barthian theology with the virtue tradition, held together by a biblical hermeneutic steeped heavily in narrative theory. While both have their strengths, I would argue that due to Yoder's stance of withdrawal from the world (granted that this is for the sake of the world), which he of course subscribes to as a Mennonite, Hauerwas provides the best example of a Barthian theological ethics. George Hunsinger has written a helpful article concerning Barth and Yoder titled "Karl Barth and the Politics of Sectarian Protestantism"; see Hunsinger, *Disruptive Grace*, 114–28. Of course, Barth would be a bit uncomfortable, though I believe sympathetic, with Hauerwas' teachings on, say, nonviolence. In particular, Barth would probably object to Hauerwas' staunch position of nonviolence, arguing that Hauerwas

The resonance between the command of God versus direction of service debate and Barth's firm critiques of natural theology should be clear: Barth is opposed to any claim of knowing God in a totalizing way outside of, or prior to, Jesus of Nazareth. So, since Jesus does not speak on the issue in the manner of a command of God, we simply cannot make the direction for service He gives us into a command of God. Furthermore, as Jesus avoids handing this down as a command of God, one must entertain the possibility of a gray area, or a time when the Spirit would guide someone to defend an accosted person, for example, in a way that does in fact utilize violence to restrain a wicked person. It is not because God is unknown that this back door, so to speak, must be left open, but rather it is precisely because God is known definitively in the person of Jesus and because God did not provide a "command" on this issue that Barth believes we must at least allow for God's freedom to will and command something that might seem contrary to the direction of service of nonviolence.[18] In short, unless God makes it resoundingly obvious, Barth believes we must always maintain the distinction between God and ourselves. God is God and we are not. Any claim to an exclusive or exhaustive knowledge of God, one not offered very directly and in command form in Scripture, puts us at risk of claiming to know more of God than is possible—and thus we become, in a very real sense, more important than God! Barth wants to avoid this at all costs and runs the risk of looking strikingly similar to nominalism, though I would argue he remains clear of it.

For Barth, ethics is dogmatics. In particular, ethics is, or should be, a christological category. What we are to do, and what we are not to do, is all wrapped up in the revelation of God in Jesus of Nazareth. Ethics is about following the command of God; it is about faithfulness to Christ Jesus. Barth's life and work is a testimony to his understanding of the

---

had crossed the line from a "direction of service" to a "command of God" view of the matter. Taking into account Hauerwas' complex but well-argued position on just war theology, for example, and his exchange with Paul Ramsey in particular, I think that Hauerwas's position can be seen as, perhaps, "open" enough for Barth's liking. See Hauerwas, "On Being a Church Capable of Addressing a World at War," in *Hauerwas Reader*, 426–58; Ramsey, *Speak Up for Just War or Pacifism*. A further suggested resourse on Paul Ramsey is Long, *Tragedy, Tradition, Transformism*.

18. Personally, I'm not sure why Barth doesn't view teachings such as the Sermon on the Mount, in general, and passages like Matthew 5:21–22 and especially 5:38–48, in particular, as commands of God. I do not believe this makes him a nominalist, perhaps just overly cautious.

interconnectedness between theology and ethics. From his early commitment to socialism to his strong anti-Nazi stance, seen especially in the Barmen Declaration, Barth's commitment to the ethical requirements of the Christian faith is clear. It is further the case that his *Church Dogmatics*, in many ways, might be seen as the paramount theological-ethical work of all time. Had he been able to complete it, the sixth and final volume, *The Doctrine of Redemption*, would have been Barth's ethical *piece de résistance*. In this final volume, Barth was to discuss redemption, which, as he stated clearly in a previous volume, has already been accomplished for all in Christ Jesus.[19] It is my contention that the realized nature of Barth's doctrine of redemption is the basis for his strong commitment to and focus upon theological ethics. The question, "How then are we supposed to live?" would be at the heart of Barth's discussion of the doctrine of redemption. For Barth, Jesus' life, death, resurrection, and ascension—and centrally speaking the cross—accomplished once and for all the forgiveness of sins as well as the possibility of living a faithful and ethical life. It made possible, in short, sanctification. Thus while Barth would like to avoid an overly developed *theologia gloriae*, the impact of his doctrines of election, atonement, and redemption should not be underestimated.[20] For Barth, because of Christ's great sacrifice on the cross, we can and should live lives of love, of justice, and of obedience—obedience to the God who is very known (and thus very much *not* unknown) by both ourselves and by all the world, in the person of Jesus of Nazareth, and especially on the cross.

Ecclesiology

Just as ethics is a christological category, for Barth, ecclesiology is a christological category as well. This is not to say, as someone like Henri de Lubac would claim, that the Church is Christ, or the extension of Christ, in the world.[21] Rather, for Barth, the Church is something more like

19. Barth, *CD* IV.1, 288. Rather than earn redemption in any way, Barth identifies the contemporary human predicament as being whether or not we will accept Jesus' redemption, His becoming sin for us and thus His redeeming us beyond sin and death.

20. Precisely because of Barth's doctrines of election, atonement, and redemption, I believe that Barth and John Wesley have much in common in terms of sanctification and holiness.

21. Quoting Bossuet, de Lubac describes the Church as "Jesus Christ spread out and communicated." De Lubac, *Catholicism*, 48.

"the provisional representation of the whole world of humanity justified in Him."[22] In this way, the Church is not Christ, but rather a body that claims and depends upon Christ as its head. The Church, with Christ as its head, points therefore to the consummation of the kingdom, according to which all people are brought into relationship with Jesus. The Church is not the kingdom of God; it is rather a foretaste or perhaps a signpost on the way to the *parousia*. The Church is broken and sinful, but at least it exists in such a way that illuminates both its own brokenness and the atoning and justifying work of Jesus. Broken as it may be, the Church, Barth believed, stands as a witness to what God can do, to the fact that lives can be changed, that forgiveness and reconciliation can take place, and that Jesus will return. The task of the Church, then, is to point toward the reality of Jesus and of His kingdom.

> The task emerges immediately from the fact that the one and only Word of God has once for all been uttered, for all men to heed, in the fact of the Incarnation: in the man Christ Jesus, in whom the sin of all men, their contradiction against God and their own inner self-contradiction is done to death, taken away, forgiven, and exists no more. The task from which the Church derives its being is to proclaim that this has really happened and to summon men to believe in its reality. It has therefore no life of its own, but lives as the body of which the crucified and risen Christ is the Head; that is to say, it lives in and with this commission. The same thing is true of each individual who is a member of a body. It is this task and commission which fundamentally impels and compels us to ask after the unity of the church.[23]

Jesus Christ is the unity of the Church. The Church's job, then, is to point toward Jesus, and to the real power of His death and resurrection. In pointing toward Jesus as the head of the Church, the Church also points to Him as the head of the world, of history, of the future—indeed of all things.

And yet, if the Church points toward Jesus Christ, whom do the many churches point toward? The churches that kick and scratch each other, the churches that argue and bicker, the churches that fundamentally disagree with each other over major social, political, and doctrinal issues—whom do these churches point toward? Similarly, what is the relationship between the Church and the churches? If ecclesiology is at

22. Barth, *CD* IV.1, 643.

23. Barth, *Church and the Churches*, 10.

its core a christological category, then these questions are of paramount importance. Barth has said that the Church is a witness. It follows, then, that that which the Church witnesses to will be affected by the quality and character of the witness of the Church. We might ask the questions, "Can the unifying power of Christ be attested to by a divided church?" and "Can a loving God be revealed through a judgmental Church?" I believe that Barth was increasingly preoccupied by these questions, and in the remainder of this work, we will turn our attention with him to this very important issue.

In Ephesians 4:5, the Apostle Paul beautifully described the core teachings of Christianity in the following way: "There is one body and one Spirit, just as you were called to the one hope of your calling, one Lord, one faith, one baptism, one God and Father of all, who is above all and through all and in all." Unity in Christ Jesus is to be the core attitude and description of the Church, according to Paul, as he states over and over again in virtually all of his epistles. For this reason, the Church affirms in the Nicene Creed that it is *una, sancta, catholica, apostolica*, or one, holy, catholic, and apostolic. With this profession, "the Christian believes—and there is—only one Church."[24] Despite all seeming contradictions to this statement, Christians believe in (and there can be only) one Church. Yet clearly the Church is not one today. With the Great Schism, the Reformation, and the almost ceaseless splitting and factioning within Protestantism, how can Christians believe in or claim one Church? To navigate this topic, Barth employs his understanding of impossible possibilities or paradox.

For Barth, there is one Church, as there is indeed only one Christ. The existence of multiple churches, then, bears witness not to the reality of multiple churches, but rather to the false reality of multiple Lords.[25] Barth puts it thus: "I repeat: Jesus Christ as the one Mediator between God and man is the oneness of the Church, is that unity within which there may be a multiplicity of communities, of gifts, of persons within one Church, while through it a multiplicity of churches are excluded."[26]

Therefore, all Christians, if they are indeed followers of Christ, are necessarily part of one and the same Church, and the head of that Church is Jesus Christ Himself. Included, and thus united together in this

24. Barth, *CD* IV.1, 668.
25. Ibid., 675.
26. Barth, *Church and the Churches*, 14.

one Church, are both Roman Catholicism and Protestantism.[27] As Jesus Christ is the one, true Lord, the road toward Christian unity, then, leads directly through Jesus. Barth is quick to point out that what is needed for all Christians, Roman Catholics and Protestants in particular, is conversion to Christ: the unitary Lord and head of the Church. It follows then that most Christians are united in the one Church, though they are unaware of and even resistant to this unity. For Barth, there really is only one Christian Church.

Reinhard Hütter labels Barth's complex and complicated ecclesiology "dialectical catholicity." "Dialectical catholicity," says Hütter, is "the concrete strategy through which this critical principle [the inner dialectic of the community] takes shape in light of the opposing principles of neo-Protestantism and Roman Catholicism."[28] Hütter rightly points out Barth's desire for oneness. In fact, I would argue that Hütter's understanding of Barth's ecclesiology is perhaps one of the most accurate that has been offered to date. Aside from Christology—not that it is possible to truly separate ecclesiology from Christology and still remain in the realm of faithful Christian theology—ecclesiology is perhaps Karl Barth's biggest doctrinal preoccupation, his greatest concern. Evidence of this is seen throughout Barth's corpus. In light of Hütter's argument, it makes sense that Barth's *magnum opus* is the *Church Dogmatics*, not the *Christian Dogmatics* or the *Dogmatics*, both of which he toyed with as titles. Just who is that Church? The answer, it would seem, would be the Church—all who would claim to be under the lordship of Jesus, in other words. Karl Barth wrote the *Church Dogmatics* because he truly believes there is one Church and because he hopes to assist that Church in faithfully following its one Lord, Jesus. "In substituting the word Church for Christian in the title, I have tried to set a good example of restraint in the lighthearted use of the great word 'Christian' against which I have protested. But materially I have also tried to show that from the very outset *dogmatics is not a free science. It is bound to the sphere of the Church, where alone it is possible and meaningful.*"[29]

---

27. Of course, Orthodoxy should be and is included here, but it would be a bit anachronistic for Barth to address this issue. As a Protestant, it makes more sense to deal first with the problems stemming from the Reformation, leaving the issues stemming from the Great Schism to a later date.

28. Hütter, "Karl Barth's 'Dialectical Catholicity,'" 147.

29. Barth, *CD* I.1, xii–xiii.

Barth is not interested in factious churches or theology, except in their conversion to the one Christ. He does not believe that Luther or Calvin intended faction, nor does he believe that the Protestant Church as it stands today is the desired result of either Reformer. Pursuing unity, then, requires Barth to reengage the great Reformers and their goals, along with the Church they were trying to reform. In doing so, all Christians, especially Protestant Christians, must ask themselves if, and to what extent, they are the Church.

> Catholicism becomes this question to us because in its presuppositions for the Church, in spite of all contradictions, it is closer to the Reformers than is the Church of the Reformation so far as that has actually and finally become [Neo-Protestantism]. It becomes this question to us because, if any of the concern of the Reformation is still ours in spite of [Neo-Protestanism], we cannot deny that we feel more at home in the world of Catholicism and among its believers than in a world and among believers where the reality about which the Reformation centered has become an unknown or almost unknown entity.[30]

Neo-Protestantism, which Barth virtually equates with liberal Protestantism and liberal individualism, is clearly to be opposed. Going further, addressing whether liberal Protestantism was the desired end for the great Reformers, Barth says, "If I today became convinced that the interpretation of the Reformation on the line taken by Schleiermacher-Ritschl-Troeltsch (or even by Seeberg or Holl) was correct; that Luther and Calvin really intended such an outcome of their labours; I could not become a Catholic tomorrow, but I should have to withdraw from the evangelical Church. And if I were forced to make a choice between the two evils, I should, in fact, prefer the Catholic."[31] Barth was not happy with the direction that much of the Reformation had taken. And yet, what makes Barth so unique and intriguing is his singular support of so many of the reforming principles of Luther and especially Calvin. Barth believed in one Church, but he believed that that one Church was in desperate need of reform, of conversion to Christ. The Reformers, he would say, had the right motive and agenda, but their efforts went astray. The challenge now is to continue the work of reform alongside the work of reunification.

30. Quoted in Hütter, "Karl Barth's 'Dialectical Catholicity,'" 141.
31. Ibid.

While this might sound well and good, Hütter for one calls Barth's ecclesiology "dialectical catholicity" and describes it as "transcendental ecclesiology" in that it is based upon an ideal—that is, non-real—Church.[32] In sum, Hütter says, "Neo-Protestantism and Roman Catholicism represent alternative ecclesiological principles which constantly need to be engaged in order to be critically overcome through a transcendental critique that is reflective of the sovereignty of God's activity in Christ."[33]

Hütter's worry is that the picture of the Church that emerges from Barth's ecclesiology is simply a name given to the constant oscillation between Protestantism and Roman Catholicism. The result is a church void of any real ecclesial roots or substance.[34] This is no real Church at all, according to Hütter.

I believe that Hütter's brief article is a tremendous help in terms of understanding Barth's theology and especially his ecclesiology. While I certainly share Hütter's worries over any form of transcendental ecclesiology, I wonder if this is the only way of understanding Barth's complex ecclesiology, wherein he believes there is only one Church despite the multiplicity of churches.[35] Barth's ecclesiology cannot help being viewed as transcendental if it is indeed predicated upon such a dialectical understanding as Hütter has chosen. However, this understanding places more reality on the broken than the whole, more emphasis on the perception of multiplicity of churches than the unity of the Savior. No matter how illogical it might seem to some, Barth always begins with Christ and not with humanity—in this case, with the unity of Christ, not with the multiplicity of the churches. Barth does not ask what it means to say that there is one Lord because there is a multiplicity of churches, but rather he asks what it means to say that there is a multiplicity of churches because there is only one Lord. As I have often argued in this work, perhaps it is best to push further, into the confusing arena of paradox, rather than to give in to a dialectical understanding of Barth's theology.

For Barth there is one Church, precisely because there is only one Lord. Christ Jesus, as the head of the Church, is the head of a body—one body. This is the reality from which Barth seeks to understand the Church. Unity must be given more credence than multiplicity. To do so

32. Ibid., 148.

33. Ibid., 151.

34. Ibid., 144.

35. I would certainly include the nonsensical and disastrous doctrine of the "invisible church" here.

is not to make a transcendental move, unless to claim that Jesus Christ our Lord is one, that He is the head of the Church, and that His death and resurrection are singularly efficacious for all of humanity once and for all, is likewise transcendental.[36] If we begin with Jesus, therefore, with His oneness, with His lordship, with the efficacy of His blood and with the universality of election wrought in Him, then the claim to one Church makes a bit more sense. In my opinion, this is the logic of Barth's ecclesiology. Nowhere is this logic more on display than in the curious way Barth discusses the relationship between Israel and the Church.[37] The argument that there is one Church, despite the multiplicity of churches, will succeed or fail based upon the even more complex claim to unity between the people of Israel, God's chosen people of the covenant, and the Church, those grafted into that covenant.

As I have already discussed, the sole factor driving all of Barth's ecclesial musings, and therefore the *Church Dogmatics* as a whole, is the classic paradoxical Christian confession *credo unam ecclesiam*.[38] The

36. Here I intend the term *transcendental* in the same manner as Hütter. In particular, by transcendence, I mean an intellectual or spiritual movement, jump, or going beyond. As such, transcendental, as used here, would be the opposite of realism, the concrete or the mundane. Hütter believes Barth's ecclesiology is an intellectual or spiritual ecclesiology, and not one based in reality.

37. Interestingly, Hütter cites Nicholas Healy's critical remarks of Barth at this point as further evidence that Barth's so-called dialectical ecclesiology is actually "transcendental ecclesiology." Hütter, "Karl Barth's 'Dialectical Catholicity,'" 149. See Healy, "Logic of Karl Barth's Ecclesiology"; Healy, "Practices and the New Ecclesiology."

I do, of course, disagree on this point, though I take seriously the claim that Israel's identity is constituted by a distinct set of practices, beliefs, norms—in short, a way of life. Any attempt to connect the Church and Israel through Christ must not eradicate or divorce the people Israel from those practices that constitute their very identity. I do not believe Barth does this, but he also does not treat this concept with the care and intentionality that those like Healy and Hütter call for.

38. Barth's ecclesiology, and in particular who he intends when he says "Church" (as in *Church Dogmatics*), is an interesting and highly debatable subject. I believe that when he refers to the Church, he has in mind the body that confesses the classic Christian confessions. Thus, I do think that he has a sort of idealistic and severely paradoxical Church in mind. All Christians, therefore, who confess to be one, holy, catholic, and apostolic, Barth lumps together as the Church—despite the glaring reality that at best there are only fleeting glimpses of this unified Church, and at worst there really is no such thing as ecclesial unity at all. It must then be taken into account that as Gentiles have been grafted into the vine that is Israel, Barth also believes that Jews stand as a part of the Church despite their ignorance to this fact and their continued identity as the people of God who have rejected their Messiah. When all this is taken into account, Barth's understanding of the Church is beautiful and problematic, idealistic in

affirmation of one Church—a Church that is unified, that is—in this modern era is problematic, to say the least. Even before the Reformation, this classic affirmation was problematic; after the Reformation, it seems downright foolish. The Church is split, it is broken, it is marred, and the possibility of reunification of all Christians seems almost laughable. Leaving this very serious issue aside, Barth's thoughts about the "the Jewish question" reveal just how far he wants to go with his notion of the Church, and Church unity in particular.

Illustration of the Reality of Ecclesial Unity: Israel and the Church

To borrow a term from George Hunsinger, one that Hunsinger employed to explain Barth's ecclesiology, the relationship between Israel and the Church, as Barth saw it, might best be described as a *"koinonia* relation."[39] A *koinonia* relation, as Hunsinger explained, is one of mutual indwelling. A *koinonia* relation parallels the perichoretic inner relationship of the Holy Trinity. As such, a *koinonia* relation is one characterized by unity-in-distinction and distinction-in-unity.[40] In such a relationship, one party is not privileged above another, nor are the parties defined by conflict, difference, or oscillation. Rather, such a relationship is understood to be a fundamental harmony, with difference and/or distinction drawing its very understanding from the more fundamental unity, and not the other way around. A *koinonia* relation is not a dialectical relationship, but rather it is much closer to the concept of paradox I've been working with. This *koinonia* relation is an accurate description of the relationship within God, and therefore of the relationship between God and creation. As such, *koinonia* relation is also one of the best ways of understanding the christological relationship between the churches, and between Israel and the Church.

The so-called Jewish question, as Barth likes to call it—the question of the relationship between the Church and Israel—is perhaps the most complexly tenuous relationship founded upon God's covenantal grace that we can speak of.[41] The very ongoing identity of the people of

---

a very realistic way, and, in short, paradoxical to say the least.

39. Hunsinger, *Disruptive Grace*, 256–61.

40. Ibid., 258.

41. Katherine Sonderegger has written an extremely profound and helpful text

Israel—in relationship to the Church, that is—is as the covenant people of God who rejected God's Son. Unlike pagan peoples who persist in the belief of other deities, Israel is characterized by the belief in the Father and the rejection of the Son. Yet, as the Apostle Paul told his readers in Rome, God will maintain the covenant, even if Israel does not, so that ultimately "all of Israel will be saved." As such, the Jewish question serves as a case study of sorts of the complex logic of God's love, as well as serving as an example of the possibility of reconciliation for all people through Christ Jesus. What it means to talk about unity amidst the multiplicity of churches is, therefore, probably a reflection of what it means to talk about unity between the Church and Israel.

The Church stands above and apart from all other religious institutions. By this I mean to say that the Church, unlike groups such as the Baha'i, Zoroastrians, and the Unity Church, is characterized by exclusive claims centering around the person and work of Jesus of Nazareth. The Christian Church is not polytheistic, nor is it syncretistic, but rather its sole allegiance is to Jesus Christ Her Lord. As such, the Church is aptly described as a missionary community, in that the Church, especially its more evangelical members, seeks to call men and women out of false religious communities, "to call them from false gods to the true God."[42] The Church cannot call Jews out of the synagogue, for the synagogue exists in worship to YHWH, the God and Father of all. Christians cannot exist in a missionary relationship with the people of Israel, who were aware of the good news and the covenant long before we Gentiles were. Yet, despite all of this, the synagogue exists today, perhaps more than anyplace else, as a place that has made a very intentional and ongoing decision to reject the claims of lordship and divinity of Jesus Christ. "But this being the case, the existence of the Synagogue side by side with the Church is an

---

on this issue. In short, she argues that "the *Church Dogmatics* is irreconcilably anti-Judaic—though not anti-Semitic—because the actualism of Barth's theology demands it." Sonderegger, *That Jesus Christ Was Born a Jew*, 174. Ultimately, she documents that Barth is not concerned with Judaism as a religion, as he believes that it doesn't exist. Rather, he is concerned with the Jewish people, and even with the State of Israel. Barth's is a theology that blends a comprehensively dogmatic account of Israel as a part of the Church, and yet one that also takes seriously the ongoing plight of the Jewish people. Thus, theologically speaking, Barth is anti-Judaic (he negates Judaism) and yet decidedly not anti-Semitic (he does not discriminate against, but rather seeks justice for, Jewish people). For a more critical view of this topic, see Bader-Saye, *Church and Israel after Christendom*.

42. Barth, *CD* IV.1, 671.

ontological impossibility, a wound, a gaping hole in the body of Christ, something which is quite intolerable."[43]

The continued existence of Judaism is as a people in outright rejection of Christ Jesus as their Messiah and God. God remains faithful to God's covenantal relationship, even if that relationship is one-sided. In Jesus of Nazareth, Emmanuel, the great Mediator, Israel was opened up, allowing for the salvation of Gentiles by opening up this covenantal relationship to all the world. The Church, as it has been grafted into Israel, is the visible sign of this covenantal relationship between God and creation. This visible sign is one of unity despite the intolerable existence of the synagogue alongside of the Church, something that Barth calls, "a gaping wound in the body of Christ."[44] The Jewish question, then, the continued faithfulness of God to God's unfaithful people, is a paradoxical thorn in the flesh of *credo unam ecclesiam*. As Barth has rightly said, the Jewish question is also the Christian question: a statement that I believe displays Barth's highly paradoxical way of understanding ecclesial unity.

Amidst this tenuous relationship remains the fact that Jesus was Jewish and that he was therefore the Jewish Messiah. His status as Messiah is not dependent upon whether or not most or all accept Him as such. As Gentile followers of Christ, therefore, it makes sense to say that since we have been grafted into the vine that is Israel—that is, God's covenant—we must seek not to convert Israel, but to be in unity with Israel. Though this unity might seem impossible or idealistic, according to Barth, who here leans very heavily on the Apostle Paul, this unity is nonetheless already existent. Because of Jesus, the synagogue and the Church are one, and inextricably so. Understood in this light, the long and often bloody history between the Church and Israel must be seen as deeply sinful—nothing more, nothing less. The people of God's covenant are to be people of reconciliation, not division. Christians, as those who believe in Jesus Christ, should lead the way in this, not because they desire to convert their Jewish brothers and sisters, but because they believe in the teachings of Scripture about God's place alongside and indeed amidst the people of Israel. The only real way of evangelizing the Jews, therefore, is to "make the Synagogue jealous."[45]

43. Ibid. Barth is here using "and yet" language—what I have argued is the language of the absurd possibility of the absurd.

44. Ibid.

45. Barth, *CD* IV.3.2, 878.

The gaping wound in the body of Christ that Barth describes must be healed, and this cannot be accomplished unless the Church takes on as one of its primary tasks the call to embody the loving teachings of Jesus toward Israel. This requires the acceptance of the bewildering claim to unity amidst such an ancient and enormous disagreement—that of the very person and lordship of Jesus of Nazareth, the second person of the Trinity, God's only and eternal Son. "'Jewish Missions' is not the right word for the call to remove this breach, a call which must go out unceasingly from the Church to these brethren who do not yet know their unity with it—a unity which does not have to be established but is already there ontologically, who will not accept what they already are, and what they were long before us poor Gentiles."[46] Human logic and understanding do not allow any reality to such a unified relationship between the Church and Israel. After all, where does such a relationship empirically exist? And yet, this unity is not caused, or based upon, or even affected by either the Church or Israel. Rather, the unity of the covenant peoples of God is established and rooted firmly in none other than Jesus Christ, and therefore it is as real and true as can be understood. This relationship is idealistic, therefore, only if Christ Jesus is idealistic. If He is ontologically the one, true Lord, however, if He is the only and eternal Son of God, by whose blood all have been elected and set apart by God for the hope of salvation, then the unity wrought by Him can likewise be trusted and can be said to be ontologically true and real as well.

Paul, the self-proclaimed "apostle to the Gentiles," states in Romans 11:26, "All Israel will be saved." Of course, in saying this, Paul is simply affirming that God keeps God's promises. God promised to rescue and bring salvation to God's people Israel; their acceptance of Jesus as Messiah was not required for the fulfillment of this promise. God's covenant with Israel was not subject to dependent clauses. In Romans, Paul affirms that God's covenant with Israel is not an if-then contract. Though Israel might become the enemies of God, God has promised to remain faithful to Israel no matter what. In fact, "the history of Israel continues to be a history of the faithfulness which Yahweh maintains in relation to Israel in spite of Israel's failure and unfaithfulness."[47] Through the gracious outpouring of God's reconciling love, Paul tells his readers, the Church has been grafted into Israel. The same is not true in reverse. The Church is the

46. Ibid.
47. Barth, *CD* IV.2, 775.

new Israel, as it is an inclusion into and a transformation of the old Israel. Thus, there is to be unity between Jews and Christians, as both parties are in reality one body. "To try to deny this would be to deny Jesus Christ Himself," says Barth.[48] Therefore, for Barth, the Jewish question is none other than the Christian question. Both questions, ultimately, are christological questions—questions of unity, of the unity of the two natures in Jesus, and the unity wrought between God and humanity on the cross. The issue of unity is anything but idealistic when rooted in Christ Jesus. In Christ Jesus, reconciliation comes to the unreconcilable and creates unity by overcoming distinction and conflict with unity and love.[49]

Conclusion: Karl Barth and Roman Catholicism— A Way Forward?

Much like everything else, for Karl Barth ecclesiology is subsumed under the broader, definitive category of Christology. It is Christ Jesus who instituted the Church, after all, and it is Christ Jesus who holds it all together. Apart from Christ, seen from an immanent, worldly perspective, the Church is broken and splintered. Seen from a christological perspective, and thus one that is transcendent in such a way that is radically immanent at the same time, the Church is one and can only be one because of the unity of Christ. This claim to oneness is not idealistic or transcendental; instead, it is christological, and therefore concrete. Ultimately, the Church is a statement about God and not humanity.

Barth's ecclesiological teachings—indeed, the highly ecclesiological nature of his entire corpus (his *magnum opus* is the *Church Dogmatics*, after all)—is often ignored. Many Protestants seem unsure of what to do with the ecclesial nature of Barth's work, often treating it in the offhand, even careless way in which they deal with ecclesiology in general. Paul Jones and Bruce McCormack are guilty of this, in that they treat ecclesiology as a sort of afterthought for both Barth and their work with Barth.[50]

---

48. Barth, *CD* IV.1, 671.

49. In addressing another topic, one that is also often categorized as "idealistic"— the love of enemies—Barth says, "Turning the other cheek" does not reveal a different God or teaching. The whole history of Israel is proof that God loved God's enemies. Ibid., 172.

50. McCormack's work is surprisingly silent on the issue of Barth's ecclesiology. Jones is a bit more complex. For Jones, ecclesiology plays a central role in Barth's work, in that Jones argues that Barth was uninterested in the classic or orthodox tradition of

Moving closer to the mark, I would argue, is someone like John Webster, who despite some of his concerns about recent ecclesio-ethical movements in theology (i.e., not explicitly christological), sees in Barth a true and solid foundation for ecclesiology in Christology. After making critical remarks about much of contemporary ecclesial and ethical theology, Webster says this of ecclesiology: "This is not, of course, to deny that the practice of the ecclesial community is of importance, nor to fall into the error of ethical nominalism in which human action *cannot* refer to divine action. It is simply to urge that what holds the ecclesial community together is not common moral activity but attention to the Gospel in which existing reconciliation is set before us both as—shocking, revolutionary, unpossessable—reality, and also as task."[51] Perhaps best of all Barth's interpreters in the arena of ecclesiology would be those postliberal readers such as Hans Frei, George Lindbeck, and John Howard Yoder. The paramount effort of this group can be seen in Stanley Hauerwas's Gifford Lectures, *With the Grain of the Universe: The Church's Witness and Natural Theology.* Much like Barth, Hauerwas is apt to talk about the Church in nonspecific, and therefore united, terms: *the Church.* Hauerwas employs such terminology in spite of the various splits and factions—in short, in spite of the multiplicity of churches. Like Barth, Hauerwas accepts as real the unity of Christ, rather than the disunity of humanity. About the *Church Dogmatics*, Hauerwas says,

> at least at one level Barth understood the *Church Dogmatics* to be a training manual for Christians, a manual that would instruct us that the habits of our speech must be disciplined by the God found in Jesus Christ.
>
> For Christians to relearn the grammar of their faith requires, from Barth's perspective, nothing less than the recognition that, as Frei puts it, "the whole substance of Christian theology could be mirrored in a distinct way in every one" of the church's major and quasi-independent topics.[52]

---

the Church, but rather with a radical reconstruction of the Church via Barth's doctrine of election. So for Jones, it could be said that ecclesiology plays a central role for Barth, but that role was to strip it bare and decentralize it! Jones, *The Humanity of Christ*.

On the contrary, Kimlyn Bender has written a recent work on Barth's ecclesiology that is thoroughly comprehensive and quite helpful. Bender, *Karl Barth's Christological Ecclesiology*.

51. Webster, *Word and Church*, 228–29.

52. Hauerwas, *With the Grain of the Universe*, 179–80.

The *Church Dogmatics*, as Hauerwas describes it, is nothing less than a story; it is a part of the ongoing story of the people of God, the Church, as they attempt to live faithfully in obedience to their savior.[53]

Unlike many Protestant scholars, Barth's Roman Catholic interpreters seem to quickly latch onto the ecclesial quality of Barth's theology. Rather than dismiss Barth's talk of *the Church*, these scholars find serious fault in Barth's system of thought, precisely because he sees the divided Church as one and, amidst his desire for unity, does not in any way subscribe to some of the most basic tenets of Roman Catholicism. It is precisely because they hold Barth's theology in such high regard that this group of scholars nonetheless remains so entirely critical of his ecclesiology. This group of Roman Catholics includes, to name only a few, Nicholas Healy, Reinhard Hütter, Emilien Lamirande, Erich Przywara, Gottlieb Sönghen, and, of course, Hans Urs von Balthasar. For this group, the importance of Karl Barth, seen especially in his christological challenge to the Church, cannot be underestimated. In fact, one could argue that Barth is one of the primary theologians, if not the primary theologian, who helped inspire the grand and sweeping changes made by the Roman Church at Vatican II—changes that are still taking place today.[54] All of this is due to the singular driving focus that Barth placed on Christ Jesus and the need for all Christians to be converted to Jesus. Much of the influence of Karl Barth can be traced back through Hans Urs von Balthasar, one of the greatest contemporary Roman Catholic scholars. Von Balthasar described Barth's work in this way: "Rarely has Christendom heard God's love sung with such infinite melodious beauty as in his life's work."[55] In fact, near the end of his life, von Balthasar is supposed to have said that "he wrote every word of his theology for Karl Barth!"[56]

One thing should be clear: Barth has left an enormous and lasting impression on the Church, especially the Roman Catholic Church. With this in mind, in closing this examination of the effect of Barth's work on the modern/postmodern world, I think that the logical place to turn is to a possible way forward for Barth studies. While there are, of course, many fruitful avenues that Barth scholars can pursue for years to come, none of these is more fruitful—none can offer more to the Church and to our

53. Ibid., 180.

54. Henri de Lubac is the other primary figure whose theology can be shown to form a basis for many of the reforms of Vatican II.

55. Balthasar, *Theology of Karl Barth*, 169.

56. Betz, "Analogia Entis as a Formal Principle of Cathlic Theology."

Lord Christ, in my opinion—than the road toward theological and practical ecclesial convergence. Surely it is only Barth—who could maintain
utter rejection of all things Roman and yet at the same time be perhaps
the most catholic of all Protestant scholars—who can offer hope for just
such a convergence.

As Barth himself said, "In the sixteenth and seventeenth centuries,
Catholics and Protestants still looked each other in the eye—angrily, but
in the eye. They talked to each other, sharply and harshly; but they really
talked."[57] Such a conversation, painful as it might be, was always at the
fore of Barth's mind. The Church, if there is any hope for it at all—and
Barth believed there was—must engage in such discussions. It was always
and increasingly Barth's hope that the Church, all the Church—both Protestant and Roman Catholic—would be converted to Christ Jesus. After
Vatican II, this was not merely a hope for Barth; it was something that he
was optimistic about.[58] It is possible, then, that reading Barth alongside
of Roman Catholic scholars who are, like Barth, christologically oriented
is the best way forward for contemporary Barth studies. There are three
primary reasons for this suggestion.

First, such a way forward makes sense in light of looking back. Barth's
vast theological knowledge, his grand vision for reform, and his ability to
pull from the very best Roman Catholic resources prior to and after the
Reformation—as well as his similarly great, if not greater, knowledge of
Protestant theology—make such a way forward intelligible. Though quite
cognizant of the ongoing splitting and factioning within Protestantism
and its drifting further and further away from Roman Catholicism, Barth
understands the historical roots of the Church to lie in Rome, and he is
willing to claim those roots as his own.

Barth's theology is a story, as Hauerwas has stated. It is a story built
upon a vast and complex history, and with that history comes all the beliefs and practices that constitute the story or narrative as such.

As we have already seen, part of this story entails a belief in a revealed
God over and against the notion presented by many, mainly within Protestantism, of a hidden God or the *Deus absconditus.* Barth's God is not
hidden, but fully revealed in Jesus of Nazareth, in whom the fullness of
God was pleased to dwell. Any talk of God's hiddeness, or of God's veiling, or of God's "No" in Barth's theology must always be subsumed under

57. Quoted in Lamirande, "Roman Catholic Reactions to Karl Barth's Ecclesiology," 29.

58. Hütter, "Karl Barth's 'Dialectical Catholicity,'" 138.

and within God's decisive revelation of God's self in Christ, that is, God's unveiling, or God's "Yes." There is no mistaking this point, and it cannot be forgotten. Barth's is not a hidden God but a revealed God. Barth's is not a veiled God but an unveiled God. Barth's God does not ultimately speak a "No" to creation, though creation indeed deserves a "No," but rather God speaks a glorious and unmistakably clear "Yes," once and for all, in Jesus Christ the crucified, resurrected, and ascended one. Though Barth does indeed display many nominalist tendencies or worries, he can never be declared a nominalist along with Luther, Scotus, Ockham, Ghent, et al., precisely because of this decisive and yet misunderstood aspect of his theology.

As a result, connections can easily be drawn between Barth and someone like Maurice Blondel, and the Roman Catholic *ressourcement* theologians who came after him, including especially Henri de Lubac, Erich Pryzwara, and Hans Urs von Balthasar. As stated in chapter 2, through the likes of Blondel, and his alternate understanding of dialectics in particular, many within the Roman Catholic Church experienced a very different version of modernity than did most Protestants. Though Luther and the other Reformers did indeed have many positive effects on the world and Church, the belief in a supertranscendent God, one who is virtually unknowable for all God's hiddeness, resulted in a very untraditional—I would argue heretical—view of God known as nominalism. This in turn helped give birth to the secular and, consequently, nihilism. Meanwhile, though some of the more apophatic strands of Roman Catholicism come fairly close to nominalism and the God of nominalism, the *Deus absconditus*, the majority of Roman Catholicism tended away from such leanings, preferring a God who is not hidden but revealed.[59] In short, Barth stands firmly entrenched in the same tradition that his Roman Catholic brothers and sisters do, and he claims that tradition as his own.[60] As a result, Barth avoids many of the mistakes of his ancestors, both Protestant and Catholic, in his attempt to follow faithfully Christ Jesus and to instruct the Church in doing the same. In Barth's work, one finds a genuinely faithful attempt to read Scripture and follow the life

59. Note, this does not take away from the mystery of God, but rather requires a slightly more complicated way of understanding God so as to affirm both the mysterious nature of God as well as the revealed nature of God.

60. Remember, Barth says, "It would seem that Church history no longer begins for me in 1517. I can quote Anselm and Thomas with no sign of horror." Barth, *CD* I.1, xiii.

and teachings of Jesus in such a way that this pursuit serves as a foundation for everything else. Barth's theology is nothing short of a complete and well-thought-out theological metaphysics rooted exclusively in the person of Jesus of Nazareth.[61] Though this is perhaps not evident at first glance, I believe this is very much in line with much of the best of Roman Catholic scholarship.

The second reason why such a way forward in Barth scholarship is plausible is the high quality of much of contemporary Roman Catholic scholarship, particularly as influenced by Barth. Barth's call to conversion to Christ has perhaps been heard and obeyed nowhere more clearly than within Roman Catholicism. Beginning with Vatican II and continuing into the present, the Roman Catholic Church's mission of *aggiornamento* through *ressourcement* is an impossible task if it is not a deeply christological endeavor. Of course, not all facets of this program are directly influenced by Barth and, strictly speaking, christological, but much of the program is. Theologians such as Henri de Lubac, Hans Urs von Balthasar, Hans Küng, Gustávo Gutiérrez, Thomas Guarino, Robert Barron, and of course Pope Benedict XVI, to name only a few, have all contributed to a new and still changing version of Roman Catholicism that owes much of its renewed christological vision to Karl Barth.[62] As perhaps the Reformation's truest son, Barth has become one of the major interlocutors for contemporary Roman Catholic scholarship.

An older friend of mine once had the opportunity to translate for Hans Küng, who was giving a lecture. Afterward, Küng told him the story of meeting Pope Paul VI at the Second Vatican Council. The story goes that the pope asked Küng about his studies, having heard that he was studying under Karl Barth. The pope said to Küng that in his opinion, Barth was the greatest example of true Reformed theology since Calvin, perhaps greater even than the Genevan reformer himself. Upon relaying this statement to Professor Barth, Küng says that Barth replied, "Maybe there really is something to the whole infallibility business after all!"[63]

61. Hauerwas, *With the Grain of the Universe*, 184.

62. Eugene Roger's outstanding book *Barth and Aquinas: Sacred Doctrine and the Natural Knowledge of God* could easily be added here, except that he is not Roman Catholic. Despite this, his is a perfect example of what I am proposing: a serious engagement with Barth's theology alongside Roman Catholic theology, such as in the case of St. Thomas. I consider this work of high importance as a signpost for future Barth scholarship.

63. Thanks are due to my dear friend and brother in Christ Rev. Thomas Findlay for relating this story to me, which he in turn was told by Hans Küng.

Situations like this one, funny though it might be, indicate the seriousness with which Roman Catholics regard Barth's theology and the challenge he presents to any theology that would call itself Christian. A quick survey of recent Catholic scholarship would indicate that Barth's influence is still very prominent—much more so, I would argue, than in Protestantism. I believe this will be increasingly true as forms of Protestant liberalism continue to grow in stature and influence in much of the Protestant world. Increasingly, Barth's theology will be seen as outdated and even oppressive due to the singular, salvific, and revelatory significance he places on Christ Jesus. Interestingly, christocentric theology has become more and more marginalized by much of contemporary Protestantism, with many preferring more inclusive and dare I say "relative" central themes to base their faith upon. While contemporary Roman Catholicism certainly has its share of major theological and practical problems, the opposite is increasingly the case: Roman Catholicism is returning to a position where Christology is seen as central.

Finally, one more reason that I believe justifies and indeed begs for such an endeavor is Barth's own well-documented and growing preoccupation with his Roman Catholic commentators, be they fans or critics. In the preface to his brief statements on baptism with both the Holy Spirit and with water that he consented to have published as *Church Dogmatics* IV.4, Barth notes that this little conclusion to his great work will most certainly draw him criticism. But, he says, "the day will come when justice will be done to me in this matter too. I hazard the paradoxical conjecture that this will perhaps come about earlier, not on our side, but among Roman Catholic theologians who to-day are questioning almost everything—unless a new Pius IX blights the present hopes of blossom."[64] Though I am not sure that Barth's finale has warranted such justice, the rest of his theology certainly has. It is curious that even then Barth believed that Roman Catholics would catch on to his theology and the christological impulse he maintained, more so than even Protestants. Barth was, dare I say, consumed by Roman Catholicism.

He begins his great *Church Dogmatics* by joking about his label as a "crypto-Catholic," and he proceeds to discuss the one reason, and the only reason, why he cannot assent to Roman Catholicism. Barth remains concerned with Roman Catholicism throughout his *Dogmatics*, often carrying on lengthy "discussions" with various Roman Catholic colleagues

---

64. Barth, *CD* IV.4, xii.

and/or critics in the small print sections. In particular, he heaps great praise upon his colleague Gottlieb Söhngen's doctrine of the *analogia fidei*, which seemingly fixes for Barth the one issue preventing his conversion to Roman Catholicism. Here it is only because he is skeptical as to whether or not Söhngen's position is truly reflective of historical Catholic spirit and doctrine that he does not fully relent his own critical position. In the preface to volume IV.2, Barth again carefully addresses where he differs from various Roman Catholic doctrines, but in a way that reveals his desire to effect change within the Roman Catholic Church. The same cannot be said for Protestant liberalism, and much of Protestantism in general, which he seems to almost completely disregard. Barth says he is increasingly charged with "ascribing too much to man"[65]—something that, according to Barth, places him even closer to the Roman Catholic camp and even further away from Luther than he previously was. This would only solidify during and after Vatican II.

A suitable place to conclude, therefore, can be found in Barth's comments upon the occasion of his trip to the "threshold of the apostles" on September 22–29, 1966, to meet with the pope and other leading Roman figures in lieu of his postponed trip to the final two sessions of the Second Vatican Council.[66]

In this short account of his trip, the "old man from Basel" relays his grateful thoughts about his Roman hosts. Barth boasts to having had a fabulous time while in Rome, and of course Barth made sure to engage in as many theological discussions as possible! Much of the book, as a result of the nature of the visit, consists simply of Professor Barth's notes and the questions that he posed to leading Roman Catholic scholars, including critical questions about Mariology posed to Pope Paul VI himself! Barth's personal thoughts about the trip provide good insight into the state of Barth's thinking on ecclesiology, the relationship between the Protestant and Roman Catholic Churches in particular, and Barth's role in the ongoing discussion that is the Church.

> As a result of the trip I gained a close acquaintance with a church and a theology which have begun a movement, the results of which are incalculable and slow but clearly genuine and irreversible. In looking at it we [Protestants] can only wish that we had something comparable, if it could avoid a repetition

65. Barth, *CD* IV.2, x.

66. Barth, *Ad Limina Apostolorum*, 12. Barth was forced to forego his invitation to the concluding two sessions of Vatican II due to illness.

of at least the worst mistakes we have made since the sixteenth century. I would be happy to see the words "Protestant" and "Protestantism" disappear from our vocabulary—and along with them the backwoods article of exception in our Swiss Constitution. The Pope is not the Antichrist! The apparatus of all the anathemas directed at us by the Council of Trent is now to be found, with all sorts of other old weaponry, only in Denzinger. *Ultra montes* I met so many Christians with whom I could not only speak candidly and seriously, but also join in hearty laughter, that I could not think without pain of certain dwarfs in our own theological backyard. Any optimism about the future is automatically excluded. But calm, brotherly hope is called for, together with a willingness in the meanwhile to conduct in both great and small affairs a thorough housecleaning of our own. "Conversions" from us to the Roman Catholic Church or from there to one of our churches have as such no significance (*peccatur intra muros et extra!*). They can have significance only if they are in the form of a conscientiously necessary "conversion"—not to another church, but to Jesus Christ, the Lord of the one, holy, catholic and apostolic church. Basically both here and there it can only be a matter of each one heeding in his place in his own church the call to faith in the one Lord, and to his service.[67]

For Barth there is only one Church because there is only one Lord. Increasingly, Barth is interested not in conversations with the "theological dwarfs" of Protestantism but in real and sustained conversations with Roman Catholics. Barth concludes by saying, "anxious souls on our side may here at last see that I returned from Rome just as stubbornly evangelical—*I would really rather say, evangelical-catholic*—as before."[68] Evangelical and catholic, Protestant and catholic, always both, never one without the other—that is the way that Barth chose to identify himself as a theologian, and as a child of God, in one of the last things he ever wrote.

It would seem, then, that as Barth was not concerned with being Protestant, or Reformed, or Roman Catholic, or even evangelical—in terms of the systems of thought known by such identifiers—then Barth's theological progeny, and Barth scholarship as a whole, should be similarly unconcerned. Barth was interested in being a theologian amidst an ongoing discussion of what it means to be the Church. Likewise, it should now be very clear that Barth's God was not the God of nominalism, the *Deus*

67. Ibid., 18.
68. Ibid.

absconditus, which has been shown to be the dominant God of modernity. Any attempt to move forward, then, in faithfulness to Barth's theological teachings will likewise reject any claims to a hidden or unknown God in favor of the God radically, unilaterally, and eternally revealed in the Son, Jesus of Nazareth. The Church, according to Barth, is a discussion, a story, and as such it is framed and given meaning by the primary character in the story: Jesus Christ our Lord. The Church, therefore, cannot be faithful to its call—it cannot even be itself—unless it realizes that each side, Protestant and Roman Catholic, is only one part of the broader discussion. Neither can be faithful on its own. Any theology that intends to be Barthian, then, will move forward only in constant discussion with Roman Catholicism, or it will not move forward at all.

Bibliography

Adams, Marilyn McCord. *William Ockham*. 2 vols. Notre Dame: University of Notre Dame Press, 1987.

Anselm, Saint. *The Major Works*. New York: Oxford University Press, 1998.

Athanasius, Saint. *On the Incarnation: The Treatise* De incarnatione Verbei Dei. Crestwood, NY: St. Vladimir's Seminary Press, 1977.

Bader-Saye, Scott C. *Church and Israel after Christendom: The Politics of Election*. Boulder, CO: Westview, 1999.

Balthasar, Hans Urs von. *Mysterium Paschale: The Mystery of Easter*. San Francisco: Ignatius, 2000.

———. *The Theology of Henri de Lubac: An Overview*. San Francisco: Ignatius, 1991.

———. *The Theology of Karl Barth: Exposition and Interpretation*. San Francisco: Ignatius, 1992.

Barron, Robert. *The Priority of Christ: Toward a Postliberal Catholicism*. Grand Rapids: Brazos, 2007.

Barth, Karl. *Ad Limina Apostolorum: An Appraisal of Vatican II*. Translated by Keith R. Crim. Richmond: John Knox, 1967.

———. *Anselm:* Fides Quaerens Intellectum. London: SCM, 1960.

———. *Die Christliche Dogmatik*. München: Chr. Kaiser, 1927.

———. *The Christian Life: Church Dogmatics IV.4: Lecture Fragments*. Grand Rapids: Eerdmans, 1981.

———. *The Church and the Churches*. Grand Rapids: Eerdmans, 2005.

———. *Church Dogmatics* I.1. New York: T. & T. Clark, 2004.

———. *Church Dogmatics* I.2. New York: T. & T. Clark, 2004.

———. *Church Dogmatics* II.1. New York: T. & T. Clark, 2004.

———. *Church Dogmatics* II.2. New York: T. & T. Clark, 2004.

———. *Church Dogmatics* III.1. New York: T. & T. Clark, 2004.

———. *Church Dogmatics* III.2. New York: T. & T. Clark, 2004.

———. *Church Dogmatics* III.3. New York: T. & T. Clark, 2004.

———. *Church Dogmatics* III.4. New York: T. & T. Clark, 2004.

———. *Church Dogmatics* IV.1. New York: T. & T. Clark, 2004.

———. *Church Dogmatics* IV.2. New York: T. & T. Clark, 2004.

———. *Church Dogmatics* IV.3.1. New York: T. & T. Clark, 2004.

———. *Church Dogmatics* IV.3.2. New York: T. & T. Clark, 2004.

———. *Church Dogmatics* IV.4: *The Foundation of the Christian Life (Fragment)*. New York: T. & T. Clark, 2004.

———. *The Epistle to the Romans*. New York: Oxford University Press, 1968.

———. *Ethics*. New York: Seabury, 1981.

————. *The Göttingen Dogmatics: Instruction in the Christian Religion.* Translated by Geoffrey W. Bromiley. Edited by Hannelotte Reiffen. Grand Rapids: Eerdmans, 1991.

————. *How I Changed My Mind.* Edinburgh: Saint Andrew, 1969.

————. *The Knowledge of God and the Service of God according to the Teaching of the Reformation: Recalling the Scottish Confession of 1560.* Translated by J. L. M. Haire and Ian Henderson. Aberdeen: University of Aberdeen Press, 1938.

————. *Der Römerbrief.* Zürich: TVZ, 1940.

————. *A Shorter Commentary on Romans.* Richmond: John Knox, 1959.

Barth, Karl, Emil Brunner, and Peter Fraenkel. *Natural Theology.* London: Centenary, 1946.

Bauerschmidt, Frederick Christian. *Julian of Norwich and the Mystical Body Politic of Christ.* Notre Dame: University of Notre Dame Press, 1999.

Bauerschmidt, Frederick Christian, James J. Buckley, and Trent Pomplun, editors. *The Blackwell Companion to Catholicism.* Malden, MA: Blackwell, 2007.

Beintker, Michael. *Die Dialektik in der "dialektischen Theologie" Karl Barths: Studien zur Entwicklung der Barthschen Theologie und zur Vorgeschichte der "Kirchlichen Dogmatik".* Munich: Kaiser, 1987.

Bender, Kimlyn J. *Karl Barth's Christological Ecclesiology.* Burlington, VT: Ashgate, 2005.

Berkman, John, and Michael Cartwright, editors. *The Hauerwas Reader.* Durham: Duke University Press, 2001.

Betz, John R. "The Analogia Entis as a Formal Principle of Cathlic Theology." Paper presented at the Analogy of Being Symposium, held at the John Paul II Institute, Washington, DC, April 2008.

Blondel, Maurice. *Action: Essay on a Critique of Life and a Science of Practice.* Translated by Oliva Blanchette. Notre Dame: University of Notre Dame Press, 2003.

Busch, Eberhard. "God Is God: The Meaning of a Controversial Formula and the Fundamental Problem of Speaking about God." *Princeton Seminary Bulletin* 7 (1986) 101–13.

————. *Karl Barth: His Life from Letters and Autobiographical Texts.* Eugene, OR: Wipf & Stock, 2005.

Cunningham, Conor. *Genealogy of Nihilism: Philosophies of Nothing and the Difference of Theology.* New York: Routledge, 2002.

Cyril of Alexandria, Saint. *Cyril of Alexandria.* Translated by Norman Russell. New York: Routledge, 2000.

————. *On the Unity of Christ.* Crestwood, NY: St. Vladimir's Seminary Press, 1995.

Davies, Oliver, and Denys Turner, editors. *Silence and the Word: Negative Theology and Incarnation.* New York: Cambridge University Press, 2002.

Descartes, René. *The Philosophical Writings of Descartes.* Vol. 1. New York: Cambridge University Press, 1984.

————. *The Philosophical Writings of Descartes.* Vol. 2. New York: Cambridge University Press, 1985.

Dillenberger, John. *God Hidden and Revealed: The Interpretation of Luther's deus absconditus and Its Significance for Religious Thought.* Philadelphia: Muhlenberg Press, 1953.

Dupré, Louis. *Passage to Modernity: An Essay in the Hermeneutics of Nature and Culture.* New Haven: Yale University Press, 1993.

Farrow, Douglas. *Ascension and Ecclesia: On the Significance of the Doctrine of the Ascension for Ecclesiology and Christian Cosmology.* Edinburgh: T. & T. Clark, 1999.

Feuerbach, Ludwig. *The Essence of Christianity.* Amherst, NY: Prometheus, 1989.

Frei, Hans W. *The Eclipse of the Biblical Narrative: A Study in Eighteenth and Nineteenth Century Hermeneutics.* New Haven: Yale University Press, 1974.

———. *The Identity of Jesus Christ: The Hermeneutical Bases of Dogmatic Theology.* Eugene, OR: Wipf & Stock, 1997.

Gillespie, Michael Allen. *Nihilism Before Nietzsche.* Chicago: University of Chicago Press, 1995.

———. *The Theological Origins of Modernity.* Chicago: University of Chicago Press, 2009.

González, Justo L. *A History of Christian Thought.* Rev. ed. 3 vols. Nashville: Abingdon, 1987.

Guarino, Thomas G. *Foundations of Systematic Theology.* New York: T. & T. Clark, 2005.

Gunton, Colin E. *The Actuality of the Atonement: A Study of Metaphor, Rationality and the Christian Tradition.* Edinburgh: T. & T. Clark, 1988.

———. *The Barth Lectures.* New York: T. & T. Clark, 2007.

Hart, David Bentley. *The Beauty of the Infinite: The Aesthetics of Christian Truth.* Grand Rapids: Eerdmans, 2003.

Hart, Kevin. *Postmodernism: A Beginner's Guide.* Oxford: Oneworld, 2004.

Hauerwas, Stanley. *With the Grain of the Universe: The Church's Witness and Natural Theology.* Grand Rapids: Brazos, 2001.

Hauerwas, Stanley, and Frank Lentricchia, editors. Special Issue of *The South Atlantic Quarterly* 101.2 (Spring 2002) 245–439.

Healy, Nicholas, M. "The Logic of Karl Barth's Ecclesiology: Analysis, Assessment, and Proposed Modifications." *Modern Theology* 10 (1994) 253–270.

———. "Practices and the New Ecclesiology: Misplaced Concreteness?" *International Journal of Systematic Theology* 5 (2003) 287–308.

Hegel, Georg Wilhelm Friedrich. *Lectures on the Philosophy of Religion.* Berkeley: University of California Press, 1988.

———. *Phenomenology of Spirit.* New York: Oxford University Press, 1977.

Horkheimer, Max, and Theodor W. Adorno. *Dialectic of Enlightenment.* New York: Continuum, 1972.

Hunsinger, George. *Disruptive Grace: Studies in the Theology of Karl Barth.* Grand Rapids: Eerdmans, 2000.

Hütter, Reinhard. "Karl Barth's 'Dialectical Catholicity': *Sic et Non.*" *Modern Theology* 16 (2000) 137–57.

———. *Suffering Divine Things: Theology as Church Practice.* Grand Rapids: Eerdmans, 1997.

Jenson, Matt. *The Gravity of Sin: Augustine, Luther and Barth on Homo Incurvatus in Se.* New York: T. & T. Clark, 2006.

Johnson, Keith L. *Karl Barth and the Analogia Entis.* New York: T. & T. Clark, 2010.

Jones, Paul D. *The Humanity of Christ: Christology in Karl Barth's Church Dogmatics.* New York: T. & T. Clark, 2008.

Jüngel, Eberhard. *Barth-Studien.* Zurich: Benziger, 1982.

Kalantzis, George. "The Sovereignty of God and Divine Transcendence: Two Views from the Early Church." In *The Sovereignty of God Debate*, edited by D. Stephen Long and George Kalantzis, 27–41. Eugene, OR: Cascade, 2009.

Lamirande, Émilien. "Roman Catholic Reactions to Karl Barth's Ecclesiology." *Canadian Journal of Theology* 14 (1968) 28–42.

Lewis, C. S. *The Lion, the Witch, and the Wardrobe*. New York: HarperCollins, 2001.

Lindbeck, George A. *The Nature of Doctrine: Religion and Theology in a Postliberal Age.* Louisville: Westminster John Knox, 1984.

Long, D. Stephen. *The Goodness of God: Theology, the Church, and Social Order*. Grand Rapids: Brazos, 2001.

——. *Tragedy, Tradition, Transformism: The Ethics of Paul Ramsey*. Eugene, OR: Wipf & Stock, 2007.

Löwith, Karl. *Meaning in History*. Chicago: University of Chicago Press, 1949.

Lubac, Henri de. *Augustinianism and Modern Theology*. Translated by Lancelot C. Sheppard. New York: Crossroad, 2000.

——. *Catholicism: Christ and the Common Destiny of Man*. Translated by Lancelot C. Sheppard and Elizabeth Englund. San Francisco: Ignatius, 1988.

——. *The Mystery of the Supernatural*. Translated by Rosemary Sheed. New York: Crossroad, 1998.

——. *Surnaturel: Études Historiques*. Paris: Aubier, 1946.

Luther, Martin. *Commentary on the Epistle to the Romans*. Grand Rapids: Zondervan, 1954.

——. "The Disputation Concerning Man." In vol. 34 of *Luther's Works*, edited by Lewis W. Spitz, 133–44. Philadelphia: Muhlenberg, 1960.

Lyotard, Jean-François. *The Postmodern Condition: A Report on Knowledge*. Minneapolis: University of Minnesota Press, 1984.

MacIntyre, Alasdair. *After Virtue: A Study in Moral Theory*. Notre Dame: University of Notre Dame Press, 2007.

——. *Whose Justice? Which Rationality?* Notre Dame: University of Notre Dame Press, 1988.

Manchester, William. *A World Lit Only by Fire: The Medieval Mind and the Renaissance*. Boston: Little, Brown, 1992.

The Matrix. Produced by Joel Silver. Written and edited by the Wachowski brothers. Warner Brothers, 1999. DVD.

Milbank, John. *The Suspended Middle: Henri de Lubac and the Debate Concerning the Supernatural*. Grand Rapids: Eerdmans, 2005.

——. *Theology and Social Theory: Beyond Secular Reason*. Cambridge: Blackwell, 1993.

Milbank, John, and Slavoj Zizek. *The Monstrosity of Christ: Paradox or Dialectic?* Cambridge: MIT Press, 2009.

McCormack, Bruce. "The Barth Renaissance in America: An Opinion." *The Princeton Seminary Bulletin* 23 (2002) 337–40.

——. "Christology and Metaphysics in Paul Tillich and Karl Barth." *Wesleyan Theological Journal* 45 (2010) 42–80.

——. *Karl Barth's Critically Realistic Dialectical Theology: Its Genesis and Development, 1909–1936*. Oxford: Clarendon, 1995.

——. *Orthodox and Modern: Studies in the Theology of Karl Barth*. Grand Rapids: Baker Academic, 2008.

———. Review of *Barth's Ethics of Reconciliation*, by John Webster. *Modern Theology* 13 (1997) 273–76.

McCormack, Bruce, K. Sonderegger, and C. Wolff. "Karl Barth and the Impossible Possibility of Theology." *Harvard Divinity Bulletin* 25 (1996) 10–11.

McGinn, Bernard. "*Vere tu es Deus Absconditus*: The Hidden God in Luther and Some Mystics." In *Silence and the Word: Negative Theology and Incarnation*. Cambridge: Cambridge University Press, 2002.

Oakes, Kenneth. "The Question of Nature and Grace in Karl Barth: Humanity as Creature and as Covenant-Partner." *Modern Theology* 23 (2007) 595–616.

Oberman, Heiko. *A Harvest of Medieval Theology: Gabriel Biel and Late Medieval Nominalism*. Cambridge: Harvard University Press, 1963.

———. *Luther: Man between God and the Devil*. New Haven: Yale University Press, 1989.

———. "Some Notes on the Theology of Nominalism: With Attention to Its Relation to the Renaissance." *Harvard Theological Review* 53 (1960) 47–76.

Olthuis, James H., and James K. A. Smith. *Radical Orthodoxy and the Reformed Tradition: Creation, Covenant, and Participation*. Grand Rapids: Baker Academic, 2005.

Pelikan, Jaroslav. *The Christian Tradition: A History of the Development of Doctrine*. 5 vols. Chicago: University of Chicago Press, 1971–89.

Pius XII, Pope. *Humani Generis*. Online: http://www.vatican.va/holy_father/pius_xii/encyclicals/documents/hf_p-xii_enc_12081950_humani-generis_en.html.

Pullman, Philip. *The Amber Spyglass*. New York: Knopf, 2002.

———. *The Golden Compass*. New York: Knopf, 1995.

———. *The Subtle Knife*. New York: Knopf, 1997.

Ramsey, Paul. *Speak Up for Just War or Pacifism: A Critique of the United Methodist Bishops' Pastoral Letter "In Defense of Creation: The Nuclear Crisis and a Just Peace."* University Park: Pennsylvania State University Press, 1988.

Rogers, Eugene F., Jr. *Thomas Aquinas and Karl Barth: Sacred Doctrine and the Natural Knowledge of God*. Notre Dame: University of Notre Dame Press, 1995.

Rumschscheidt, H. Martin, editor. *The Way of Theology in Karl Barth*. Allison Park, PA: Pickwick, 1986.

Schröer, Henning. *Die Denkform der Paradoxalität als theologisches Problem. Eine Untersuchung zu Kierkegaard und der neueren Theologie als Beitrag zur theologischen Logik*. Göttingen: Vandenhoeck & Ruprecht, 1960.

Scotus, Duns. *Ordinatio* II.,d.3.1.2.48. Online: http://individual.utoronto.ca/pking/translations/SCOTUS.Ord2d3p2q2.trns.pdf.

Smith, James K. A. *Introducing Radical Orthodoxy: Mapping a Post-Secular Theology* Grand Rapids: Baker Academic, 2005.

———. *Who's Afraid of Postmodernism? Taking Derrida, Lyotard and Foucault to Church*. Grand Rapids: Baker Academic, 2006.

Sonderegger, Katherine. *That Jesus Christ Was Born a Jew: Karl Barth's "Doctrine of Israel."* University Park: Pennsylvania State University Press, 1992.

Taylor, Charles. *A Secular Age*. Cambridge: Belknap Press of Harvard University Press, 2007.

Toulmin, Stephen. *Cosmopolis: The Hidden Agenda of Modernity*. New York: Free Press, 1990.

Turner, Denys. *Faith, Reason, and the Existence of God.* New York: Cambridge University Press, 2004.

Vattimo, Giovanni. *The End of Modernity: Nihilism and Hermeneutics in Postmodern Culture.* Baltimore: Johns Hopkins University Press, 1988.

Webster, John. *Barth's Moral Theology: Human Action in Barth's Thought.* New York: T. & T. Clark, 2004.

———, editor. *The Cambridge Companion to Karl Barth.* New York: Cambridge University Press, 2000.

———. *Confessing God: Essays in Christian Dogmatics II.* New York: T. & T. Clark, 2005.

———. *Word and Church: Essays in Christian Dogmatics.* New York: T. & T. Clark, 2001.

White, Thomas Joseph. *The Analogy of Being: Invention of Antichrist or Wisdom of God?* Edited by Thomas Joseph White. Grand Rapids: Eerdmans, 2010.

Wright, N. T. *Resurrection and the Son of God.* Minneapolis: Fortress, 2003.

Yoder, John Howard. *For the Nations: Essays Evangelical and Public.* Eugene, OR: Wipf & Stock, 2002.

———. *The Politics of Jesus.* Grand Rapids: Eerdmans, 1994.

Index of Names

Abelard, Peter, 23
Adams, Marilyn McCord, 24
Adorno, Theodor W, 35
Anselm of Canterbury, 41, 43, 44,
  58, 59, 70, 73–82, 83, 85, 87,
  96, 104, 106, 110, 187
Aquinas, Thomas, 13, 62, 63, 100,
  105, 200
Arnoldi, Bartholomaeus, 28
Athanasius, 13, 122–23, 130
Avicenna, 14

Bacon, Francis, 9, 26
Bader-Saye, Scott, 180
Balthasar, Hans Urs von, 41–42, 73,
  107, 110, 185, 187–88
Barron, Robert, 188
Barth, Karl, vii–192 (see Table of
  Contents for list of subjects
  covered.)
Bataille, George, 11
Bauerschmidt, Frederick Christian,
  14
Beintker, Michael, 42–43, 49–54
Bender, Kimlyn, 184
Benedict XVI, 188
Bernard of Chartres, 9
Betz, John, 185
Biel, Gabriel, 18
Blanchot, Maurice, 13
Blondel, Maurice, 35–37, 125, 187
Bloom, Harold, 13
Bonhoeffer, Dietrich, 167
Bossuet, Jacques–Bénigne, 172
Bradwardine, Thomas, 18

Brunner, Emil, 44, 58, 74, 86–91,
  105, 167
Bultmann, Rudolph, 44

Calvin, Jean, 13, 38, 88–90, 105, 130,
  166, 176, 188
Candler, Peter, ii
Cervantes, Miguel de, 9, 11
Cicero, 21
Cunningham, Conor, ii, xii, 14,
  16–18, 21, 26, 33, 170
Cyril of Alexandria, 13, 21, 122, 123

Denzinger, Heinrich Joseph
  Dominicus, 191
Descartes, René, 9, 14, 26, 30, 86
Dupré, Louis, 17–19, 22

Eckhart, Meister, 20–21, 25–27
Fehr, Jakob, 100
Feuerbach, Ludwig von, 3, 94, 152
Feuling, J. B., 100
Fichte, Johann Gottlieb, 26
Findlay, Thomas, 188
Fraenkel, Peter, 58, 88–89
Frei, Hans, 184

Galilei, Gallileo, 9
Gifford, Adam Lord, 92
Gillespie, Michael Allen, 9, 12–16,
  19–26, 73
Gogarten, Friedrich, 44
González, Justo, 28
Gregory of Rimini, 18
Guanilo of Marmoutiers, 76
Guarino, Thomas, 188

Index of Names

Gutiérrez, Gustavo, 188

Hart, David Bentley, 9, 34
Hart, Kevin, 13
Hauerwas, Stanley, 13, 35, 93, 170–71, 184–86, 188
Healy, Nicholas, 178, 185
Hegel, Georg Wilhelm Friedrich, 3, 26, 34, 130
Heidegger, Martin, 12
Henry of Ghent, 14, 23, 187
Heraclitus, 21, 34
Hermann, Wilhelm, 83
Hobbes, Thomas, 9, 26, 34
Holcot, Robert, 18
Holl, Karl, 176
Homer, 9
Hopkins, Gerard Manley, 18
Horace, 21
Horkheimer, Max, 35
Hoskyns, Edwyn C., 67
Hume, David, 26
Hunsinger, George, 161, 170, 179
Hütter, Reinhard, 13, 165, 175–78, 185–86

Jenson, Matt, vii, 108
Johnson, Keith L., 104
Jones, Paul, 13, 183, 184
Jüngel, Eberhard, 42, 60

Kalantzis, George, 130
Kant, Immanuel, 26, 68, 73, 99
Kierkegaard, Søren, 48, 112, 119
Kirschbaum, Charlotte von, 157
Knox, John, 92–93
Küng, Hans, 188
Kutter, Hermann, 159

Lamirande, Emilien, 185–86
Leibniz, Gottfried Wilhelm, 26, 36
Lewis, C. S., 8
Lindbeck, George, 184
Locke, John, 9, 26
Long, D. Stephen, vii, 170–71
Lubac, Henri de, 32–33, 86, 172, 185, 187–88
Lucas, George, 25

Luther, Martin, 1, 2–5, 9, 13–14, 17, 21, 27–32, 34, 37–39, 61, 63, 68, 71, 73, 90, 99, 102, 114, 164, 167–168, 176, 187, 190

Malebranche, Nicolas, 26
Manchester, William, 27
Marcion, 29
McCormack, Bruce, 4–5, 13, 39, 40–56, 74, 110–14, 130, 151, 161, 163, 168, 183
McGinn, Bernard, 26
Milbank, John, 4, 17, 25–26, 35–37, 170
Mill, John Stewart, 26
Möltmann, Jurgen, 13
Montaigne, Michel de, 9

Nestorious, 122, 125
Newton, Isaac, 9
Nietzsche, Friederick, ii, 75

Oberman, Heiko, 14, 18, 28, 30
Ockham, William of, 4, 14–18, 20–21, 23–26, 32, 38–39, 164, 187

Paul VI, 188, 190
Pelikan, Jarsoslav, 29, 80
Peterson, Erik, 42, 60
Petrarch, Francisco, 20–23, 26
Pius XII, 32
Plato, 34, 66, 99
Pryzwara, Erich, 86, 187

Quenstedt, Johnannes Andreas, 100

Ramsey, Paul, 171
Reiffen, Hannelotte, 69, 73
Ritschl, Albrecht, 83, 176
Rogers, Eugene, 62
Roscelin, 23
Rumscheidt, Martin, 75

Schleiermacher, Freidrich Daniel Ernst, 83, 84, 176
Scholz, Heinrich, 75